Marlene J. Zett.
715-266-4604

Out of Dr. Bill's
Black Bag

From Northern Wisconsin . . .
A Country Doctor Looks Back
(1941 · 1991)

WILLIAM B.A.J. BAUER M.D.

OUT OF DR. BILL'S BLACK BAG

From Northern Wisconsin . . .
A Country Doctor Looks Back
(1941–1991)

William B.A.J. Bauer, M.D.

Copyright ©1994 by Brother Bill's Publishing Co.
P.O. Box 9158
Rochester, MN 55903

Printed in the United States of America

ACKNOWLEDGMENTS

This book would never have been completed without the constant persuasion and continuous efforts of my wife, Gussie, who repeatedly said, "Our grandchildren should know what their grandfather did." Her long experience of being a doctor's wife, with delayed meals, interruptions of family events and social affairs, and her ability to overcome these graciously, made her a very special critic. Thus, word by word and page by page, her thoughtful and sometimes severe criticism forced many a chapter to be rewritten and retyped many times. Since Gussie did all of the typing, this was an arduous task for her.

Acknowledgment must also be made to an English teacher, Lois Bauer Remmer, my sister, who punctuated the first drafts of my manuscript with what appeared to be endless black marks, but which proved to be positive suggestions of syntax, word choice, and grammar. I am deeply appreciative of her many contributions.

Therefore, this book is dedicated to my wife, Augusta Ahrens Bauer, and my sister, Lois Bauer Remmer.

FOREWORD

In 1942, a well-educated young physician with a Brooklyn accent opened his medical practice in an unlikely place, a small town on the banks of the Flambeau River in sparsely populated northern Wisconsin.

A bronze plaque with the words, "William B.A.J. Bauer, M.D.," hung beside his downtown Ladysmith office door for thirty-four years. His shingle indicated he was a physician, but he also was a philosopher and counselor. The plaque is gone, but Dr. Bauer's imprint remains on the community and in the lives of the patients touched.

A tall, imposing man, Dr. Bauer commanded the trust and respect of his patients. But in some respects, his stature belied his nature. Although he was strong-willed, he was a quiet, principled man who treated his patients with compassion. His subdued voice was reassuring, and his warm bedside manner comforting. He knew his patients as friends and neighbors, and they sensed that his caring was genuine.

In this era of specialization in medicine, it is hard to comprehend how a rural family doctor could have done so much, from delivering babies to making house calls (home-calls) to handling all kinds of emergencies. Dr. Bauer shares many of these experiences in the chapters of this book. His observations also indicate how the demands of the job affected him and his family.

Dr. Bauer's gift for writing provides readers with a rare glimpse into the life of a country doctor. You will share in the joy of his triumphs, feel the agony of his losses, and, above all, develop respect for a vanishing breed — the rural family practitioner.

—John Terrell, Editor
Ladysmith News

PREFACE

Why this book? A dozen years ago my wife, Gussie, said, "You should write a book about your practice so our grandchildren can know what their grandfather did with his life." After several similar promptings, I wrote a few chapters and then complained, "No one will be able to read my scrawl, and since I can't type, I guess it's a lost cause." Always ready with the right answer, Gussie exclaimed, "You can't get out of it that easily! Like the druggist, I'm accustomed to your scrawl. I'll type it."

And so the long process began, a seemingly unending process, because so many fascinating experiences had happened to me. Each time I thought of one, several others would come to mind.

One day a close friend stopped by and asked what I was doing, surrounded by piles of paper, some my scrawled notes and others that Gussie had neatly typed. I explained my mission to share my medical life with my grandchildren.

"Let's have a look," he said and started to read one of the typewritten sheets.

His comments and those of others who read some of the chapters were enough to spur me on: "I never realized what a doctor went through." "It's not as I thought." "Doctors don't have much of a home life." "It must feel real good to see someone get well and feel you helped, but it must make you feel awful when someone suffers or dies." Don't you get tired of getting up in the middle of the night?"

As the comments continued, a new concept was added to my original purpose. I still wanted to leave my grandchildren the story of how much their Grandpa enjoyed his life as a country doctor, but it occurred to me that others might also enjoy knowing the feelings that possessed me for my 50 years of practice — my moments of joy as well as despair, knowing human nature as it is, good and bad, serious and humorous; the living and the dying — and to reveal it from behind the scenes, from the physician's point of view.

I hope by demonstrating the multiple problems of private practice with its many anxieties also to reveal the many rewards. These rewards did not fill the billfold; they filled the heart. Often they were delayed, subtle, or even absent. As a whole, however, they were commensurate to the time and effort I expended in my relationships with my patients.

Names have been changed and descriptions altered to avoid hurt to anyone.

The first part of this book touches on the imprints of my childhood, education, marriage, professional training, and the most difficult part of my career —

the first worrisome year as a solo physician.

The second and third parts deal with my gradually growing confidence, modified by the constant reminder of how much more there was to learn. During those years, I was constrained from doing some things and forced by circumstances to do others. My experiences varied from consultations with parents and teenagers to tense moments in the operating or emergency rooms.

The fourth part is more or less philosophical. After many years as a physician, I still find there are many unanswered questions, concerning the mystique of healing, the power of the mind over body, the power of love and hate, approaching a patient suffering from cancer, and a patient's right to die with dignity. One of the most difficult questions involves why the public in general, and lawyers in particular, assume that medicine is an exact science.

The fifth part is a farewell to my 50 years of medical practice — a reflection of what those years revealed to me. The book ends with words of affection from a patient.

INTRODUCTION

Ladysmith, a town of four thousand people, is embraced by a large oxbow of the Flambeau River. Once primarily a lumbering town, it has gradually added several industries but has had little change in population.

Ladysmith is the seat of Rusk County, Wisconsin, the population of which also remains somewhat stable, vacillating between 15,000 and 18,000. The county's only hospital also serves parts of three bordering counties.

In addition to the jobs created by the industries, there are the jobs provided by the usual businesses, such as banks and retail stores — drug, hardware, clothing, jewelry and supermarkets. But the greatest number of jobs are due to the dairy farming industry, which is the backbone of this community. A small liberal arts college, Mount Senario, adds not only jobs but also an opportunity for obtaining an advanced education and enjoying cultural activities.

The remoteness of this community in northwestern Wisconsin, with its readily accessible outdoor pursuits, attracted me, but the caring attitudes of the doctors toward their patients made me sure that this was where I wanted to practice.

After an 18-month partnership with one established physician, it became obvious that we had dissimilar philosophies. When office space above a drugstore on Miner Avenue, our main street, became available, I decided to go into practice by myself. At first, the need for patients to climb stairs to reach my office seemed a disadvantage. But, on second thought, I welcomed it for I reasoned that if patients climbed that flight of stairs, it was because they really wanted to see me. As time went on, this move proved a blessing, for I was able to create not only my own individual office arrangement but also my own individual office atmosphere.

With minor carpentry changes, the upstairs office developed into two adjoining waiting rooms with a children's play area and six bassinets in which mothers could lay their infants, three examining rooms, and a consultation room. Usual types of reading materials and scrapbooks of special medical stories and articles I had accumulated were available. Wise thoughts, like those of Abraham Lincoln, were framed and hung on the walls. I collected pathological specimens such as tumors and diseased organs and preserved them in jars of formaldehyde. These were on shelves in my consultation room. Patients could see examples of their surgical problems. A skeleton, X-rays of fractures in various stages of healing, and drawings that clearly demonstrated the anatomy became tools of explanation. As for comfort in the summer, my second-floor office could get very hot, but it was ten years before I could afford window cooling units.

The final but most important part of having my own say in the office was the choosing of office personnel. I wanted workers who were intelligent, compassionate and discreet. I was most fortunate to find women who met all three requirements.

As most young men starting out, I felt my way gingerly, making decisions warily, much more uncertain of myself than I dared to admit.

More than 50 years later, I have never regretted, nor has my wife, that we made Ladysmith our home.

PHOTO ALBUM

Dr. Bill as an intern.

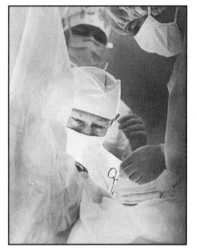

Dr. Bill at surgery.

I stand entranced by my grandchildren while they attempt to catch trout in our North Pool. One of the pools I dug by hand.

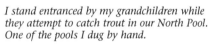

At my office desk.

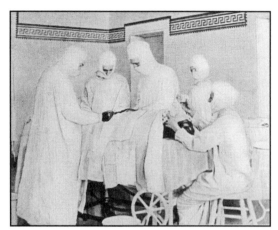

My father, Dr. John L. Bauer, operating in Wycoff Heights Hospital in Brooklyn, NY. Note the old fashioned operating gowns.

Napping, covered by my afghan made by my "Pin-Up Girl." (See Chapter 15.)

This is a sketch of me drawn by a young patient, Byron Pickering, who was awaiting his turn to be seen. He had only momentary glimpses of me as I came to the waiting room door. His talents led him to become one of the best seascape artists in the country.

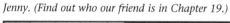

Jenny. (Find out who our friend is in Chapter 19.)

St. Mary's Hospital, now Rusk County Memorial Hospital.

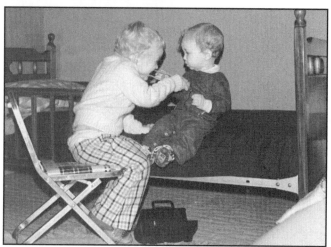

My grandchildren, Chris and Aaron, playing doctor when they were very young.

My granddaughter, Kari Williamson. She is now in medical school to become our fourth generation doctor.

Part One

Looking back, I appreciate the many good influences of my childhood, education, marriage, and professional training. These influences often came to my aid at unexpected times.

Table of Contents

Part One

BORN TO BE STUBBORN

My father liked to tell the story of my birth. "Bill was destined to be stubborn," he would start. "During his months in his mother's womb, he refused to stand on his head. He sat with his bottom down."

Then Mother in her pleasant way of mitigating harsh situations would interrupt. "Yes, Bill is stubborn but he is also caring and that is natural too. Just before I went into labor, there was a great commotion inside of me. You see, Bill didn't want me to suffer from a breech delivery. He cared, so he turned himself around in my womb."

Although I didn't appreciate it during my youthful years, I was blessed with my parental team. With his stern discipline my father taught me to be exact and to complete a job. Often in the process, my behind and his razor strap managed to collide because I found his rigid rules difficult to follow. My mother, on the other hand, mixed compassion and understanding with her discipline. Although she never compromised her principles and never wavered in her objectives, her discipline did not destroy her children's self-confidence or their self-image. My father's method took its toll. Actually, he was the loser. Though his stern discipline made all seven of his children toe-the-mark, unfortunately he never really developed a closeness with any of us.

Thus, during much of our early years, my siblings and I resented his stern discipline. Slowly, as we became adults, we forgave him. We realized this was the only method he knew. This was the method, the old German method, under which he had been raised.

Our home was in Brooklyn, New York, but we spent our summers at Bayport on Long Island, where we lived in a sprawling white house situated on 40 acres of woods, meadows and swamp. My father, who was a physician, drove the 50 miles to be with his family on most weekends.

Here, at Bayport, I was in my glory. Painfully thin and painfully shy, but full of energy and ideas, I found I could escape by being elsewhere. Soon after an early breakfast, I would set out for a day of adventures with my dog, Brownie, a wire-haired fox terrier. Dressed only in a thin pair of khaki shorts and no shirt, we explored and became familiar with every inch of our 40 acres, including the turtles, frogs, fish, crabs, snakes, birds, woodchucks, and opossums that dwelt thereon. Even the spiders, crickets and grasshoppers became my friends. My arms, legs and chest turned a dark brown, mottled with countless freckles and furrowed with irregular scratch lines from blackberry briars.

My feet became hardened almost like leather but were pitted with various cuts from clam and oyster shells. To top off my odd appearance, my hair turned almost snowwhite. Yes, I was in my glory, seldom returning home till the sun was ready to set.

My constant companion was Brownie, who inadvertently saved my life by her unwavering faithfulness. I was down at Brown's Creek, where the salt water ran up the creek during incoming tides from Great South Bay. With a long-handled net, I was catching crabs that clung to underwater posts and the walls of docks.

It was a long time ago but I clearly recall speaking outloud to Brownie, "I never saw such a large crab." In my enthusiasm, I leaned out too far and fell in. The sensation of going down, down, down, is still very vivid, very real. When I hit bottom, I bent my knees and sprang upward. I don't recall being afraid. When I reached the surface, there was Brownie. She had leaped in after me. She came to me, nudged me with her nose, licked my face, and then dog-paddled towards shore. I was not yet five and I didn't know how to swim, but I imitated her dog-paddling. Brownie turned, came again to nudge me and started once again for shore. I followed as she repeated this procedure several more times.

When we reached the reed-covered shore, Brownie shook herself thoroughly, as I seized the reeds to pull myself through the knee-deep swamp.

My net was gone. My khaki shorts were soaked. I knew I would have to present myself to the homefront, the parental court. What would they say? What would they do? Would they put me to bed for a day? I found this was the worst punishment of all. It was Saturday so my father would also have to be faced.

Trembling, not from my experience, but in fear of punishment, I found a large thick bush, took off my khaki shorts and hung them on top of the bush to dry. I crept under the bush and hid there in my birthday suit until my shorts were dry. I put them on and started home. My mood was bittersweet. Bitter, because I feared to let my parents know I had fallen in. (A few years later I learned it was 16 feet deep at that spot.) Sweet, because I felt an overwhelming sense of conquest, even at my young age. On the way home, I picked some wild flowers to offer Mother as a peace offering, even though this didn't always work. Another ruse I often tried but which never worked was to promise my mother my first million dollars, a promise I never kept.

Although painfully thin and painfully shy, I was full of inexhaustible energy and spunk and was constantly in trouble. Undoubtedly, I deserved the frequent bouts with my father's razorstrap. In time, I made a pact with myself not to cry out, not to give him any satisfaction. This drove my father to apply extra strokes. The result was that sitting down on a blistered bottom became more painful than the actual spanking.

There is little doubt that my father's discipline fortified my life, but there is little doubt that it was excessively severe. One day, crawling over a barbed wire fence, I ripped my khaki shorts beyond repair. In no uncertain terms, I was told that I would have to pay for a new pair, 2 dollars. Often when depressed I would retreat to my secret wild strawberry bed to munch on their sweet flavor. I did so on this day. After savoring a few, I decided to pick enough to sell. At 5 cents a pint, I managed to make a whole dollar, but this depleted my secret strawberry bed.

The following day, I went down to Brown's Creek to fish. The tides shunted many kinds of minnows up the creek from the bay. With this plentiful food supply, the fish, the bass in particular, grew to a large size. On this day, I was especially lucky: I caught 5 or 6 largemouth bass that were better than 4 pounds each. Pulling my little wagon throughout the neighborhood, I sold the entire catch for 5 cents a pound, netting me my second dollar.

I wince when I think of what my Mother had to put up with. On the surface, washing my clothes would appear simple enough since I wore only the short khaki trousers. But Mother never knew what she would find in my pockets: dead minnows, worms, grasshoppers and at times, snakes. And the snakes were not always dead. Mother handled all this with such self-possession that it left a lifelong impression upon me.

When I think of the countless hazards I encountered in my youthful innocence, I marvel at my good fortune. I am now grateful for the value of my early background which plunged me into a close alliance with nature, the outdoors and God, perhaps planting seeds of courage, confidence and self-reliance.

At firsthand, I soaked up a love for the land and water and those who lived thereon and therein, developing an association that can only be called all-absorbing and almost spiritual. It was here I found God. The outdoors became my temple, my cathedral for solace and worship.

CHAPTER 2

"GIVE HIM ANOTHER ONE, DOC"

Ten inches of snow had already fallen and, driven by a northeasterly wind, more was threatening to accumulate. It was time to be indoors, a time to relax and muse in front of a flickering fire.

While my wife fried raw potatoes and onions, I broiled a venison steak over the open fire. We moved our handmade pine and maple table close to the fire so we could bask in its glow as we ate. Our five children were called and eagerly gathered to share the warmth. It was a peaceful time, a special family time.

"This must be the way the Pilgrims felt on a stormy night, " said Christine. "We're all snuggled in but can hear the wind howl outside."

"The fire is very pretty," said Cathi. "Look how the blue flames look like swords and the yellow flames are the knights holding the swords."

"No, Cathi, those are dinosaurs. Look, you can see the Tyrannosaurus chasing the stupid Brontasaurus," interrupted Mark.

"What an imagination you've got," said Billy. Those are just flames from the logs that are burning."

"Gee, sure is nice to be inside tonight, and those potatoes and onions taste great, Mom," said Tim. And then, as an after-thought, not to leave me out, "Steak is good too, Dad."

Contentment oozed out of every pore. I certainly was in no mood to face the elements, but circumstances contrived otherwise.

The phone rang several times before I answered. My hesitation was deliberate.

"This is Huck Lybert. My wife, Shirley, needs you. She is in awful pain. Hurry up, Dr. Bill!"

"Whoa, Huck, I remember you and your wife and three children, but I've never been to your place. Give me some directions. What's the matter with your wife? How long has she been sick?"

"Oh she's not sick, Doc; she's having a baby. Hurry, please, she's having terrible pains."

This was hardly the time to scold him for not having brought his wife for prenatal care. When sure of the directions, I told him to light a kerosene lantern and put it by his mailbox.

The roads were heavy with snow and the going was slow. It required 40 minutes of exceptionally cautious driving to cover the dozen or so miles. The lantern beside the mailbox, acting as a beacon, marked the entrance to the Lybert farm. As I turned into the drive I was unable to differentiate the trees from power poles or the house from the barn, for there was no yardlight. Through the rapidly falling snow, I finally noticed a dim light, and as I drew closer a house made almost entirely of logs slowly took form in the glare of the headlights. The dim light I had noticed was coming from a single tiny window.

Reaching behind the front seat, I grabbed my obstetrical bag and quickly made my way to the door. After knocking loudly, I opened the door and entered. On the other side of the large single room was a wooden table, around which were sprawled three youngsters who looked up as I burst in.

Dripping snow, I removed my overcoat. The three youngsters, one boy and two girls, rushed to see who had stormed their home. All three were less than six years of age.

"Mom is having a baby. Are you the doctor?" asked the oldest, the boy.

"Pop is out in the barn. I'll get him." said the four-year-old. "I'm Doris. I'll go get him right away."

"Mom hurts a lot. Can't you help her?" asked the youngest, possibly three, as she twisted her little face into an anxious look. "Can't you help her, please?"

As Doris put on a worn coat and went to get her father, the boy said, "I'm Dan, and my sister here is Sue. I'll take you over to Mom. Follow me."

Actually this was not necessary, for in that single room I could clearly see and hear Shirley Lybert where she lay on a bed moaning with each labor pain.

Dan took me by the hand and we went to the bed—all three of us, for Sue followed along.

Mrs. Lybert was a pleasant-faced woman in her early 30's with brown hair and hazel eyes that clearly were appealing for help. "This is my fourth baby, and it pains more than the other three put together. Please help me, Dr. Bill. I know I should have come for prenatal care, but we thought this time it wasn't necessary."

Just then Doris and her father burst into the room. "I see you made it, Dr. Bill. What can I do to help?" Huck asked.

Looking around the room, I took in the sparse furnishings, the bare walls, only three small windows, and a stairway to a second floor. "What's up there?" I asked.

"Two bedrooms where the children sleep," Huck said.

"Well, the first thing you can do to help me is take the three children to a neighbor, " I said.

"Too far, Doctor, especially in this storm."

I tried again: "Huck, hard to say how things will go. Really, they shouldn't be here."

"They gotta get used to these things, Doctor. You know, on the farm they happen all the time."

"At least take them upstairs, " I pleaded. "They are really too young."

"Too cold up there. We only have this one wood-burning stove to heat the house. They might as well learn early."

I was dismayed. In those days the modern idea of having children in the delivery room had not yet surfaced. What if Shirley should hemmorhage or have some other serious compication? Moreover, should the mother be the object of her children's curiosity? I made a final appeal. "Huck, I can't believe this. Can't you at least take them upstairs and put them to bed?"

"Come on, Dr. Bill, they gotta get used to it"

Shirley, whom I had delivered three times before in the hospital, was really in pain. She was having a frank breech delivery—the baby's bottom coming first with the legs extended straight toward the head.

With Huck's assistance, supports were made to hold Shirley's legs. These supports were fastened to overhead logs. All this time the children were inquisitively eyeing the entire proceedings.

After preparing Shirley, I put on sterile gloves and draped the area. Feeling as if I were in a small arena with the three children and husband surrounding me, I tried to encourage Shirley to cooperate. And she did. She managed to push with her pains and relax between them despite her extreme discomfort. This was a difficult breech presentation and the baby was large, so it threatened to be a long, hard session, the outcome of which could not be predicted. I feared the baby might not make it and was most apprehensive about possible hemmorhaging.

I enlarged the birth opening by performing an episiotomy.

"What'cha doin', Doc?" Doris asked.

I didn't answer. I was deeply concerned. Shirley's efforts, though good, were not making satisfactory progress, and the breech was too far down to turn the baby around. The audience of children had been forgotten by now and Doris' question, though heard, was like a distant voice.

Repeatedly I urged Shirley to push harder, to hold her breath longer. "Come on, Shirley, you can do it. The baby is a boy but he needs your help. Push, Shirley, hard, harder — hold your breath and push."

The struggle seemed interminable but finally I was able to bring down one of the baby's legs and then the other. Not long afterward the buttocks delivered and then the head.

The baby's face and neck were dark, almost black. He was not breathing. I gave him a good whack on his bottom. I did it again and again. The baby did not cry and he did not breathe. The room was silent now, save for the sound of my whacking the baby's bottom.

Suddenly the baby gasped, then gasped again, and then made a feeble cry followed by another. Then came a lusty wail, and with that wail came a child's voice, Dan's voice: "Thatta way, Doc. Give him another one. He shouldn't have crawled up there in the first place."

SCHOOL and COLLEGE

I was born in 1911 and hints that I might someday become a doctor surfaced at an early age. Though I often teased my three sisters, as boys are wont to do, they always called on me to doctor their dolls who they frequently insisted needed medical attention. My father, Dr. John Leopold Bauer, often took me on his house calls in Brooklyn, New York, where we lived. Sometimes, while my father was with his patients, I would sit for hours in his car, quietly observing the pedestrians. Even at an early age, I was intrigued by the variety of people — their many different faces, the way they walked and dressed. My early fascination with people has continued to this day.

Although the family spent each summer at my parents' country home at Bayport, Long Island, the family returned to Brooklyn for the winter months. Here I was most unhappy and , at times, caused my parents great concern by running away. They soon learned where to find me — back in the country I loved.

I grew rapidly in height (eventually reaching six-feet-four inches) but not in weight, and though I looked over the heads of most boys my age and older, I was a prime target for bullying. When I was 11, I was determined to put a stop to this frequent threat, so the following summer I obtained the job of removing five large oak trees per day, roots and all. In the evening, I would row five miles. When I returned to the city with my added weight and newfound strength, I was able to withstand the attacks of the bullies, who soon left me alone. This made it easier for me to tolerate city life.

When I was 12, my Dad allowed me to witness an operation. Though I fought to prevent it, I passed out. This gave me the notion that I could not cope with the blood and gore that doctors must face. I decided to become a naturalist.

One early morning, while walking the railroad track on Long Island, I came upon a human body that had been badly dismembered by a train. It is difficult to explain why my reaction to this grisly spectacle convinced me that I should become a doctor, but suddenly the significance of life struck me: nothing could be done for the dismembered victim, but for those with life still in them, doctores were needed. From then on, my yearning to become a doctor never faltered.

I was still a problem to my parents, however, perhaps for many reasons, but mostly because I hated city life. My parents then made an excellent decision. In 1928, at the beginning of my junior year of high school, they sent me to Phillips Exeter Academy in Exeter, New Hampshire, where I flourished in a country atmosphere of serious learning. Here the student was understood and encouraged. In my first two months there, I flunked five of the six required subjects and passed one with a D-. Mr. Edward Cushwa, my advisor, called me to his office. Anticipating that I would be discharged from the school, I sat, inwardly shaking, beside his desk. Busily examining my record, Mr. Cushwa muttered a bit to himself, then turned to me.

"Bill, you study as hard as anyone, I know," he said in kindly tones. "You'll make it. Just think of the hundreds of lads who have graduated from this school. You may be no smarter, but you are no dumber either." He said no more.

In the following month, I passed all six subjects, and with a C+ in English, won a prize for the greatest improvement in English. Mr. Cushwa's words gave me new confidence, which gradually increased my sense of self-worth. Years later I passed on his message to many patients who were afraid or ready to give up, altering the words slightly to fit their particular concern: "Did you ever think how many thousands of women have had babies? You may not be any better, but your are just as good." I used such words to many frightened pregnant women.

I graduated from Exeter in 1930. Williams College, nestled in the Berkshires of New England, in Williamstown, Massachusetts, became my home for the next four years. Like Exeter, the college had high standards and a faculty of understanding teachers. The surrounding mountains and valleys, carpeted with lush green during most of the year and white in winter, made it a haven for this country-loving boy.

At the end of my first year, I was faced with the decision of choosing a major. Courses like physics and chemistry struck me as 'dead' subjects, whereas biological courses seemed 'alive' and fascinated me. But I needed a great deal of chemistry to meet the requirements for medical school. I decided to consult Dr. Walter King, chairman of the Chemistry Department whom I respected highly but held in awe.

"What can I do for you?" he asked.

"I'd like to major in chemistry, " I answered uncertainly.

"What?" he barked. "You a chemistry major! You belong in biology. In biology you get all A's but in chemistry you have a B and a C."

I had expected this but had thought it out before consulting him. In my short lifetime I had discovered that things I did not like must be met head-on. I did not like chemistry but needed it; so with a touch of assurance, I asked, "Couldn't I try a chemistry major for one semester? You know I want to be a doctor and will need to know chemistry."

Dr. King looked at me intently and after a long moment said, "All right, Bill, but after one semester, if you don't keep your grades up, you should change to a biology major."

I agreed and left the chemistry building concerned but with high hopes. In the three years that followed, I successfully completed my chemistry major. There were times when I doubted the wisdom of my choice: The long afternoon hours in the chemistry laboratory five times a week were tedious and usually made me late for practice in sports, which I enjoyed. In fact, sports were a refuge from the daily grind of classes, laboratories, lectures, and books, and I did well enough in sports to letter in four of them.

There were a diversified sprinkling of liberal arts courses among the scientific courses I was taking. I often wondered why medical schools looked more favorably at students who included such courses in their curriculum. What advantage could there possibly be to have read Keats, Shelley, Wordsworth, Longfellow, and Frost? To have a reading acquaintance with Boswell, Samuel Johnson, and Joshua Reynolds? To be able to read German, French, and Spanish? To labor over Caesar and Cicero? To have a knowledgeable background of the world's history? Years later I understood and was grateful to have entered into the lives and been exposed to the philosophies of many thinking people and to have looked into human origins and development. I believe this humanities background helped to soften my approach to my patients.

Graduation came at last. Several hundred strong, the class of 1934, garbed in long black robes and mortarboards, marched to the austere-looking Alumni Hall, fronted with tall marble pillars. Once within, we settled comfortably into the tiered seats, uncertain of what was to come and eager to get it over with, yet stirred by tradition and the formality of the building itself. We fell into a solemn mood and listened attentively as our futures were decreed and prophesized in sumptuous terms. To us, the program seemed longer than necessary and we itched to get our hands on our sheeps-skins, the diplomas that verified we had completed four years of personal effort to the satisfaction of the same professors now appraising our futures in laudatory but overly-long terms.

Following the final speaker, it was announced that we would regroup in the gymnasium. Most of us, unfamiliar with the program of graduation exercises, were dismayed. What now? Why the gymnasium? We later learned it was traditional to hand out diplomas in the gym. To my father, this was an invitation to josh me. As I came off the stage, diploma in hand, my father left his seat and eagerly shook my free hand. I will never forget his words. "Bill," he said, "I knew they would have to come to the gym to give you your diploma."

CHAPTER 4

MEDICAL SCHOOL and HONEYMOON

One evening in 1935, while attending the Long Island College of Medicine in Brooklyn, New York, I planned to spend an hour or so at the Montague Street Library to study anatomy, but my plans were suddenly changed. On the steps of the library, two blonde heads were rapt in conversation. One belonged to my youngest sister, Lois, and the other to her closest friend, Augusta ("Gussie") Ahrens. There was no use trying to duck them. They had seen me.

Though I enjoyed female company, I was no ladies' man. With one exception, I had never taken any girl seriously, but there was something about my sister's friend that attracted me. I had never liked the name Gussie, but that didn't seem to matter, nor did the fact that she was a bit short, only five-feet-five inches tall. I had frequently observed her in my sister's company but had avoided her. After all, she was six years younger than I. I came to realize that avoidance had been a mistake.

"Gussie, this is my brother, Bill," Lois said. "He is a first year medical student."

"How's the air up there?" Gussie asked with a mischievous grin.

"Fine, fine," I said. "Nice to meet you." I looked deep into her blue eyes, bluer eyes I had never experienced before. But at the same time, I was so chagrined by her casual greeting that I was desperate to retreat.

"I've got some studying to do," I said and leapt up the library steps, two at a time. For an hour I glanced blankly at Sobbata's excellent anatomy drawings, but the image of Gussie's face continued to appear before me. For study, the hour had lost its value.

I was basically content as a first-year medical student, but my feelings were mixed. The clop-clop-clop of the horse-drawn wagons, the cries of the street vendors, the overhead clatter of the elevated trains, the rushing pace of cars, trucks and people — all denied me the peace and quiet of the country. On the other hand, as the multiple systems of the human body began to integrate in my mind, my fascination blocked out much of the rush and noise of the city. Anatomy, physiology, and chemistry had new meaning as I began more clearly to understand and appreciate the incomparable wonders of the human body and the mechanisms that make it function.

The Depression had left its mark on my parents. Their well-planned financial structure collapsed. Five of their seven children in college or graduate school became a real burden. I was in my prime at 24 and decided to help. I contracted with a hospital to do emergency laboratory determinations at night in exchange for room and board. In the summer months, I taught swimming, lifesaving, and tennis during the day and tutored high school subjects in the evenings. It was my first real step towards independence, and I liked it.

Medical School was a challenge in more ways than one. There was so much to learn from books, lectures, and just listening and feeling the vibrations from professors and fellow students alike. At times I felt as though I had been tossed into a tempestuous sea in whose waters I was completely insoluble. There was little doubt that each of us was completely on his own and it took some time before friendships developed. But, in time, they did, which gave a warm comfortable glow to the medical school as a whole and to the cold anatomical dissecting room in particular.

The dissecting laboratory was cold, not just in temperature (necessary to help preserve the cadavers) but to all the senses. Spending hours and days dissecting the bodies of fellow humans with the strong odor of formalin that permeated the laboratory, made an enormous impact on us, both male and female students. Here we were at the acme of youthful enthusiasm and at the incipiency of maturity. We had just completed our introduction into the serious task of absorbing knowledge, which we learned at college. Most, if not all of us, were sensitive to the physical pains of our fellow men. This had drawn us to the medical profession. Our philosophical and religious thoughts had been nurtured by courses in ethics and philosophy and by the efforts of various clergymen.

Yet, we were raw young men and women, trying to convince ourselves that this was really our calling. Carving these cold cadavers did not lend itself to the conviction that this was our forte.

Before one particular day came to a close, I was almost convinced that I was in the wrong profession. For six hours my three teammates and I were busy dissecting the rib section of our cadaver's chest. We had uncovered the ribs, the thoracic muscles, the intercostal muscles, blood vessels and nerves, even the small perforating mammary nerves.

Exhausted physically and emotionally, I took the long elevated train and trolley ride home. Soon after arriving home the dinner bell rang. Our family, all nine of us sat down. Mother served each of us. Occupying the center of each plate were spare ribs.

As Mother handed me my plate, her eyes searched my face. I was feeling somewhat queasy as I thought of my day's rib dissection. She hesitated before setting down my plate. "What's the matter, Bill?" she asked.

I did not answer, but somehow Mother knew. She picked up my plate and disappeared into the kitchen. She returned in ten minutes with two poached eggs and toast. Later I thanked her. I am far from a squeamish person but I was eternally grateful for Mother's substitution.

Fred, Joe and Emil were my three dissceting teammates. Each cadaver had four "surgeons". We stood at the head of the class alphabetically and thus were chosen for cadaver number one.

After a week together, dissecting, learning each other's traits, background and beliefs, we became relatively comfortable as a team. Fred was quiet, a good listener, and patient. He was of the Mormon faith. His father owned a large department store and a bank. Emil was talkative, loved to tell jokes and was a good student. He was Catholic and his father had terminal cancer. Joe was indifferent to our joshing each other and did his share of the work without comment. He loved to discuss religion. He was not an agnostic, but was still searching for a sect that would satisfy him. Joe managed, without stirring up resentments, to discredit the Mormons, the Catholics and my religion as Protestant.

Several months went by. We visited each other's homes. We were impressed with Fred's magnificent home. We were distressed with the meager furnishings of Emil's home and the poor condition of Emil's father, slowly being eaten by his unrelenting cancer. At Joe's house we were served an eight course Italian dinner. Joe's father was rotund, still active as an eighty-six year old physician. They lived in a typical brown-stone house. The entire block was similarly built.

Examinations, both oral and written, both announced and unannounced, kept us on our toes. However, it was time for the mid-year examination. Not all, but most of our grades, would depend on the result of this examination which would last for a full three hours.

Of necessity, class members had to sit in rather cramped style so that all 108 of us could crowd into the relatively small room. The congestion was disturbing and the room soon became overheated. I wondered why we hadn't been seated in one of the large amphitheaters. The shuffling of nervous feet did not lend itself to concentration. There were three roving professors, ostensibly to answer questions, but just as ostensibly to survey students for possible cheaters.

Twenty minutes into the examination, I saw and heard Fred turn to Emil, "I can't tell you, " he said. "Both of us could be expelled from medical school."

"Come on, Fred," Emil said. "no one is looking."

Once more Fred turned to Emil, "Please, Emil, one of those professors will catch us. Do the best you can."

As Fred's last words left his lips, a heavy hand fell on Fred's shoulder and a stern voice said, "All right, that's enough. You come with me."

Fred was taken to the head office and told that his medical school days were over. "We don't allow cheats to remain in this school," he was told. "Doctors must be trustworthy."

Having overheard the whole conversation and as president of my class, I felt the responsibility to intercede. But to no avail. Fred would not say a word in his own defense.

Joe, Emil, and I agonized over this unfairness. Emil was ready to admit his guilt and Fred's innocence but Fred said, "No.". We often discussed the situation, wondering why Fred refused to stand up for himself.

One day I was again invited to have an Italian dinner at Joe's home. While there I brought up the unfairness of Fred's dismissal from medical school. Joe's elderly father usually spoke with a firm, solemn voice. What he said was more solemn than usual:

"Fred is an unusual person. He will go far in this world and yet not be recognized. Like Jesus, Fred is self-sacrificing. We need more men like that in our profession."

These words remain indelibly on my mind, but it took years before I fully appreciated Fred's generous attitude in this situation. Undoubtedly, Fred recognized the poverty of Emil's family and how devastating Emil's expulsion would be to Emil's father. Emil's parents were living on a pittance compared to Fred's family.

Yes, all these circumstances were reasons for Fred's generous attitude, but at what a potential cost to Fred. He went to a European medical school for a year before returning to the United States to complete his medical education at a Western medical school. Fred's father could afford the extra cost but Emil's father could not. No matter how you look at it, Fred went far beyond what most of us would have done. However, in doing so, Fred, the first Mormon I ever knew, has left a heritage of generosity for many of us to follow.

During this time it gradually dawned on me that the girl with the mischievous smile from the Flatbush section of Brooklyn was getting under my skin. Though on a tight schedule, whenever I had a rare night off from my lab duties, I took the long subway ride to spend a few short hours at Gussie's home. Sometimes, this developed into an awkward situation, for exhaustion often overcame me and I'd fall asleep. This was hardly an acceptable method of courting a girl.

Our togetherness became even less frequent when Gussie went to Wellesley College. We surrendered to this separation unhappily. By now, we had agreed that we would settle in a small town, but we needed more time to communicate and exchange other ideas. Letters and phone calls were poor vehicles for discussing our hopes for the future. Our infrequent times together were swamped with ideas each of us stacked up. Too much to talk over in too little time. Discussions often became disputes, at times heated. The home we planned to build some day became a major source of friction. Gussie wanted to remodel an old house and I wanted to build a new one, a New England colonial. By the way we talked, a listener might have thought we already had a half dozen children.

By then, it was obvious that both of us were strong-willed. The difference in our dreams of a house almost separated us before we were even married. Yet, many a time I have been grateful that Gussie is strong-willed. Though clashes were frequent, her strengths surfaced. These strengths later had a great influence on me as a practicing physician.

We still think of June 1939 as a hodge podge of events. Final medical school exams, state board exams and my graduation from medical school were all meshed in with Gussie's final exams, her graduation form college and our wedding.

Somewhere among all of these, we had a five-day honeymoon in New England. On one of our honeymoon nights we planned to sleep in our Nash Lafayette, whose back seat converted into a bed. An afternoon of fishing on Moosehead Lake in Maine had left us exhausted from paddling a canoe against a stiff wind. We ate our supper and prepared for bed. The car was parked in a wood-ed area and the open car windows were covered with portable, fine-meshed screens.

Gussie climbed into bed. As I changed into my pajamas in the front seat of the car, I could hear her bouncing about and slapping. "The bugs are terrible," she said.

"Can't be," I answered rather positively. "We have screens in the windows. Even little bugs can't get through those screens." With that I climbed into the back, but before I could get under the covers, bugs swarmed over me too.

"Wow, let's get out of here," I shouted. I removed the screens and quickly climbed into the driver's seat. I drove briskly up the road, hoping to blow the no-see-ums, as they are called in Maine, out of the car. They were so small that they must have flown through the screens without pause.

At the first hotel we came to, I hopped out of the car, and dressed only in paja-mas, entered the lobby, walked up to the desk and asked for a room. The room clerk, apparently too astonished to protest, made no comment, but the hotel guests seated in the lobby were aroused from their lethargy and stared at me as I shamelessly went to get my bride. When I reappeared with Gussie, who had put on a raincoat over her nightgown, the lobby was a beehive of conversation. We were, without doubt, the center of attention.

CHAPTER 5

HOSPITAL YEARS

Our honeymoon over and state boards completed, on July 1, 1939 we moved into Brooklyn State Hospital where I began a six-month residency in psychiatry. This hospital treated a wide variety of mental patients for it was the largest mental hospital in the United States. Daily visits with dozens of mental patients taught me to react to them as to normal people and not to talk down to them.

At that time there were few malpractice suits and I was unaware of even those few, but some doctors were already wary. With my newly acquired medical degree, I felt a responsibility for my patients that my position as a resident physician did not warrant. When Alfred Martin, a manic-depressive patient, developed a bloodstream infection, he was given sulfadiazine by mouth, but it wasn't helping him. I had read an article in a medical journal that stated that sulfadiazine given intravenously had saved the lives of some patients suffering from bloodstream infections. With boundless enthusiasm, I approached my superiors, seeking permission to give my patient sulfadiazine intravenously. It was emphatically denied.

"We can't take the chance of being sued," one of my superiors informed me.

"But look at the article in this medical journal. Sulfadiazine has been used intravenously, " I pleaded. "Alfred is going to die if we don't give it a try."

Something within me refused to be satisfied. I went to the top — Dr. Bellinger who was the hospital administrator. He was a large, kindly man, highly respected by his staff.

As I entered his office, he asked, "What can I do for you, Bill?" He looked at me as a father looks at his son, which gave me renewed confidence.

"One of my patients will die if we don't do something." I showed him the article in the medical journal.

"But the manufacturer's label warns against using sulfadiazine intravenously. If we use it, we are liable for suit." Dr. Bellinger leaned his huge frame back in his chair and looked at the ceiling.

"But my patient will die if we don't. What difference would it make if he died of sulfadiazine or died of septicemia? At least he would have a chance if we tried, and we have the medical backing of this article."

For several long minutes, Dr. Bellinger stared at the ceiling. Then he stood up, put a hand on my shoulder and spoke firmly. "Ok, Bill, you have a point and it seems logical. Try the sulfadiazine intravenously. I'll sign a permission slip for it. But keep me informed."

Alfred Martin made it and my budding medical career was given a boost.

Another time, a schizophrenic patient, Peter Ogden, offered me an unusual challenge. Trying to complete a mental history on him was frustrating. It seemed impossible to hold his attention. Apparently absorbed by auditory and visual hallucinations, he kept turning his head and talking to someone who was not there. Suddenly, a possible solution flashed in my mind. When he turned toward me again, I asked, "Peter, do you think it is polite to talk to two people at the same time?"

Peter cocked his head to one side and gave me a questioning look. Then he turned away and said to his imaginary friend, "Excuse me, I have to talk to the doc."

We completed the history without further interruption.

Our next move was to Minnesota, where I served a rotating internship at Minneapolis General Hospital for eighteen months. Dr. Erling Platou, a pediatrician, took us under his wing and helped us to find a small, affordable room close to the hospital.

Our fifteen-dollar-a-month room was on the third floor of a building overlooking Portland Avenue in Minneapolis. A pair of windows opened onto a roof, which on warm evenings became our private terrace. The room boasted a rocking chair, a wobbly straight chair, a small table, a dresser, and a single bed. When people came for a meal or a game of cards, the bed and a board on the radiator became our third and fourth chairs. Some three hundred-pound hulk must have slept in that bed before us, for even without an occupant the mattress was permanently shaped into a canyon where Gussie and I met on those rare nights when I was off duty. The walls seemed to have been constructed merely of wallpaper tacked onto two-by-fours, for we could easily hear the conversation of our neighbors. Their most frequent remark was, "You can get used to hanging if you have to."

Our room was irregular in shape. Under the eaves was a closet of inadequate dimensions which, along with our kitchen area, was barely five feet high. Gussie cooked on a two-burner gas stove with a top-of-stove ovenette. Washing our few pots, dishes, and eating utensils we used our gallon thermos jug and water from the common bathroom.

Our meals were truly simple; vegetables, fruit, milk, and bread were the main ingredients. Meat was out of our economic range. When possible, however, we managed to catch crappies and northerns in small lakes close to the city. The flavor of these fish was distinctly earthy, so we boiled them first and then fried them.

Our meals were modest, our quarters small, our privacy inadequate, and our income paltry. We lived on our savings and my pay of seven dollars and fifty cents a month, but our aspirations were huge and our spirits high. Besides, we were together.

During my rotating internship I was exposed to a variety of specialties that stirred conflicting ambitions. Surgery was both technically and dramatically seductive. Psychiatry held a strange allure but seemed somewhat vague. Pediatrics offered the special joys of working with children, while obstetrics was surrounded by the mystique of birth. Each speciality had its own attraction. No wonder this rotating internship nourished my already-strong notions of becoming a country doctor, where I would touch on all specialties.

This growing desire to become a country doctor was further fostered by the special consideration given to me by some of the attending doctors. They encouraged me to take on responsibilities, to try my hand under their expert guidance. Dr. James Polzak, an urologist, would say, "Go ahead, Bill, you do the job. I'll be right here next to you."

"But I've never removed a kidney before," I'd interject.

"There has to be a first time for everything," he'd say.

"Remember , I'll be standing here ready to take over. I wouldn't let you do it if I didn't think you were ready."

OUR FIRSTBORN

We had been married almost two years and were still childless. The stress of my long and arduous hours had taken its toll, but uncertain that this was the cause, we consulted Dr. William Lang, head of the obstetrics and gynecology service at Minneapolis General Hospital, where I was interning. After a few tests, he confirmed the opinion that stress and fatigue were responsible.

It came as a pleasant surprise, but shortly after this consultation, Gussie showed unmistakable signs and symptoms of pregnancy. We were elated, but our elation was short-lived. At six weeks, the pregnancy was threatened. We again sought the assistance of Dr. Lang.

"Most spontaneous abortions are bad eggs. If it's a bad egg, better your wife lose it," was his succinct response.

Dr. Lang was kindly as well as knowledgable and his statement should not have irritated me, but it did. I felt he must know what could be done to save the pregnancy, yet he offered only the statement as solace for our threatened loss.

I was young and medically inexperienced. I desperately wanted to be a father. Gussie fervently longed to be a mother. Little did I really know about abortions, spontaneous or otherwise. I recalled Professor Alfred Beck's last obstetrical lecture at medical school. His eyes moist with sincere emotion, he spoke gravely on all types of abortion. Scanning his audience of would-be doctors, he implored us never to induce an abortion, except to save a life. Then, attempting to demonstrate the importance of a baby to a woman, he ended his lecture with these words, "A women's menstrual flow is a sign of a woman's body shedding bloody tears because she is not pregnant."

Gussie and I earnestly sought to sustain the pregnancy. She stayed in bed for two weeks till the bleeding stopped. On two such other occasions, she had to take to her bed for a week or two. Somehow, the pregnancy remained and became our firstborn, a healthy and normal baby girl. Was it because of the enforced inactivity? From luck? Or because it was meant to be?

I have often considered that if our oldest child was a bad egg, bad eggs can't be all bad. However, one day I came across a medical article that helped me to appreciate Dr. Lang's quietly spoken words. The article stated that more than 70 percent of spontaneous abortions have severe deformities. I realized that Dr. Lang, in his own kindly way, was trying to salve our feelings.

Before our baby was born and at the end of my internship, we left Minneapolis to fill in for Dr. Frank Atkins in Ladysmith, Wisconsin, during July and August, 1941. Two months as a country doctor eroded my enthusiasm for any of the specialties and convinced me that general practice was my forte and my fate.

At the end of August, Gussie and I went to Long Island, New York, where I had spent my childhood. A singular opportunity to share a practice with three well-established physicians had come up. Several advantages beckoned us: my parents offered us the use of their country home, I would not have to rent office space, and all three physicians had influential positions on the hospital staff. One was chief of the medical department.

After several weeks, I learned there were disadvantages too. Under the guise of what was best for the patient, beginning doctors until they had been in practice for a year, regardless of their training, were not allowed to enter patients into the hospital. Thus, any patient needing hospital care had to be referred to an established physician. Nor were beginners allowed to deliver babies or to assist at surgery until they had been in practice three years. One physician, who had been in practice for a full two years and had five years of training as a surgical resident, was still not permitted to assist at surgery.

Apparently belonging to a group practice with influential staff members gave me special privileges, for I could enter my patients into the hospital, assist at surgery, and deliver babies. But I was disillusioned by the political manipulations that gave advantage to those in power. I saw that the chief of surgery commanded a constant flow of surgical cases that kept him busy and his coffers full while excellent surgeons stood by and hungered for work.

Uneasy about my favored postion, I discussed the possibility of returning to Wisconsin with Gussie. But plans for our future had to wait, because Gussie was now eight months pregnant. Although I had been providing her prenatal care, we had yet to decide who would deliver our baby. Somehow Gussie and I had avoided any discussion of it. The subject seemed taboo.

But one day at lunch, we did talk. All morning, while making house calls, I had been worrying about it and had resolved that the decision must be made that day. With firmness, I brought up the subject. "I'll get Dr. Alfred Beck, my obsterics professor, to deliver our baby," I said.

Gussie shook her head. "No, I want you to do it." she said.

"Doctors don't deliver their own children. They don't treat their own families. You know that."

"But I want you to do it. Some fathers who aren't even doctors deliver their own children."

"That's different," I said. "They do it for emergency reasons."

"But I really want you to be the one. It's something special for me. I have confidence in you, not some professor." Gussie reached out and touched my hand.

"Honey, don't you see, doctors shouldn't because they are too emotionally involved. If something goes wrong, they could be so emotionally involved that they might not do the right thing at the right time," I pleaded.

"You just don't understand. I want this baby. I've fought hard to hold it. I have a big investment in it. I trust you, not some stranger. As a doctor, you are concerned for all your patients. I want to be your patient, not someone else's." In her eagerness, her blue eyes filled with tears.

"Most doctors do care. Most want the best for their patients," I answered.

"Yes, I understand, but it's not the same. I have faith in you, and that eases my fear of delivery. I want you there."

With that, I got up from the table. Neither of us had eaten the lunch Gussie had prepared. Gussie sat and looked up at me, her eyes appealing to me, her cheeks wet with tears.

Shaken and wanting to satisfy the woman I loved but fearful of breaking unwritten medical rules, I felt the need to think, to reassess my thoughts.

"I'll be back," I said kissing her tenderly. I hurried out the door and into the woods behind the house — the house where I had spent my summers as a child. Every tree, pine or oak, was an old friend. I walked down the pine-needled path to the bluff, an abrupt drop-off from the woods to the meadows. I sat down on the remnant of a woodpile, now nearly decayed. Down below, a creek meandered through the meadow, a stream of bass and pickerel, where I had often fished as a boy with my dog, Brownie.

For a long time I sat, half enjoying nostalgic glimpses of my youth, but I knew I was avoiding the situation that troubled me and forced myself to face it. Great men admonished that a physician's judgment could be warped by emotional involvement. If I attended Gussie and something happened to our baby or my wife, I'd be overwhelmed by guilt and remorse. But would I not feel guilt if something happened and I had not followed her request to attend her? Was her need for me at this time crucial? Was that need greater than the hazard of my own emotional involvement? Her words kept echoing in my mind: "I have faith in you. I want you there."

Suddenly I knew the answer, an answer that set the pattern for all my years of practice and a standard for making decisions about my patients. I walked into the kitchen and said, "I'll do it. I'll deliver our child." The smile on Gussie's face, the look in her eyes, and the relief she conveyed supported my decision.

Ever since that decision was made, I have followed this simple standard as a doctor: I would ask myself — if the patient before me were my wife or any other member of my family — how would I treat her or him? For this standard, I am indebted to my partner, Gussie.

Thus, we had our baby together. In some ways, it was a trying time for both of us; in others an especially happy time of togetherness. This was in early November on Long Island. In late December, we moved back to Ladysmith.

CHAPTER 7

SOLO PRACTICE AT LAST

Our three-room apartment was cold, but it wasn't until we heard the weatherman announce the morning temperature that we realized how cold it was outside. It was forty-two degrees below zero.

"Sounds like Siberia," Gussie said, ducking back under the covers.

"Couldn't be that cold," I remarked, rationalizing that the weatherman must have made a mistake.

After breakfast, I walked the short block to begin my first day in my own office. The thought possessed me: my own office, not one that belonged to three other physicians, as on Long Island, nor to Dr. Adkins here in Ladysmith, but my own.

The sight of a man holding a hose with water running out of it interrupted my thoughts. As the water hit the sidewalk, it froze instantaneously, then piled up like a stalagmite. Unconsciously, I pulled up my collar and accelerated my pace. The weatherman must have been right when he said that it was forty-two below zero.

I reached my destination and I bounded up the stairs to the second floor – a four-room apartment I had transformed into a doctor's office. I proudly surveyed the secondhand furniture, the two examination tables, the sterilizer, and a few other absolutely essential tools of my trade. It wasn't much of a showing, but it was a start.

A long two hours passed. It was eleven o'clock, and no hoped-for steps of approaching patients broke the unbearable silence of the empty rooms. I began to pace back and forth, wondering what kind of person would seek the services of a young doctor, a newcomer to the community. Random thoughts popped into my mind. Was I ready for this solo country practice? My basic training in medicine and surgery was sound. My wife, although city bred, endorsed this change to country life. but I was in debt. Already thirty years old, I owed more than seven thousand dollars and Rusk County had the lowest per-capita income in the state.

Suddenly, the acid truth hit me. It wasn't the money that worried me – I had been in debt before and had worked my way out of it. It wasn't that I was a stranger to this town or these people. After all, I had spent a summer in Ladysmith caring for Dr. Atkins' practice. It was the insecurity of knowing that I was entirely on my own with no one to back me up.

After another twenty minutes of inner turmoil, I decided to settle down. The Ladysmith News had written an article announcing the opening of my office on this January day, so there was little I could do but wait. I opened a medical journal to read, but I couldn't concentrate. My attention was focused entirely on listening for a patient's steps on the stairs. Thus, I really did hear the very first sounds of people coming up to my office, and I quivered with eagerness. A moment later, the door at the top of the stairs opened, and there stood Mr. and Mrs. Henry Matthews.

"I heard you were back. I'm glad." Mrs. Matthews spoke with the same easy candor that I remembered from the previous summer when she had come to see me at Dr. Atkins' office.

"I'm sure glad to see you back, Doc," Mr. Matthews added. "My wife's been in a tizzy ever since you left last summer. Several doctors advised her to have her womb removed, but when she heard you were coming back, she decided to wait."

"Matter of fact," Mrs. Matthew's broke in, "Neighbors pushed me to go to Rochester, so we went. The doctor there wanted to operate at once, said I had fibroid growths. You told us that, but said I might be pregnant. So here we are."

It was an awkward moment. I could feel myself flush. Was their confidence in me justified? Although Mrs. Matthew's' abdomen was enlarged, was she really pregnant?

"I can't tell you how happy I am to see you. Please come in." I said, opening the door to one of the examining rooms.

I had recognized her at once, and clearly recalled last summer's office visits. She had complained of heaviness in her pelvis and had skipped three periods, but had no morning sickness. I had examined her and found her uterus enlarged and knobby with fibroids, not at all suggestive of a pregnancy. During an internal examination, however, I had noticed signs that indicated pregnancy.

I also recalled our dialogue after I told her of my findings.

"You're not telling me I'm pregnant, are you?"

"No, but I'm not telling you that you aren't pregnant, either. You have some positive signs of pregnancy."

"But I'm 45 years old, been married better than 13 years and never skipped a period till now." Then, with a guileless, almost childlike look, she murmured, "Wouldn't it be wonderful if I was?"

I had done a pregnancy test. It was negative. But I had been so impressed by the signs of pregnancy that I had advised her to follow up such a possibility with Dr. Adkins when he returned. I had also suggested that she not worry about the fibroids unless she developed bleeding.

Now, here she was in my office, hoping that my diagnosis had been correct. She was in the closet I had designated as a dressing room. The door had been removed, and a sheet hung on a curtain rod. This provided privacy. Soon she appeared in one of the white tie-behind-your-back gowns I had recently bought.

"Don't you think I look cute?" she asked, laughing as she lay back on the examining table.

I found her physical condition to be excellent. Using a head stethoscope, I thought I heard a fetal heartbeat. After several more attempts, I was certain. Upon examination, I found her uterus to be the size of a full-term pregnancy, but it was still covered with fibroids. Later, a single X-ray taken at the hospital revealed a baby's skeleton.

Trying to control my excitement, I announced, "I have good news for you. You are going to be parents."

Mr. Matthews, who had been standing during the examination, sat down. "Can't believe it, he said." I just can't believe it."

Mrs. Matthews' face broke into a smile. For a time she said nothing. Then she looked at me as though I were a saint who had produced a miracle, and in whispered tones said, "Me? I'm going to a mother. At my age, do you really think I can? What about the fibroids?"

"Of course you can. You are a very young forty-five," I said with the hope of putting off a discussion of her fibroids till another time.

Mrs. Matthews was an unusually perceptive individual, and when she again asked, "What about the fibroids?" I knew it was time to lay all the cards on the table.

I opened Beck's obstetrical textbook and Sobatta's pictorial anatomy book and explained the situation. "Come, look at these pictures," I said, pointing out pictures of the layers of the uterus and the placental attachment of the infant to the innerlayer. "The uterus is a cradle that stretches and grows as your infant grows. The infant is nourished by this same cradle to which it is attached. Now look at this picture. Notice that the uterus has three layers. Each layer has a purpose. The inner layer to which the placenta is attached is to feed the baby. The muscular layer helps the baby to be born during labor. The third layer is the covering that prevents the cradle from sticking to other organs."

Both of them seemed to understand so I went on." It seems apparent that the fibroids on your uterus have not grown into the inner layer or you would have bled. I do not believe they have penetrated deeply into the muscular layer; but if they have they could interfere with the muscular contractions necessary for labor."

"What do you suggest?" asked Mrs. Matthews.

"In spite of your excellent physical condition, because this is your first baby and at age forty-five, and because of the fibroids, I suggest a Cesarean Section."

Both agreed to this, and we set a date for the section. Since she was close to term, it seemed wise to have Mrs. Matthews come to Ladysmith from her home twenty miles away and stay at a hotel so she could be close to the hospital should she go into labor before the date we had chosen.

When the time came, Mrs. Matthews was delivered of an eight-pound girl under local anesthesia. What that baby meant to her parents requires no imagination to understand. She was an only child, but she brought great happiness to her parents. Now they are proud grandparents of three grandchildren.

CHAPTER 8

I COULDN'T WIPE AWAY MY FEARS

Although it was a bright, sunny day when I entered the white clapboard house, I found myself in a dark room with the shades drawn and only a single kerosene lamp burning. A fully bearded man of sixty or so gradually took form as my eyes accommodated to the semi-darkness. He sat propped up in bed, breathing rapidly. Profuse spittle covered his beard and was frequently replenished by recurrent coughing episodes. Even in the dim light, I could see the bearded man was as pale as death. Only his eyes seemed alive.

"Hello," he whispered hoarsely and started to cough anew.

I stood at the foot of his bed and glanced about, trying to take stock. His dark brown eyes spoke as they followed my every move: pleading for help, begging for relief, wondering what I would do. There was no semblance of order in the dark room. The sparse furniture was hidden under clothes, pillows, blankets, magazines, and newspapers. Unwashed dishes and paper plates were scattered here and there, most of them on the floor.

As I released a chair from its assorted burdens, a rear door opened and a man's shape took form. With his huge features and scars on his face and neck, he looked grotesque. As he came closer, dragging his left leg, I recognized Stuart Eberly, a bachelor farmer who had been mutilated by a bull. This was the man who had summoned me.

Stuart smiled and reached out his huge hand. "Sure happy you came, Doc," he said.

I was relieved to see Stuart, for I had wondered how I could gather information from the patient whose every whisper produced paroxysms of coughing. "Mighty glad to see you too, Stuart," I said. "I need you to tell me about this man. How long has he been this way? I've never seen him before."

"This is Irvin Manoske," Stuart said. "He's been in bed six weeks. Neighbors been trying to help. They brought him food, washed him and tried to get him to a doctor. He kept getting worse, but he wouldn't let them call a doctor; so they came and got me. When I realized how bad he was, I told him I was going to call you. He told me not to, but I did anyway. I told him you fixed me up pretty good after the bull got through with me."

Putting the chair beside the bed, I sat down to examine Irvin. I looked at his sad eyes, his pale face, its thinness hidden under his beard. When I opened his shirt, I saw his ribs that were markedly exposed and warped from childhood rickets. I began to feel very uncomfortable, for he looked so helpless. His pleading eyes tracked every movement I made, yet he didn't try to speak. The room was filled with the sounds of his short, labored breathing and his spells of coughing. To reassure him I tried to explain everything I did as I tapped his chest and listened with my stethoscope. Now that I was close to him I observed red specks of blood in his sputum-covered beard. Pneumonia, tuberculosis and lung cancer – all were possibilities. While tapping on his chest, I heard a hollow tympanic sound. In the same spot, through my stethoscope, I heard the sound of a tinkle, like a tiny bell. These were signs of a cavity. I felt sure that Irvin had tuberculosis (TB).

For a long time, or so it seemed, I sat there, swallowed up by the eeriness of the room, the harsh loneliness of the patient, and my own responsibility. Propped up in this bed was a man probably dying of TB, a man who had refused medical aid too long. I was here only because of the insistence of the man who had called me.

My introspection was broken by Stuart's voice, "I gotta go, Dr. Bauer. I'll call you tomorrow morning. Hope you can persuade Irvin to go to the hospital."

Speaking slowly and calmly, I tried to explain to Irvin the seriousness of his illness, the need for X-rays and sputum tests, and the advantages of hospital care. Tightening the muscles of his face, Irvin whispered, "No, I've been sick so long, I might as well stay in bed here at home."

I was desperate, but I saw it was no use, so I collected sputum for staining at the office. When I was finished, I sat down again and looked into Irvin's eyes. "Irvin," I said, "everyone is concerned about you. Your neighbors and friends have tried to help you. They want you to get well. Why won't you let us help you?"

Irvin looked back into my eyes. An intangible something passed between us. Suddenly, he leaned forward, wrapped his arms around me and kissed me profusely many times – beard, spittle and all.

The outer discomfort of the spittle plastered on my face and lips was minor compared to my inner fear of contracting TB. But how could I withdraw from Irvin's embrace, his way of demonstrating gratitude for my concern? I withdrew slowly but fearfully, though I tried not to show it. In moments, my exit was complete.

Once outside, I frantically wiped my face and hands with gauze from my medical bag and snow from the north side of the house, where it had evaded the sun. Breathing deeply, I said a silent prayer and started back to Ladysmith. I went directly to my office, scrubbed myself thoroughly , threw away my shirt and tie, and put on white pants and top from an obstetrical pack I kept in the office. I hung up my suit outside, where I left it for a week. I called Gussie, explained the situation, and went home. I showered longer than usual, trying to wash off my imaginary ills as well as any real ones. For several days, I kept away from my wife and baby girl, praying more often than I had for some time.

Two days later, Irvin entered the hospital, his reluctance overcome by a massive hemorrhage following a violent coughing spell. His sputum was positive for TB and an X-ray revealed a large lung cavity. Within a week, I transferred him to a sanitarium in Eau Claire, Wisconsin, where he was treated with fresh air supported by a wholesome diet. In those days, there were no specific antibiotics to treat TB. Sixteen months later, Irvin, having made a satisfactory recovery, returned home.

Though I never mentioned it to others and tried not to admit it to myself, Irvin's hug and kisses made an impression that long remained. For weeks, I squirmed with the thought of the potential hazard of this intimate contact, and I still squirm at the thought of it.

CHAPTER 9

PEGGY

I had lain in bed an extra hour, thinking about my growing practice with a certain pride yet troubled because I sorely needed help – an office girl to sign up patients, to handle the telephone, to keep the books, and, most important of all, to be present when I examined female patients. Small towns do not have large classified ad columns, and I wasn't sure I wanted to advertise. What would I say? Wouldn't it sound a bit odd to advertise for a smart girl who could be warm and friendly towards patients, but discreet? I munched on the thought all day.

It was a special Saturday in Ladysmith – Maxwell Street Day. Merchants spread wares that had not sold well, on carts and tables in front of their shops. A full-faced sun had warmed the cold, bracing air and drawn farmers and their families to town in droves. Street and sidewalks were crowded with people, many of whom climbed my stairs and filled my waiting room, further accentuating my urgent need for help. By four o'clock, I went home and sank into a chair, exhausted. Christine, just short of a year, came crawling to me, cooing delightedly. I reached down, picked her up, and chatted with her as fathers do. The "tete-a-tete" with my daughter was more relaxing than a massage, and as my wife placed Christine into her high chair, I fell asleep.

I was awakened by the sound of Christine happily tapping her little feet against the footrest her highchair. A wave of gratitude passed over me as I watched my wife feeding our daughter. All thoughts of my need for office help and of my debts evaporated as I appreciated what I had.

Impulsively, I asked, "How would you like to go out tonight?"

"I surely would," Gussie said, then added, "but can we afford it?"

"Let's go whole-hog tonight. It's been a long time since we've been out." We both knew what going whole-hog meant: a local movie, a milkshake and a baby-sitter.

I immediately called Peggy Smith, a recent high school graduate and the daughter of a patient. Peggy was a bright young lady with a pleasing disposition.

I had heard she was good with children.

When Peggy arrived, I went though a list of what and how we expected things to be done. We were still overly careful, having been through so much stress to obtain our firstborn. Peggy murmured assent, and Gussie and I went off to our movie and our milkshakes.

On our return, Peggy was rocking Christine.

"Why isn't she in her crib?"

"I'm rocking her to put her to sleep."

"We don't want you to do that. We want Christine to learn to go to sleep without being rocked."

Peggy looked up but continued to rock Christine. With her brown Irish eyes looking straight at me, she retorted, "If you don't trust my judgment, I'll never babysit for you again." Taken aback, I said no more. After Peggy left, I turned to Gussie and said, "Maybe she's the answer."

"What are you talking about?"

"About help for the office. Peggy is like you. She has a mind of her own. I was impressed with her conviction that rocking Christine was the right thing, but she wasn't the least bit disrespectful."

"Oh, you want to ask her to be your office girl? Bill; she has had no training, not as a bookkeeper, a secretary, or nurse."

"Perhaps that will be an advantage . I can train her . Did you see how she handled Christine? There's something special about her. She is a person who cares, and a caring person would be a plus in any doctor's office."

I mulled the question over in my mind for several days and then decided to see if Peggy was interested. After completing my office hours, I called her, and she came at once.

We discussed the situation thoroughly – the long hours, the bookwork, the sterilizing and the many other necessary tasks. She admitted she had much to learn but was undaunted.

With some hesitation, I asked, "How are you at keeping secrets?"

"What do you mean, Dr. Bauer?"

"There are some people who don't feel adequate unless they share everything they know. No matter what it is, they must tell someone. What you learn in this office about other people's lives is and must be kept inviolate, as though it were sacred."

"Of course, I would never say anything," Peggy said with a trace of hurt showing in her eyes.

"Fine, then you can start tomorrow."

Within a month, I felt a great relief. My office began to hum with this young girl's multiple activities. She kept the books, attended to the patients' records, and helped me bandage wounds and put on casts. Minor details received her attention. She also took over the ordering of office supplies. She ran the office; I worked there.

Starting out in practice, with its awesome responsibility, had been trying. Having the load of office details lifted from my shoulders was an undisguised blessing. It was not only Peggy's efficiency that I blessed, however; it was also her manner of caring for people that gave my office a special warmth.

CHAPTER 10

HOSPITAL SISTERS

Sister Joseph should have been the mother of a large family. She would often say, "I have just made some fresh bread I want you to try," or "It just so happens I have baked a cake. Wouldn't you like a piece?" She certainly mothered me. There was nothing imposing about her, but she was the epitome of wholesome goodness and brightened my night visits to the hospital with her quiet, amiable disposition.

Sister Joseph also possessed an unusual gift. Without physical examination, she could tell when to call a physician for an expected delivery. In fact, her call to come was so reliable that once I realized Sister Joseph had this talent, I was spared many hours of waiting in the hospital. I also learned not to ignore her call.

It was three months since I had started my solo practice, and yet I still felt ill-at-ease in my daily association with the hospital sisters. It was Sister Joseph's warm manner that helped to release me from the artificial constraints imposed by their long black robes and starched collars. Within those religious habits were some very fine women. As the masking effect of their habits wore off, I recognized that each sister had her own personality, character and ambition. I began to relate to each individually. Most were amiable, fun-loving, and sincere, earnest in their life's work, and eager to spend time and effort to attain the goals of their order, the Servite Order of Mary.

Even as I felt more comfortable with the sisters, I grew to respect their remarkable restraint in the face of adversity and their drive in the pursuit of their religious beliefs. After all these years, I still retain feelings of admiration, awe, and wonder for these dedicated women. As in all segments of society, however, there were some among the sisters who did not measure up.

Several weeks after I amputated her gangrenous leg, Adela Simpson, a woman of 60, was admitted to the hospital in a diabetic coma. Within three days Mrs. Simpson was her old self. Readjusted by diet and insulin, she was lavishing her humor and inflicting her domineering spirit on fellow patients in her ward – a sure sign of recovery.

On the afternoon of Mrs. Simpson's fifth hospital day, Sister Margaret telephoned me at the office. In a plaintive voice, she told me that she had given Mrs. Simpson a second dose of 85 units of insulin too soon after the first. "I made the error." she said. "I didn't look at the chart. It's all my fault." Realizing the imminent danger of insulin shock, I hurried to the hospital at once, telling Peggy to reschedule the patients who were in the waiting room.

For the next three hours, I attended Mrs. Simpson. Though not in shock, she was sweating profusely. Her face was pale and her hands trembled. "I'm afraid it's over for me. I'm going to die," she repeated over and over again in a hoarse whisper. I gave her intravenous fluids containing glucose and observed her constantly.

When I felt secure that the excess insulin had been balanced, I approached Sister Margaret. Taking her hand in mine, I said, "Thanks for letting me know. It must have been hard to admit you'd made such a mistake. It was good that you called me at once. I appreciate it. The results could have been disastrous if you hadn't."

At the moment, Sister Margaret seemed totally dejected. Her normally erect posture and self-assurance were gone. She drooped like a flower wilting in the sun. Looking into her eyes, I sought some response, but she said nothing, so I continued, "Sister Margaret, anyone can make a mistake. It takes a good person to admit it, but please try to be more careful."

Exhausted, I went home to a late supper that was especially enjoyable because of Mrs. Simpson's recovery. I feared to think what might have been.

The next morning I was seated at the nurse's station studying charts when I heard a commotion. It began with the spilling of a pail of water and was followed by the sound of a loud, scolding voice, which I recognized as Sister Margaret's. Glancing down the hall, I saw a cleaning woman mopping water in a frightened and inept manner. Hovering over her, Sister Margaret repeatedly shouted, "How can you be so stupid, so careless?" Each time Sister Margaret shouted, the cleaning woman appeared to be more distraught and her mopping more clumsy.

Perhaps I should have let it pass unnoticed, but the extra dose of insulin on the previous day had been branded on my mind. I walked down the hall and firmly grasped Sister Margaret's arm and led her to the room behind the nurse's station. "Sister," I said, "that was an uncalled-for demonstration. Yesterday you made a serious error, which, fortunately, you admitted. Now the cleaning woman has made an error too, but a very mild one. If you can be excused for a serious error, why should she be so harshly chastised for spilling a bucket of water?"

At first Sister Margaret appeared defiant. Her eyes narrowed and the corners of her mouth dropped, but she said nothing.

Fleetingly, I recalled my awe of the sisters. For the moment, I was silent as I considered my position. Although I was not Catholic, I had been kindly received by this sisterhood. Its members shared experiences of life and death with me. Their faith often sustained me.

Taking a deep breath to cover my embarrassment, I reminded Sister Margaret that she was a symbol of Christ, who stood for forgiveness. I expected her to challenge me. Instead, tears started down her face as her defiance melted.

After this event, Sister Margaret became on of my staunchest supporters.

THE LAST RIGHT?

Syringe in hand, I was about to enter Alice Murphy's hospital room.

"Wait, young man, I must go in first," spoke a gray-haired man of the cloth as he hurried up to the door. "I must go in to save her soul."

"I must go in to save her life," I said, blocking the doorway with my large frame.

"But her soul is more important than her life!" The man with the white collar tried to push past me.

"I think we can save both," I said, the large syringe in my hand dripping fluid as I swung around to face him. "So I will go in first."

"Oh, no, her soul comes first!" he shouted loud enough to startle two sister nurses passing by.

Of course, the religious man did not know what I knew – that right-sided heart failure is dramatically responsive to treatment. I was about to explain this when he seized my arm and blurted, "Listen, young man, I have no more time for your foolishness. Besides, I have a golf date."

I couldn't believe what I was hearing. That was it. I set down the syringe and forcibly removed him from the doorway. "Any more protests from you and I will report you to your superiors."

Mrs. Murphy was gasping for breath, her chest was heaving and the dilated vessels in her neck were pulsating rapidly. The obese woman looked as though she was ready to depart this earth. I could well understand why the nurse had called for the priest to administer the last rites.

The syringe I had prepared contained 50 percent glucose, which by osmosis would draw excess fluid from the blood. I knew it would work, but upset by my confrontation with the priest, I had difficulty getting the needle into Mrs. Murphy's vein. Her gasping didn't make the situation any easier, for the arm I was trying to enter kept moving with her rapid respirations. After several unsuccessful attempts, I began to worry. Should I have let the priest give Mrs. Murphy the last rites? What if she dies? What would the sisters think? I was sure that my conversation with the priest had been overheard.

In the midst of my struggle, my new friend, Sister Margaret, came in. "Can I help?" she asked.

"Sure can," I answered. "Hold her arm still." I was about to say "damn arm" but caught myself just in time.

My own heart was pounding nearly as fast as Mrs. Murphy's. As Sister Margaret immobilized Mrs. Murphy's arm, I entered the large needle into her vein and slowly administered the hypertonic glucose. Ten or fifteen minutes dragged by – minutes that seemed like hours – before Mrs. Murphy's breathing slowed. Gradually her heartbeat slackened, as did mine. In another half-hour, when the patient appeared to be relatively comfortable, I asked Sister Margaret to call the man of God.

He passed me without a glance or word. I left him to his task, also without a glance or word, but I choked back several unprofessional words with difficulty. Though it was not customary to be in the room during the administration of the last rites, I remained to observe my patient. Fearing the procedure might startle her, I hoped he would notice the change in her condition and perhaps find it unnecessary to give her the last rites. He proceeded, however, with all the grim reality associated with it, and the patient, apparently exhausted from her bout of heart failure, slept through it all. When he finished, the priest, looking straight ahead, left the room without comment.

I never heard another word about the incident. The sisters never referred to it, and the priest, for whatever reason, left the area soon after.

CHAPTER 12

DIGNITY and the MUSHROOM HERNIA

A late June hay maker beat down unmercifully as I sweltered in a suit, shirt, and tie. Most of the local people dressed quite informally in hot weather; certainly farm folks did. But I was anxious to look as professional as possible, like the town's two older doctors who always wore suits. Just why they did, I couldn't say, because the two middle-aged doctors dressed informally and were just as well received by the public.

Together these other four physicians represented many years of experience in rural practice. The attitude of all four toward the community was the same: concerned and responsible. Each exhibited a pride and competence in his profession not generally associated with rural practice. I soon learned that necessity demanded much of each member of this "medical family" and that it was common practice to share knowledge and experience. Consultations were frequent and at no cost to the patient. Deprecating remarks were rare, yet honest criticism was common. This was their way of life, and I felt fortunate to be a part of it.

It was so beastly hot in my office on that particular day that I was about to take off my suitcoat when the phone rang. "This is Dr. Collins speaking. I have a patient here at the hospital I want you to see. Come at once." Each word was spoken with deliberate care. After the command, the phone clicked dead. Mystified and curious, I went.

The hospital seemed cool by contrast to the outdoors and with its shades drawn and its insulating brick wall, it might have been. But the drawn shades made visibility poor. I followed the floor nurse down the dim hallway of the first floor. Four beds occupied by male patients cluttered the hall, for our 80-bed hospital was crammed with sick people. Ushered to one of the beds, I was brought face to face with the owner of the low, imperious voice, standing beside the bed. My mouth was dry and my palms were sweating. Why would another physician seek the advice of a young doctor just starting his practice?

He was a small, slender man in his late 80's who had retired 20 years earlier.

His hands shook with constant tremors as he seized mine in both of his. "So glad to meet you, "Dr. Frederick Collins gasped between heavy breaths "We have a problem here. This is Jack Hawkins."

The elderly physician's sparse hair was snow white. His heaving respirations suggested senile emphysema. Tremors possessed not only his hands but his head as well. All of his movements were slow and excessively deliberate, and his words, though clear, were protracted, making his speech as deliberate as his movements. Parkinson's disease had left its mark.

My initial conception of this elderly physician as arrogant appreciably changed as I perceived how he clung to the last vestiges of his strength in his concern for his patient-friend. Any resentment I may have felt at his high-handed command to come at once was quickly transformed into respect for his age and his pursuit of help for his friend, Jack.

Jack appeared to be about 70. He was completely naked; only his lower extremities were concealed by a sheet. In spite of this, he exuded an unmistakable aura of dignity that I became aware of at once. He acknowledged my presence with a quiet smile but without comment. Turning his head slightly, he searched my eyes and, seemingly satisfied, nodded a silent hello, then turned his head back. As my eyes grew accustomed to the dim light, I saw that Jack held himself rigid but uttered no sounds of pain. Then I noted a large mass, shaped like a mushroom, just above his navel. The mass was a hernia. It had a thick stem supporting a hood-like top that protruded a full three inches above the skin. The surrounding area was markedly discolored.

Jack had a typical epigastric hernia, a rupture above the navel. Dr. Collins had done what he could to reduce the hernia by manipulation, but without success. Anxiety for his patient-friend had prompted him to call me. I offered my diagnosis to Dr. Collins and then added, "Of course, Jack will need to have an operation as soon as possible." My words came out slowly, not because I was uncertain of the diagnosis, which was obvious, but because I didn't want to sound critical of the kindly old physician, who had waited so long before seeking assistance.

I turned to leave. "I must get back to my office," I said.

Dr. Collins, his head shaking more than ever, said, "No, no, you can't go. You will have to operate." In spite of his shaking, he looked at me steadily.

After a long moment, uncertain of what to say, I blurted, "The patient has not asked me to."

Jack raised his head, opened his eyes, and said, "If it's gotta be done—do it. I'd appreciate it."

I phoned the other physicians, all four of them, to find one to assist me. To my chagrin, none were available, which undoubtedly was why I had been called. And then as I realized I was entirely on my own, the weight of the full responsibility struck me. Had my many hours of reading, my days of observing, and my months and years of studying, prepared me for this? Should I ask this nice old fellow with the shaky hands to help me? This could be a difficult operation. Would he be a help or a hindrance? Rather than offend him, I decided to have him scrub up.

Within half and hour, we were in the operating room. After preparing the patient's abdomen, I infiltrated the area with a local anesthetic. As I started the operation, my elderly assistant inadvertently placed one gloved hand beyond the sterile area. His gloves needed to be changed. Then, shortly after he returned to the operating table, he reached one hand to scratch his neck. Again his gloves were changed. After a third 'break' in sterility, the operating room supervisor wisely managed to distract him while I proceeded with the surgical nurse as my assistant. Thus, I learned the priceless value of a capable surgical nurse—and of that nurse in particular, Mary Haasl.

Beneath the skin of the herniated mass lay 10 to 12 inches of gangrenous colon, partially telescoped. Next to it was a knuckle of gangrenous omentum. I cut these away, sewed the cut ends of the colon together to reform the continuity of the bowel, and then closed the incision. I finished the operation.

Jack's recuperation was uneventful. After three days, he insisted he could not afford to stay longer and went home.

Although I felt flushed with success at my first solo operation, my elation was tempered by the thought that I had been called only because no other physicians were available. But somehow I survived this indignity and Jack recovered nicely.

Several weeks passed after I operated on Jack Hawkins. One day, as I was about to leave the office, Peggy stopped me.

"Jack was here again this afternoon, " she said. "This is his second time. Each time he leaves 50 cents as partial payment on his bill. Don't you think it is a little odd to leave 50 cents?"

"Does seem strange. I wonder why he does?" I murmured and decided to pay Jack a visit. I had not seen him since I removed his stitches after his surgery.

I drove to Tony, a small town four miles east of Ladysmith. After several inquiries, I found Jack's house, a one room tarpaper shack. Jack greeted me as I stepped out of my car.

"How are you, Dr. Bill? Sure is a nice day, ain't it?" It was the first time I was ever called "Dr. Bill" and I liked it immediately. "Would you like to come in?" The poorly-fitted door squeaked on its rusty hinges as Jack opened it. "Duck your head. My ceiling is a mite low, too."

I surveyed Jack's single room as we settled into the only two chairs. The room was so small that his sleeping and eating accommodations were almost inseparable. A wood-burning stove provided heat for warmth and for cooking.

Not seeing a water tap, I asked, "Where do you get your water?"

"Come, I'll show you."

We went outside. About a dozen or so feet from the south side of the house was a barrel and just a short distance beyond that was an outhouse. Leaning against the outhouse was a stack of wood, cut and split for the stove. The stack obviously needed replenishing.

"My pump's under that barrel," Jack explained. "I have to cover the pump with gunny sacks and then put that barrel over them or the pump will freeze in the winter."

Suddenly, Jack turned toward me. "I'm feelin' just fine, Dr. Bill. I eat good and sleep good and don't have any trouble with my bowels. How come you came out to see me?"

"Just to see how you are getting along, Jack. Well, that's not the whole truth. I was curious to find out why you left 50 cents with my office girl on each of your two visits?"

Jack's eyes opened wide and his face grew serious. "That's all I can afford, Dr. Bill. But I'll pay you each week. You can count on it."

I wanted to crawl in a hole. I had not intended to humiliate him. As I looked at this man's meager living quarters, I was at a loss, wondering how to respond. Words finally came, "Jack, I wasn't worried about your payments. I was just curious, and I'm still curious to find out how you get to Ladysmith. You have no car and it is a good five miles."

"I walk. Done it for years, almost every week." Jack spoke with a touch of pride. "Sometimes, if the weather is bad, I skip a week, but you can count on it. I'll bring you 50 cents every week."

Blushing with embarrassment, I offered no further explanations and started for home. I drove slowly, still shaken by my bumbling conversation with Jack. How could I accept his money when he had so little? He needed the 50 cents more than I did. Then I recalled the first time I had met him, lying on a bed in the crowded hospital hall. Though in severe pain, he had not uttered a sound. Even though naked and hurting, Jack had been self-contained and dignified. It was clear to me then. To this man, fulfilling his responsibility to pay what he could was a need greater than any need he might have for the 50 cents.

CHAPTER 13

SMALL TOWN MYSTIQUE

It was fall and the air was crisp. The trees were aflame — the maple in red, the birch and poplar in gold. I no longer felt a stranger to the people or the land. As the days whisked by, I became content in my role as a country doctor, and as my practice grew, it reached out into the surrounding area. I discovered Ladysmith was ringed by smaller towns, much like the planets surrounding the sun. Like the sun, Ladysmith was the center, for it was the county seat.

I had arranged to give shots for diptheria, whooping cough and tetanus, and smallpox vaccinations in the basement of the Sheldon Elementary School. Though reinforced by sufficient voluntary helpers, the "shot clinic" moved slowly. More children came than we had expected, and quite a few were "allergic" to needles and required gentle persuasion.

As I gathered my medical equipment after completing the "shot clinic," the janitor approached me and said there were three men who wanted to see me in the next room.

It was already 11 o' clock and I was feeling rushed. Sheldon was more than 15 miles from Ladysmith, and I had promised to make several calls before lunch. I hurried into the adjoining basement room and found three young men standing shoulder to shoulder, eyeing me up and down as I approached them. Already upset by the lateness of the hour, I was really annoyed when one of the three stepped toward me and said, "We hear you're a good wrestler."

"Wherever did you hear that?" I asked.

"My sister brought my mother to your office yesterday, " the same man said, "and you told her."

"So we decided to try you out and see if you are really as good as you say you are," chimed in another of the three.

"You fellows have it all wrong. I did wrestle in college, but I was making conversation with your sister and mother. Your sister was telling me that her brother and two of his friends were the best wrestlers in the area. To add to the conversation, I said I had once wrestled, too."

"Well, we're going to find out how good you are, " the third young man announced, "...and right now."

I was in a pickle. I had little time and no inclination to wrestle. " Maybe some other time, " I said, with no intention of ever doing so.

"You're not getting off so easy," said the blonde one, who I later learned was Hank Caldwell, the son of the woman I had seen in my office the day before.

"No, we're going to try you out right here and now!" said the redhead, Bruce Hill, Hank's cousin.

"We're going to take turns to see how good you are," said Dan Fawcett, the brunette and the shortest one.

Actually, I towered over all three, for none of them was more than five-feet-seven or eight inches. They were farm lads, quite obviously in good physical shape. In the few seconds that had passed, I felt sure that nothing could persuade me to take on any one of them. I had summed them up — all three were in their 20's, appeared hard as nails and were overly eager to take me on. Although in my early 30's and still in good physical shape, I smoked nearly a pack of cigarettes a day and certainly didn't keep good hours.

"Well, come on, Doc," Dan said. "Strip down and I'll be your first opponent."

"Look, fellows, I've got to make some home calls. I'm already late. Besides, I know any one of you could take me, so I'll just be on my way." And with that I took two steps toward the door, but Dan and Hank stepped in front of me.

Bruce put a firm hand on my shoulder from behind and said, "No use arguing with Hank. He's the champ around here and he's determined to feel you out; so you'd better prepare yourself."

I was more determined than ever to avoid this confrontation. Sure, I was larger than each of them, not only taller but also heavier by at least 30 pounds. I wasn't afraid, but embarrassed. At best, the situation was awkward. Each one of them was determined to try me out. Perhaps I should just give in and get it over with. But I had always been a competitor and knew I couldn't do that. But then I thought, how would it look if I won? After all, I was so much larger than each of them. On the other hand, how would it look if I lost? So, with a boldness that I didn't really feel, I said, "Only one way I'm going to wrestle you three. I'm late already, and I can't afford to be much later. If you want to feel me out, all three of you will have to try me out at one time. If you agree to that, I'll strip down."

Hank looked at Dan and then at Bruce. Then he turned to me. "I think you're nuts, Doc, but if that's the way you want it OK. Just let us know when you're ready."

I took off my suitcoat, shirt and tie and stood ready in the center of the room; the three of them surrounded me, six feet apart.

"I guess I'm as ready as I'll . . .," I started to announce, but I never finished the sentence. In their eagerness, all three lunged toward me at the same moment. Instinctively, I took one step to face Hank, convinced he was the one I had to fear the most. This proved to be a blessing. Dan and Bruce crashed into each other head-on. They staggered and fell to the floor dazed. Hank tackled me with momentary vehemence, but I was able to hold him off. But when Dan and Bruce continued to lie motionless on the floor, Hank called a halt. I went to a nearby sink, filled the janitor's pail with water, and poured it over both their heads. They stirred and gradually got to their feet.

No one spoke for a few moments, then Hank said, "I don't know how you did it, Doc, but maybe we'll try you again sometime. No hard feelings?"

I dressed quickly and started for Ladysmith, still bewildered at the strange turn of events. What in the world had provoked those three to confront me? What had Hank's mother and sister said? Or, was this part and parcel of a small town's mystique?

I never did get answers to these questions, but several summers later I met my three wrestling friends once more. It was August and the Rusk County Fair was in full progress. My children, Christine and Billy, were about four and three years old, respectively, and both had begged me to take them to the fair. After a few rides on the merry-go-round and the tilt-a-whirl, we were wandering about aimlessly, just looking. Suddenly our attention was drawn by voices to our left. "Hey, Doc, come on over here. We want you to try somethin'."

As I turned my head, I noticed my three wrestling friends standing with three women. Near them rose a wooden structure with a small platform at its lower end and a bell 12 feet above. Remembering my experience in the Sheldon basement, I wondered what these three were up to. As the children and I approached them, Bruce, Dan and Hank introduced me to the three women, their wives, and then I found out why they had called me over.

"Come on, Doc," Hank beckoned. "We wanta see just how strong you are. Try hitting this and make the bell ring."

I looked at the wooden frame with the bell on top. It was supposed to measure a man's strength. A large mallet was supplied to hit a metal disc at knee height, and an indicator rose to supposedly measure the force of a hit.

Actually, I had never seen one before, so I stalled for time. "Show me how to do it, Hank."

Hank already had his sleeves rolled up. Taking a deep breath and raising the mallet high over his head, he came down on the metal disc with a tremendous lunge that started from his toes and wound up in his hands. The indicator rose halfway.

"Your turn, Doc," Bruce said.

"Why don't you show me, Bruce. Then I'll give it a try," I said, still uncertain of how this rig worked and how to go about it and somewhat embarrassed because my two children and the three women were watching.

"OK," said Bruce and taking a great swing he brought the mallet down thunderously on the platform supporting the metal disc. The indicator rose less than it had on Hank's swing.

I had been observing with great care. Supposedly, if the disc was hit with great power, the indicator would rise the full height and ring the bell. Actually, it seemed to me, if the disc was hit accurately with the center of the mallet, there was no need for strength.

"Your turn, Doc," Bruce said, and then Christi, my daughter, piped up, "You can win a prize, Daddy, if you ring the bell on top."

Fortified by my observation, I took half a swing and hit the disc firmly with the center of the mallet. The indicator hit the top, the bell rang, and the man to whom I had given my dime said I had won a prize.

"Beginner's luck," said Hank.

"Better try it again," said Bruce.

So I did and again hit the nail on the head, so to speak. The bell rang and I had won a second prize.

All three of my 'friends' looked at me uncertainly. Their wives made some flattering remarks that added to my embarrassment, but the real embarrassment came when the children and I got home. I had told Billy and Christi to choose the prizes. When they showed the prizes to their mother, I saw the prizes for the first time and was truly embarrassed. Each prize was a small mirror on which was painted a naked woman.

Interestingly, in the months and years that followed, Bruce, Dan and Hank, along with their families, sought my services as a doctor.

CHAPTER 14

A MODERN JOB

Most of us suffer the pangs of frustration. Fatigue and fright leave their mark. Yet none of these leave the indelible imprint made by tragedy. Wilhelmina was truly a modern Job, who suffered a succession of calamities that seemed endless as well as extreme. Her chain of agonizing experiences would have destroyed most people. But not Wilhelmina. Now well into her autumnal years, this modern Job has retained her mind, her spirit and her humor.

Mrs. Wilhelmina Vanderkellan came from Holland with her husband and four children. they came to this country with high expectations. Armed with enterprise and thrift, this family fit smoothly into community life. Herman, the husband and father, worked at the local mill; Wilhelmina worked at a tailor shop. Their command of English grew at an astounding rate but their Dutch accent lingered.

Two years had passed. Herman and Wilhelmina seemed content. Yet their high expectations still remained as goals to be met. They were ready to make the necessary efforts and sacrifices to reach them but little did they foresee what those efforts and sacrifices would be.

Suddenly the axe fell. The first tragedy struck. Herman developed general malaise, followed by a rapidly ascending numbness, starting with the toes. As the numbness proceeded up through his feet and legs, paralysis followed. Within three days, the numbness had reached his neck and paralysis his chest. On the fourth day Herman died.

He died from an extremely rare and ancient disease. It is chronicled in the Bible as "Creeping Paralysis." We know it as Landry's Ascending Paralysis; a disease sometimes linked to poliomyelitis. It's cause is poorly understood and treatment remains of questionable value.

Wilhelmina was in a state of collapse. Two weeks later she bounced back. Her spirit undaunted, she continued her regular work at the tailor shop and took on extra work to support her family.

45

A few years rolled on. Her older son, Jodi, joined the service. Gretchen, the older daughter, married and moved to a large city. Millie, the younger daughter attended high school. Denny, the youngest, was now in junior high.

It was Christmas. Jodi was on a week's pass from the service. His brief exposure to army life had precipitated Jodi's maturity. His mother looked at him with undeniable pride. That Saturday night the second tragedy struck. A train hit the car in which Jodi and friends were riding. Jodi was killed.

Wilhelmina VanderKellan was again devastated. But like Job in the Bible, this modern Job pulled herself up by her bootstraps. Her spirit, supported by her faith, snapped her back to face life once again.

A year later, Millie married and moved to a small town, some twenty miles distant. She soon discovered that her husband was an alcoholic. In time, Millie's husband overcame this with his wife's cooperation. Meanwhile Millie became pregnant, or so she thought. She expressed her delight to me in animated terms, yet revealed marked apprehension because of her husband's violent outbursts while under the influence of alcohol.

But Millie wasn't pregnant, as I discovered on her fourth prenatal visit. She had a reddish colored vaginal discharge. A cautious vaginal examination revealed a strange looking substance extruding from the cervical canal. It gave the appearance of a small grape. The uterus on bimanual examination (one hand in the vagina and the other over the lower abdomen) felt soft and spongy, not at all like a pregnancy. Dr. Alfred Beck, a dramatic and precise teacher, had referred to hydatidiform mole as the "grapes of wrath." Alerted by the memory of this vivid description, my suspicions led me to remove the "grape" from the cervical orifice. Another took its place and then another.

I was now thoroughly convinced that Millie had a hydatidiform mole. I sent Millie to the hospital where I emptied her uterus of a large mass of "grapes." But I could not give immediate and complete assurance that Millie would be without complications, for five percent of hydatidiform moles develop a malignancy (chorionepethelioma). This fact prolonged the concern for Millie, but fortunately Millie escaped this potential consequence.

Shortly after this distressing experience Wilhelmina sustained additional emotional trauma – a fourth tragedy. Gretchen, the older daughter, who lived in a large city, underwent surgery for appendicitis. Pathological examination revealed that the appendix was cancerous – one of the rarest of rare conditions. Treatment with radiation proved ineffectual. The cancer spread rapidly and when Gretchen was assured nothing further could be done, she came back to Ladysmith to die. She died in the Ladysmith hospital.

All this emotional upheaval was not enough for this modern Job; Wilhelmina developed her own physical ailments. She suffered from long bouts of backache which required long stints of traction for a ruptured lumbar disc. Finally persuaded that surgery offered possible relief, she underwent two back operations but never seemed to fully recover.

Wilhelmina continued to plug on. Though weary of her unending travail, though her positive attitude was interspersed with grave moments of doubt as each tragedy befell, somehow she carried on.

Determined once again to visit her homeland, Holland, to seek a nostalgic return to the place of her birth, she came to my office for necessary "shots" before departing.

We chatted perhaps for half an hour as she reminisced pleasantly. Looking forward to the land of windmills and dikes, she painted word pictures of the Holland countryside with astonishing clarity, garnished with a pleasant residual of her Dutch accent.

As she talked I could see the vast fields of tulips, hear the blades of windmills groan in the wind and hear the clop clop of the wooden shoes as she had known them in her childhood. At one point, I felt as though I had been ushered into her home and introduced to her family, each dressed in typical Dutch apparel; for Wilhelmina described them in such vivid detail.

"Patients are piling up. There's no extra space in the waiting room," broke in the receptionist. It seemed a shame to have this pleasingly descriptive monologue interrupted by such comparatively mundane considerations as returning to office work. However, the office nurse assured me, after a third call, that it was mandatory.

Wilhelmina's parting words were, "What can I bring you from Holland?"

In jest, I responded, "Bring me a windmill." Three months later, this modern Job returned. She brought with her a three foot high replica of a Dutch windmill, which she turned over to me with these words, " You wanted a windmill. Here it is."

Over the years I had tried, yet felt totally inadequate to ease Wilhelmina's sufferings. Just listening to her troubles may have helped. Somehow she managed with amazing endurance of her own. In truth, Wilhelmina Vanderkellan taught me more about facing tragedy than I taught her. It seems that one needs to face personal tragedy in order to learn how to cope with it.

CHAPTER 15

MY PIN-UP GIRL

Mrs. Rieper was five feet seven inches tall, large of frame and generously padded. She had eight daughters and one son. The latter was thoroughly and understandably spoiled. Her husband had died six years before, leaving the family with a legacy of good naturedness, but little in the way of worldly goods.

Yes, Mrs. Rieper was generously padded. Some would have called her stout. She was also generous with her humor and with all her moods, for when she chose to be dour, she was generous with that too. And when she was stern, she was generously stern. There was no halfway with Mrs. Rieper. All who knew her respected and loved her, however, and this included all her nine children

One bright, brisk spring morning, Mrs. Rieper slipped and fell on one of those abominable throw rugs (all of which deserve complete abolishment). Examination later confirmed by x-ray, revealed a subcapital hip fracture (the upper end of the thigh bone just below where it fits into the hip socket). I placed her in temporary skin traction while I considered proper long term treatment.

Even though overweight and with high blood pressure, Mrs. Rieper' s general condition appeared satisfactory. Her attitude was excellent. She understood the gravity of the problem and accepted it with dignity and optimism.

At that time (1943) the accepted method of treatment in our area was Anderson's "well-leg traction". Use of this method was considered best.

What to do? My training had included assisting at several hip "nailings," in which the broken parts are fastened together with a metallic nail inserted into the hip from the outside. This procedure offers the patient many distinct advantages. There is no encasement in plaster. Mobility is possible, patients can sit in a chair and move their legs. It permits better breathing, better heart action and all around better physiology. It also reduces the special nursing requirements.

What to do? I was a medical youngster, a new comer in this region where my colleagues had practiced for many years with skill. Would it not be best to follow the same procedure that they had used for many years, well-leg traction? Of course, I was impressed with the advantages I had been taught in my hospital training – the advantages of hip-nailing.

What to do? Even though Mrs. Rieper was overweight and had moderately high blood pressure, I reasoned she would be an excellent candidate for hip-nailing and a poor candidate for "well-leg traction." I was spurred into this decision by her optimistic attitude. My mind was made up. I approached her and three of her daughters at her bedside. I explained the two methods of treatment and my reasons for choosing "hip-nailing." They listened and asked pertinent questions and I went into elaborate details.

Their responses were enthusiastic for the surgery until I mentioned that Mrs. Rieper would have to travel to another hospital and another doctor. "Why can't you do the surgery here?" they asked repeatedly.

"In my training I assisted at many hip nailings and nailed a half dozen hips under supervision, but our hospital does not have the equipment needed to perform a 'nailing' ," I answered.

"Then we had better settle for the 'well-leg traction'," Mrs. Rieper replied and her daughters agreed. They were adamant and further arguments in favor of moving her to another hospital were all contradicted by: "She must not be moved. We three daughters can visit her regularly here, besides we want you to take care of her."

The last remark, "We want you to take care of her" was an ego booster but certainly was a poor reason to keep her in our hospital and put her in "well-leg traction" when I strongly believed she would do better with "hip nailing."

Once again I reviewed the hazards compared to the advantages, but to no avail. The women were immovable, Mrs. Rieper particularly so. As I said, there was nothing half-way about her. With this I left the room, informing them I would be back. I needed to think. I sat for a spell in the Doctor's Room, tossing thoughts of treatment about in my mind. Perhaps there was a way to nail her hip here at our hospital. With this in mind, I restudied Mrs. Rieper's x-ray's and measured the hip as if I was going to nail it. Then I went downtown and conferred with my friend Carl, who had a well equipped tool shop. I had brought three Steinman pins made of stainless steel with me. Normally, these are used for skeletal traction for a severely broken arm or leg.

Carl was a nut on precision. This fact was a great advantage to me, for he was deeply concerned to do an accurate job. He fashioned the three Steinman pins exactly the length I requested and sharpened the points of each pin to razor-sharp edges.

Returning to the hospital, I consulted a colleague who agreed to assist me, and he added a few suggestions of his own. For example, he recommended that we sterilize an ordinary carpenter's hammer, since at that time we had no such surgical instrument.

I returned to Mrs. Rieper's room to consult with the four pleasant but stubborn women. I repeated my opinion that "well-leg traction" was a poor choice and that my first choice would be to have Mrs. Rieper go elsewhere to have her hip nailed. This was again refused, so with reluctance I gave them my second choice:

I would do it here in our hospital, but explained that the equipment here for "nailing hips" was limited. The four unanimously agreed that "nailing" the hip should be done here and by me.

Mrs. Rieper went to the operating room the following day. Her attitude remained concerned but calm. She told me not to worry, assuring me that she would be all right – a reversal of the usual doctor-patient pre-operative advice. Her last words before succumbing to the anesthesia were, "I know you will do a good job, Doctor." I am certain her confident attitude was a positive factor toward the ultimate success of her treatment.

Details of the operation have no place in this story. Things went well. I placed the three pins at varying angles till the Operating Room x-rays revealed they were in satisfactory position. The wound was sutured closed. The patient returned to her room in good condition.

Two hours post-operatively, Mrs. Rieper responded with a smile and a feeble, "How did we do?" She began a series of minor exercises in bed that evening. The exercises were gradually increased in intensity and duration over the following days. In eight weeks she was allowed partial weight bearing with the help of a walker. In six months she limped with full weight bearing. A year after her original fall, she walked as before with only a minor limitation in her range of lateral motion. This gave her a slight swaying gait.

What a splendid patient she was. The nurses enjoyed her as much as I did. We were all taken in by her charm. Her children were proud of her. Her complaints were minor and prefaced by, "I hate to be a bother to you."

In the ensuing months her blood pressure responded well to medication. She lost weight, perhaps not enough; but she was an excellent cook and enjoyed her own cuisinery.

In time she faced another problem. Her youngest child, her only son, had grown up. He was getting married and leaving home. She would be alone. Together we came up with an answer which her children endorsed with enthusiasm. She would sell her house and spend the year visiting her children on a rotation basis. All would share her and she would get to visit all of them. By not remaining in one place, none would tire of her, nor she of them.

For many years, she made the rounds. The various locations and the various families of her children added spice and vigor to her life. She fared well. About every three months and occasionally more often she climbed the stairs to my office for a checkup and conversation. One or two of her daughters attended her on each trip. I came to know them all. They were beautiful women, inside as well as out. They were a tribute to their mother.

At eighty-five, eighteen years after her fractured hip, Mrs. Rieper entered the nursing home adjacent to the hospital. Unquestionably she was failing; but was still capable of getting about and in full possession of her faculties. In the following months, her memory gradually faltered. She lost a little of her weight. After a series of minor strokes, her speech slurred slightly, but she still emphasized certain words with her distinct mannerisms, such as cocking her head to one side.

Another year went by. I visited her relatively often. One day I noted she was making an afghan, a rather large one of two shades of brown. She showed it to me with some reluctance, deprecating her own efforts, stating that her fingers tired easily. In another month she was gone. A large stroke suddenly took her.

A week after the funeral, the same three daughters who had been present at the time of the hip "nailing" visited me. They referred to their mother as my "pin-up girl" alluding to the fact that their mother had often called herself, "Dr. Bauer's pin-up girl." They brought many kind and generous thoughts. They also brought a package which at their request, I opened. It was the afghan in two shades of brown that Mrs. Rieper had been making the day I saw her in the nursing home.

One of the daughters looked at me and spoke with great tenderness, "Mother made this for you. She was so afraid she wouldn't have it finished before she died."

I still use the afghan when I take my daily nap. Each time I use it, I am reminded of the extraordinary experience I shared with this unusually fine person.

CHAPTER 16

POLIO COULDN'T KEEP BESSIE DOWN

For three days a blizzard howled. Snow, driven by a blustery northwest wind, had piled drifts into beautifully contoured shapes, but had made all roads impassable. Travelers were stranded; some froze to death in, or close to their vehicles. It was a time of both fantasy and tragedy.

On the morning of the fourth day, the sun rose upon a world shrouded in white, a world ready to be at peace with the elements. The wind had ceased, the sky was blue, and the noise of machines and shovels filled the air. Shouts of joy belied some of the tragic results of the blizzard, as camaraderie joined all together in a common effort.

By early afternoon, I had dug my way out of a huge drift that had completely blocked my driveway. Meanwhile, a snow plow had made our street passable. I drove to the office between walls of snow, some high enough to completely obliterate the buildings that lay just beyond them.

As I entered the office, a tall thin man rose from a chair and cried out with obvious concern, "Bessie is sick. I don't know what the trouble is. Please come. I would have called but the phone and power lines are still down. I have a truck with a snow plow attachment. I'll drive you to my farm and bring you back."

"All right, John, let's go." With that, I grabbed my bag and we left.

John and Bessie Smedley were an interesting combination. She was a small, heavy-set woman, at least twenty pounds over-weight, with a merry disposition. John was a tall and could easily have absorbed her extra pounds. He usually had little to say.

Both were industrious, eager to improve their farm income and worked long hours to do so. They had two children, a boy, eight and a girl, six.

It was better than twenty miles to John's farm. As we sat in the cab of his truck, John told of his three day's of complete isolation. It had been a strenuous three days as he battled the drifts between his house and barn, kept his cattle clean, fed, and handstripped; and kept his wood-burning stove filled with logs. With his wife sick, he had to do the cooking as well.

Though the winds had lulled, John drove slowly, for drifts, some more than eight feet high, bordered the roads. At times it was like driving through a white tunnel, the walls of which would occasionally open.

It was a ghostly world. Even the trees were almost completely wrapped in ermine, as were the telephone and power poles. The familiar browns, yellows, and blues of houses were now white with wind-driven snow. Windrows of snow etched patterns everywhere, filling my every glance with wonder.

Had I been driving, I might have passed the farm, even though I had been there dozens of times. Recognition of camouflaged landmarks was difficult in itself, and my attention had been diverted by my complete enchantment with nature's artistry, which led to a thought of gratitude: Had I chosen to practice medicine in the city, brick walls and dirty streets would have replaced this incomparable world of white beauty.

John's voice jolted me back to reality as we turned into his farmhouse road. "Doctor Bill," he pleaded, "I'm worried about Bessie. It's not like her to stay in bed. She just can't move her legs at all."

On entering the farmhouse, I was greeted by the two children. They ushered me into their mother's room while their father checked the woodburning stove. Bessie, in her typically affable manner, made me welcome. "I'm so glad you came. Would you like a cup of coffee?" she asked. "One of the children can get it for you."

"No thanks, "I said and sat down beside her bed. Though there was anxiety in her eyes, Bessie was still her pleasant self. She whisked the children away with a few soft-spoken words, "Go on, you two. Your dad could use some help."

As the children retreated, Bessie filled me in on her troubles. Following some strange feelings, somewhat like a cold, she had developed a fever. As the fever subsided, her back felt stiff, like a washboard. She could no longer stoop, bending her back was almost impossible. Then her legs became useless, immovable. "They would not budge," she said, "and I lost all sensation in my feet and legs."

I was already convinced Bessie had poliomyelitis, but checked her carefully. As she had so clearly stated, her legs were immovable. Her story was typical of the onset of polio. Only a week before, I had diagnosed polio in a nearby farmhouse.

Polio had seized several of our Rusk County citizens in its devastating grasp. Though children were the most frequent victims, now and then adults and infants were afflicted. In one family a twelve year old, her four year old brother, and their grandmother suffered from polio. The grandmother lost the use of both legs and one arm. The disease had entered my own home, affecting one of our sons.

These thoughts ran through my mind as I turned to face Bessie.

"Bessie," I began, "you have poliomyelitis. In the early stages of polio, before your back became stiff and your legs immovable, rest might have helped, as well as extra liquids. You are now in the third stage. Hot packs and exercises might prevent further paralysis. I suggest you go to a polio care center."

With reluctance, John and Bessie accepted the suggestion. Bessie spent three to four weeks at the Sister Kenny Institute in Minneapolis, unfortunately with little change in her initial paralysis.

Meanwhile, as other polio cases developed in the county, public apathy towards vaccines was transformed into action as understandable fear entered most homes. A common foe, polio, brought individuals together in a united front. "Shot" Clinics were better attended and volunteer helpers for these clinics were more readily found.

When Bessie returned, even though confined to bed at night and a wheelchair during the day, her courage and patience grew to amazing proportions. Friends, neighbors and relatives offered generously of their time; but their efforts to help were graciously but vehemently refused. She could, she would, and she did manage without their help.

Bessie made the beds, cleaned the house, washed the clothes, cooked the meals and generally asserted herself as the capable mother of the family.

She found herself unable to garden, but managed to can many quarts of vegetables and fruits. Mending clothes, knitting and crocheting, plus liberal amounts of reading consumed most of her evenings. Under her care the family grew and the farm flourished.

One day her boundless energy and her insistence on not accepting help triggered an accident. Unable to reach an object while fastened to her wheelchair, she had tumbled forward, wheelchair and all, breaking both legs just above the knees. Inactivity had hastened osteoporosis, making her leg bones markedly fragile. External fixation, drilling pins through the bones above and below the fracture sites, and then casting both, relieved her of a long stay in the hospital. Within ten days Bessie was back tending the family with her usual concern and selflessness.

A little less than a year later, her wheelchair rolled down the church steps. The chair's brakes had not been set. This time she broke both legs just below the knees. I placed pins transversely through the bones below the knees and again casted her legs. As uncomplaining as ever, Bessie again accepted her plight and soon returned to take her due place in the household.

At times John came to the office to consult me about himself or the children, but it was seven or eight years before I saw Bessie again. John telephoned that Bessie was vomiting, had upper abdominal pains and was terribly yellow. She had been sick for three days. Knowing Bessie's usual under-estimation of her own problems, I went directly to the farm. Bessie was heavily jaundiced. Her urine was orange-colored and her stools clay-colored. These signs portrayed a typical case of common duct obstruction due to stones. With difficulty, I persuaded her to go to the hospital for surgery. Following surgery, Bessie was already champing at the bit to go home.

"There's so much I can do at home. The children need a mother. John has all he can do in the barn and in the fields," Bessie begged.

A few days later, I agreed to let her go home, if she would promise to return for dressing changes at regular intervals.

Bessie promised, and she did. The family had just bought a panel truck. A stretcher with wheels was rented from the hospital. Using two wide boards as a mobile ramp, Bessie was wheeled into the panel truck. The stretcher was then anchored to the truck by thongs attached to large screw-eyes fastened to the floor.

On one of these trips to have her dressings changed, a full realization of Bessie's selflessness and genuine concern for others struck me.

As I entered the rear door of the truck, I ducked and continued to stoop while changing Bessie's dressings.

Bessie was lying in a partially reclined position, her legs supported in their fixed position of flexion. As she looked up at me, her face broke into its typical smile. She reached her right hand towards me and said with genuine concern, "This is awful, Doctor. What can we do to make it easier for you? Stooping like that must actually hurt."

I looked at her face and noted her anxiety, but felt unworthy of her concern. Bessie was truly incapacitated by polio. She had twice broken both legs and was now recovering from biliary surgery, yet the single fact that I had to stoop to tend her made her feel concern for me.

Years have passed. Bessie has long since gone. Her generous smile frequently haunts me and I hear her selfless words, "What can I do to make it easier for you?" As always her words remind me that those who know pain and sorrow best feel for others.

CHAPTER 17

THE PRECISE MRS. GRUNDY

"This is Mrs. Grundy. I'll expect you this morning to check my ankle. Don't keep me waiting. I've some ladies coming for tea at one o'clock."

I was tempted to hang up without replying. I had already had a run-in with Lois Grundy the week before. She was a precise woman who expected all people to be equally precise and wasn't averse to making a fuss when they weren't.

"You certainly don't keep your appointments," she had chided. "You'd think a young doctor like you would want to get ahead. Do you realize I've waited 20 minutes?"

As I was re bandaging her ankle, she had rankled me further. "Young man, you should wrap that bandage counter-clockwise. That's the way my doctor did it in Chicago. You sure have lots to learn."

I was sure I had lots to learn, but ladies like her with time on their hands found it convenient to be critical. Didn't they realize that physicians found it difficult to keep even a modicum of appointments on time?

It may have been that I was overly tired. I had spent most of the previous night working on a stubborn delivery, but when she flushed me out of her house with, "Now, be sure you are on time next week," my dam of self-control burst.

"Can't say I will, Mrs. Grundy. Can't say I will." Then, raising my voice to a point that startled me as well as her, I shouted, "You'd better find a doctor who can please you" and I turned and strode off.

Apparently she had overlooked my parting remarks and decided to keep me on. While she presented a problem with her precise demands, she was among the few who paid cash, so the next time she called I decided to go, answering her request with, "I'll do my best to be on time, but believe me, Mrs. Grundy, my time really isn't my own." I hung up and went back to my immediate tasks.

The waiting room was filled with young men to be examined that day in 1942. I had contracted to do physicals for the armed services. It was a non-paying job, but one I felt strongly about doing well. Although I had been to Milwaukee to volunteer for the Navy, I was refused induction on the grounds that I was needed in Rusk County.

Going through the motions of examining these young men was in itself a learning experience. Each one reacted differently as each presented himself for examination, and each held my full attention till Peggy broke in on one of them. "We have a problem out in the waiting room. A bully is giving another fellow a hard time."

Among the 20 or so men left to be examined was one who was short, plump and shy. Each time Peggy went into the waiting room to bring in a new man for examination, she had noted this shy young man sitting alone in a corner with downcast eyes. On several occasions, she overheard a larger man with a powerful frame teasing this shy one: "Wait till you get in there and the doc brings out his needle – you'll pass out."

"What should I do?" Peggy asked.

By now I knew Peggy well. Something had stirred in her – her soft spot for the underdog. "You handle it, Peg. I'm too busy in here." Although I had all I could do to complete the examinations and make it to Mrs. Grundy's on time, I itched to see what my Irish Peggy would do. I left the door ajar and listened.

Peggy stood over the bully, looked him over thoroughly several times, and then said so all could hear, "You know, we'd better have you lay down when we draw your blood. You are just the type to pass out on us, and you are so big we'd hate to have you fall. Matter of fact, we'd better take you in now so you don't pass out here in the waiting room." With that she led him in and helped him onto the examining table, where he passed out cold when I approached him with the needle. Peggy purred contentedly. She had talked him into it.

It was already noon when we finished and I hurried to Glen Flora to Mrs. Grundy's. I knocked several times, but there was no answer, so I let myself in. Rocking gently, Bible in hand, sat Mrs. Grundy, reading aloud. Even as I approached she never looked up. It was as though she was mesmerized.

"I'm here, Mrs. Grundy. I'm a bit late but ready to dress your ankle. Has it hurt much?"

Words still trickled from her lips. Her Bible lay in her lap but her eyes were closed. Was she playing 'possum with me because I was late? I observed her frail figure, thin face, pointed features, and white hair. She was in her 70's but was as determined a wench as I had ever encountered. I didn't know what to do. At other times I had heard her reading her Bible, but her words had been clear and uttered in her typically precise manner. Had she had a stroke or was this an act to punish me for my tardiness?

For want of a better approach, I turned as if to leave and said, "I'm sorry I'm late, but I'll come back tomorrow if you want me to ."

As I glanced back, I saw her peek at me from behind half-closed eyelids. "Might as well stay and look at my leg," she said. "I'll be busy all day tomorrow."

After her leg was redressed, Mrs. Grundy, all five feet of her, stood up and smiled at me. "You know, I've gotten fond of you, young man," she said. "I've fixed you some lunch if you'll stay." It was the first time I had ever seen her smile.

Though I still had to make a home call on Paul Baker and was faced with a heavy schedule of office patients, it seemed propitious to accept her invitation. As graciously as possible, I said, "What a thoughtful gesture," and then fearing my choice of words might be misunderstood, quickly added, "I'd like that."

Mrs. Grundy led me into her dining room, and there upon a lace tablecloth was set out a full complement of china dishes for two people. At her insistence, I sat down. In moments she hobbled back from the kitchen and placed beside me a cutting board, upon which rested a freshly made loaf of bread. On her next trip, she brought a tureen of steaming vegetable soup and finally, and most unexpectedly, a large decanter of wine.

She settled herself into a chair beside me, folded her hands on the edge of the table, closed her eyes, and said grace in her characteristically precise manner. Then she looked at me and said, "All right, Dr. Bauer, get with it – serve the soup and the bread." With that, she reached for the decanter of wine and poured each of us a liberal portion.

After a few minutes of silence, she began: "My ancestors are a part of the history of this country. My grandfather was Pennsylvania Dutch and was a colonel in the Civil War. There was a second cousin of his who fought in the French and Indian War."

For the next half hour, Mrs. Grundy, fascinated by her own detailed recall, flooded the room with images of relatives who had served our country with courage and valor. I was moved by her earnestness and listened as attentively as I could, always aware that I still had to make a home call on Mr. Baker and get to the office. I was beginning to fear that she would reach back to the Mayflower in her discourse about her relatives when the phone rang. It was Peggy.

"The office is jammed. Where have you been? I called your home and your wife said you haven't been home for lunch and you haven't taken care of Mr. Baker, either. His wife called again and said he is in a lot of pain."

"I'll be along shortly. Do the best you can till I get there." Then I turned to Mrs. Grundy , "You've been most kind. I've thoroughly enjoyed the lunch and your stories, but I must go."

Mr. Baker's home was on the way back to Ladysmith. The old fellow had waited patiently, but his bladder had become overly distended. His wife had called the office again, fearing he would "burst his buttons," as she put it. An enlarged prostate had shut off his water. I slid in a retention catheter which drained his bladder and eased his pain. Mr. Baker and his wife were so apologetic for their impatience that I told them how I had once suffered with an over-distended bladder after an operation, and so I knew how he felt. After I showed them how to release the catheter clamp when he felt uncomfortable, I went on my way.

Peggy was right – the office was jammed, and starting and hour late added to the confusion. Even Peggy's calm exterior and caring attitude could not quiet the hubbub of anxiously-awaiting adults and restless children.

In the midst of this chaos, I entered one of the examining rooms. I was hardly inside the door when the patient, Therese Durkee, a good-looking woman of

28, suddenly stood up, put her arms around me, and kissed me passionately several times. I had heard tales of such confrontations but had never encountered one personally, so, of course, I was unprepared to meet it. Embarrassed and taken aback, I removed her arms from around my neck, stepped back, and said nothing. Only partially regaining my equilibrium, I excused myself and left the room. In a few minutes, I returned with Peggy and took care of Mrs. Durkee.

Later I told Peggy what had happened. "This must never happen again. Please, Peggy, make every effort to be in the room at all times when I am with a woman patient." I knew this was impossible and was not surprised when Peggy said, "How can I be in two places at once?"

Soon afterwards, I hired a full-time receptionist so that Peggy could always be present when I had to examine a female patient. This, incidentally, reduced my telephone confrontations with the precise Mrs. Grundy, but after she died in her sleep two years later, I found that I actually missed her aggravating preciseness and her irritating demands and often recalled, "You know, I've gotten fond of you, young man. I've fixed some lunch for you, if you'll stay."

CHAPTER 18

A RIDE in the HILLS

I had been so busy I had not noticed that my first summer had passed. It was September. People accepted me and I felt as though I belonged. The town no longer seemed a hodgepodge of buildings now that the streets and houses of Ladysmith were familiar. I no longer needed to use maps or to stop to ask directions for the maze of dairy farms, woodlands, streams, lakes and meadows had all taken on their separate identities. The barber was Jim, the druggist, Bob, and the banker, Fred. To many, I was 'Dr. Bill,' and that, too, felt comfortable.

As the days merged, one week ran into another. I had been increasingly involved in my work, too involved to pause long enough to savor the autumn smells, to appreciate the brilliant sunsets, or to hear the honking geese overhead. Even though I had driven many miles through the Blue Hills west of Weyerhaeuser making home calls, I had only incidentally noted the streams cutting bright ribbons through the fields and forests. So, on this enticingly warm September day, I determined to satisfy my craving to spend an hour or so driving and perhaps find a spot where I could sit alone and catch up with myself.

I chose the Blue Hills because they reminded me of New England, with its many farms among the lush rolling hillsides. Within half an hour my car was crawling over the dirt roads that wind through the hills. With my windows wide open, I was enjoying the freedom I sought. But as my car traced the road down into one of the valleys, suddenly I saw a man lying next to the road in obvious pain. I stopped and recognized at once that it was Tom Madison. I recalled that Tom was an independent soul who believed that people who didn't get things done were just plain lazy. He was a farmer who rose with the sun and went to bed soon after the sun had set. What had happened to him?

When I reached him, he told me. That morning Tom's wife, Amanda, had left for town as Tom took a corn-picker into the field. With his accustomed vigor, Tom hustled to complete the harvesting of the huge field of corn as quickly as possible. As usual, he was alone with his thoughts, the corn-picker, and his hustling. By mid afternoon, two-thirds of the field had been picked. Tom had not even stopped for lunch. He was enjoying the thought that the corn harvest would soon be completed and he would sit down to a good supper.

A strange buzzing and then a grinding sound startled Tom out of his pleasant reverie. Without shutting off the power, he reached down into the gathering-chain of the corn-picker, which had become clogged. The sleeve of his left arm became entangled, drawing in his arm at the elbow. Somehow, Tom managed to shut off the power. His arm was mangled, bone protruded through the skin, and blood spurted freely. Alone, half a mile from his farmhouse, he tore off a pant leg with his other hand and wrapped it as tightly as he could around his mangled arm.

An hour later, I arrived at the spot where Tom lay. Tom's arm was a mess. Bones protruded at the elbow and the forearm and hand were badly swollen, but the bleeding had stopped.

"Dr. Bill, thank God you came by," Tom gasped. "My arm hurts like hell. You know, it didn't hurt till just a little while ago, but now the pain is just awful."

I gave Tom a large dose of morphine, and when it started to take effect I helped him into my car and drove him to the hospital.

"Hey, Doc, are you going to have to amputate my arm?" Tom asked as he was placed on a stretcher. "How much will you have to cut off?"

"You've done a good job to stop the blood flow, Tom.," I said, patting him on the shoulder. "You can be proud of yourself." Then looking him straight in the eye, I added, "I'm not planning to amputate any of your arm, but I will need a lot of cooperation from you. To save your arm is going to take a lot of doing."

"You mean you won't have to cut any of it off?"

"That's right, Tom, but it's going to take some time before it's completely well."

"What will you have to do? I wanta know, Dr. Bill."

The morphine was working, but Tom's anxiety about losing his arm persisted, "I've gotta know, Dr. Bill. I need both arms on the farm. What are you gonna do?"

I explained that I needed to make several long cuts through the skin, parallel to the long axis of his arm.

"What in hell are you going to do that for? I'm not sure I want you to do that."

"Tom", I said, "your fingers, hand, and forearm are swollen. The skin is drawn so tight that the pulse in your arm is feeble and may soon be shut off entirely. If nothing is done, you will have a useless claw hand."

"Is that what the cuts are for?" Tom asked, still confused.

"Yes, as soon as your arm gets numb from the Novocain, I will make those cuts. They will release the pressure of the swelling that is restricting the circulation."

"What about the bones that are sticking out?" Tom looked at me anxiously, but it was obvious that the large dose of morphine was taking effect. Just then Amanda, Tom's wife, came in.

"Can't you save his arm? Please, Dr. Bill, can't you save it?" Amanda pleaded.

"I think so, but he will have to stay in the hospital for some time. I explained this all to Tom, but he's getting too groggy to understand or to sign a consent."

"You don't need that from us, Dr. Bill. Just explain to me what you gotta do."

I described to Amanda the delicate procedures I would have to do for several days to reduce the swelling in Tom's arm enough for me to set the bones. I asked if she understood.

"Not really, Dr. Bill," Amanda said,"...but if you think that's what needs to be done, go ahead. I'll wait outside."

Tom's arm was placed in traction and was irrigated every two hours with a sterile solution through the four incisions I had made. He received sulfa around the clock. A week later, when the swelling subsided, I sutured the median nerve, set the bones, and closed the wounds. Tom did well, returning to full-time work in four months.

Forty years after his accident, Tom stopped to see me. He brought one of his daughters, whom I had delivered years before.

"I just wanted to stop and see you." Tom said. "It's been a long while. Amanda died two years ago of a stroke. My kids are all grown and have their own families. Haven't been sick myself or I'd been up to see you."

We chatted for half and hour or so. As he was about to leave, he took off his jacket, rolled up his left sleeve and proudly exposed his arm. "I retired two years ago when Amanda died," he said, "but I've done all my own work for all these years."

As he spoke, I was reminded of his accident and of the enticingly warm September day when I wandered through the Blue Hills seeking to catch up with myself.

CHAPTER 19

WAS THERE SOMETHING MORE I COULD HAVE DONE?

We had celebrated our first Christmas in our home. Now the new year had begun and with it my second year of solo practice. I had seen many new faces, treated a variety of ailments, and learned some valuable lessons, yet there were times when I felt completely helpless. Even with the generous help and advice of four older physicians, going it alone was a heavy responsibility. Although consultations with one of the other doctors often relieved me of frustration and at times renewed my confidence, there were some situations for which I could find no answer, search as I would back through myriads of facts, accumulated in my years of schooling.

The liberal arts courses in college had widened my appreciation of the mind and soul. The scientific courses in medical school taught me much about the human body, its functions, and malfunctions. Training under skilled physicians during internships and residency in the hospitals helped me to assimilate and make use of many of these acquired facts. But some problems seemed to have no answers. Even the courses I had taken in ethics, logic, and philosophy were of little help.

One problem that really stumped me began with Carl and Freddy, two teenagers who had come to my office for physical exams required for a 4-H club outing. Freddy was fine but Carl was pale and short of breath. I discovered two of his heart valves were not working properly. There was no doubt in my mind that he belonged in bed, not up and about and certainly not doing farm chores – for Carl had rheumatic fever.

After the examination, I called Carl back to talk to him.

"Carl, I want you to take it easy, starting right now – today. I need to talk to your parents. Where can I reach them?"

"They are in Iowa for the weekend and won't be back till tomorrow night. I can't take it easy, though. There's lots of work to do on the farm. Freddy is helping me with the cows. We have to strip them, feed them, and clean their stalls. It's hard work...but why do you need to talk to my parents?" Carl asked anxiously.

"I want to talk to them because you have rheumatic fever. It could get worse unless you go to bed and let your heart get a rest."

"Oh, I'm all right, Dr. Bill. I just get a little tired sometimes, but it's from all the work I do."

That night I called Carl's parents in Iowa. I tried to explain the urgency of their son's condition over the phone. I stressed the fact that his heart and his life were in danger. Their response seemed indifferent. They were no more concerned about the seriousness of their son's condition than if I had told them he had a bruised finger. They would not be home till late Sunday night and would meet with me the first thing Monday.

At seven Monday morning, Carl's parents met with me. The meeting turned out to be no more than an exhausting exercise in frustration as I tried desperately to convince them of the terrible hazards of rheumatic fever.

"I have seen numerous cases of rheumatic fever and how it cripples young people," I began. "Carl has rheumatic fever; two of his heart valves are already damaged. That's why he gets short of breath and why his heart beats so fast. He needs complete bedrest to put less demand on his heart and to stop further progress of the disease."

"But we need Carl on the farm. He is a strong lad. He doesn't look weak to me," his father said, completely unconvinced.

"I know he is a strong boy and a good one, going to school and then coming home and helping with the chores, but you can't see how his heart is struggling. Because of my training as a doctor, I can."

"Perhaps we'll look into it further sometime." Carl's mother suggested. "Meanwhile, we'll see that he gets to bed earlier."

Carl's future looked dim, so I persisted. "I only wish I could make you understand how serious this is. Why not take him to another physician or even two of them and get their opinions?"

Carl's parents left, unconvinced of the shadow that hung over their son. Beaten, I returned home for breakfast, cross and moody, and aired my frustration to Gussie. I could think of nothing else but the miserable prospect of Carl's future. "Why couldn't I convince his parents? What didn't I do? Was it because I'm a young doctor and they didn't believe me?"

Gussie set a cup of coffee before me. "Maybe so, but you did your best. No one can do more."

"But my best wasn't good enough. There must be something more I could've done. At least they should have consulted other doctors."

"No, Bill, no one can do better than his best. It's when you haven't done your best that it's hard to live with yourself. His parents also have a responsibility to their son."

Several months later, Carl, who had continued to go about his daily chores, developed leakages in all four valves of his heart. He became unable to get about without a wheelchair. Again, I felt I should have been able to do or say something that would have convinced his parents. "Why couldn't my medical school and hospital training have prepared me for this?"

Again, Gussie admonished me to be reasonable. "You can only do so much. It was his parents' responsibility to act on your advice or seek other advice. You can't help it if they chose to ignore your warnings. You mustn't let it hurt you so much."

I suppose Gussie is right. A doctor can only be responsible for his part in any situation. But sometimes, as in Carl's case, how I wish I could have been more persuasive.

CHAPTER 20

ONE LONG MOMENT

Perhaps you have played tennis or golf while being observed by a professional, or gave a talk to the Lions or Kiwanis or Womens' Club with a professional orator in the audience. If so, you can appreciate how I felt during one long moment in the operating room.

Lena and her mother, Nora, were truly poor folks. After Mr. Bradford died of a brain tumor, both of them did domestic work five times a week for very small fees, barely sufficient to pay their rent and buy their groceries. After paying the hospital, doctor, and funeral expenses, there was little left except their home, a small three-room apartment with its sparse furniture.

Lena and her mother continued to come to my office for minor illnesses and once for a badly broken arm. They paid their bills without complaint, but always weeks and months later.

Once when Nora came to see me for some menopausal problems, I noticed her daughter's face was markedly swollen at the angle of her right jaw. I suggested I take a look. Reluctantly, Lena permitted me to feel the mass and finger the floor of her mouth. She had an enlarged submaxillary salivary gland blocked by a stone in the duct. It had been enlarging every day for five weeks. It was tender, painful and interfered with eating and talking. For two weeks, she had been unable to go to work.

After I explained that Lena needed to have the stone removed from the duct, Mrs. Bradford agreed they would think about it. Meanwhile, I consulted with a general surgeon and an oral surgeon in Minneapolis to determine what the total cost of hospital, operating room and doctor's charge would be. In both cases, the estimate was between $1,800 and $2,000. This was, of course, far more than these two could afford.

It was Christmas time. My wife and I had just been given our best Christmas present: We had the good news that our son, Bill, who had poliomyelitis, was left with only the slightest of paralysis – a foot drop. Thus, it seemed a natural thing to do – to give a Christmas present to the Bradfords.

I conferred with Sister Ruth, the secretary-treasurer of the local Catholic hospital. Ward rooms were $5.00 per bed. Operating room was $50.00 minimum. Figuring as closely as possible, she said the hospital cost would come to about $100.00. After a little more conferring and bartering, Sister Ruth agreed to make the total cost $55.00, provided Lisa stayed only three days and had no complications. I told her it would be my privilege to pay the $55.00 in advance.

Actually, I wanted very much to do this, blessed as we had been to have our son free of serious paralysis. I had never witnessed the removal of a stone from a salivary duct. I had removed others from the biliary system that drained the liver. I would use a T-tube to drain the salivary discharge from the submaxillary duct in the same manner as I used a T-tube to drain bile from the common duct. I knew the anatomy. The more I thought about the operation, the more my confidence grew. The day came. The procedure was going well. Just as I removed the stone from the duct, the operating door opened and a white-gowned figure entered. I paused and looked up. In spite of his white operating suit and the gauze mask, I recognized the man at once. His overly large spectacles magnified his always pleasant gray eyes. With his large ears, his cat-like approach, and his erect posture, I was certain it could be none other than Dr. Sutton, the chief surgeon of the teaching hospital affiliated with the Wisconsin Medical School.

Dr. Sutton stood behind the sister anesthetist and spoke softly, "I am Dr. Alfred Sutton. I understand you are Dr. Bauer."

I nodded. Dr. Sutton said no more then nor during the next 20 minutes, after which he left.

For an instant, I had swallowed hard. What was the chief surgeon of the Medical School Teaching Hospital doing here? Doing here, observing me? Why? What had brought him here?

Positive thoughts slowly took the place of negative ones. I sutured a T-tube into the salivary duct and made a hole in the cheek so the tube would drain outside the mouth. After dressing the cheek with large fluffs, I walked into the doctors' dressing room.

Dr. Sutton rose from his chair, set down his coffee cup and reached out his hand. "I am Dr. Sutton," he said with a twinkle in his gray eyes. "That was a nice job you did."

Soon we were engrossed in tales of trout fishing and I no longer had any residual of misgivings. Later he explained that he was visiting our hospital to determine if conditions were appropriate for students to experience rural practice.

I have often thought of this "long moment." It was a time when one wavers, feels insecure in the presence of a 'giant,' yet needs to continue with assurance. Perhaps my close alliance with nature had planted seeds of self-reliance, courage, and confidence that helped me in many a "long moment."

PART TWO

After graduating from grammar school, high school, and college, then finally, medical school, I felt like an experienced graduate. Never again, I thought, would I go through another graduation.

But I did, at least in spirit. When I finished my hospital training, my sigh of relief was balanced with a sigh of accomplishment. And again when I completed my early years of solo practice, I felt a deep feeling of accomplishment modified by a weight of responsibility.

Table of Contents

Part Two

CHAPTER 21

OUR OWN HOME AT LAST

It was crowded in our three-room apartment, and it wasn't because of Christi, the newcomer in our lives. We had accepted the limited space because the rent was low. Now that our financial situation looked more promising, we were ready to find more spacious living quarters. Thus, John Crawford's visits to my office, though unexpected, were timely. He thought I was a good prospect to buy his homestead.

John sought a price higher than I could afford. He tried to barter, appealing that this was the home where he had been raised. I assured him that his boyhood memories undoubtedly were priceless, but to him, not to me. On his second visit, he told of two buyers ready to pay more than I had offered.

"Then you should sell your homestead to one of them," I said. "Tell you what, John – take the house off the land, remove it completely, and I'll give you the same price for the land." Two hours later, I owned the deed for both the land and the house.

A lot of thought had gone into the building of the house, but it was now in disrepair. Plaster had crumbled. Some electric fixtures had been torn off the walls. Vandalism and the decay of age had left their marks. The second floor appeared to have been built as an afterthought. It might have been satisfactory for short people, but not for me at six feet, four inches. The doorway of what was to be our bedroom came only to my chin. This was in the days of the Second World War and building materials were difficult to come by. It actually took years of a little work here and a little there to make the house our home. Meanwhile, I enjoyed the increased space, and Gussie, like most women, the feeling of having roots.

We sat in front of the fireplace, the two of us, reassessing, looking back and looking forward. It was a special evening, our first evening in our own home, and we both felt it. So much had happened in so little time that our lives seemed short of breath. It was a golden moment as the rush of the past events tumbled into the present and mingled with our dreams of the future.

Our one-year-old, Christine, was asleep in her crib, a delight to both of us, but the memory of how close we had come to losing her lingered. Gussie snuggled closer and looked into my eyes. "We are going to have another child," she whispered, her blue eyes moist with joy. I leaned over and kissed her. "Wouldn't it be great if it was a boy?" I whispered back, well aware of what she would say.

"How can you say that when we have such a beautiful girl? As long as the baby is healthy, that's all that matters."

The fire crackled; a shower of sparks flew aimlessly about as a half-burned log settled into the glowing embers.

"Just think, we have our own home. Remember what it was like in Minneapolis, first crowded into that one room and then in the small apartment with the Murphy bed? Now we have a real home." Gussie spoke softly in tones of full appreciation for what we had as I recalled how well she had endured the broken-down furniture and cluttered little rooms of our past.

"It's gonna take a heap of fixin'," I said, "and even if we could afford it, we can't get the lumber because of the war. I've been to the lumberyard. The manager says he'd give us credit but he can't get the materials."

"Well, we can wait a while. We'll do a little patching here and a little painting there. That will help until we can really fix it up. Tell me, how is Peggy working out?" Gussie asked.

"Great. She's an enterprising girl, and I don't know what I ever did without her. The office runs so smoothly now I'm not nearly as exhausted as I used to be."

Yes, it was a time of great contentment, yet within me I hankered for something more. We lived in a land of forests, streams, and lakes, but I saw them only as I passed making house calls. It had been years since I had gone fly-fishing, and I drooled at the thought.

"Someday I'm going to cast a fly on Main Creek or the Weirgor River," I said, staring at the flickering flames as they licked a fresh log I had just put on the fire. "I've stopped and seen a few nice trout. I'd sure like to try to catch one of them."

"Be patient. The time will come when you can." Gussie gave me her 'what's-your-hurry' look.

I stood up and glanced out the window. Our hillside on the bank of the Flambeau River was bare of trees. Its nakedness suddenly seemed to be covered with evergreens, and among them I imagined a meandering stream. It was a bewitching moment of pure fantasy that held me in its spell.

"Gussie," I said, bursting with the enthusiasm of my wishful thinking. "What happened when Mohammed couldn't go to the mountain? Didn't the mountain come to him?"

"Whatever are you talking about?"

"We could have our own little forest and trout stream here on our two acres. When I came home it would be like being in the woods."

"You're a dreamer," Gussie said, slowly shaking her head.

My fanciful thoughts stayed with me. Within a week I had interrogated several farmer patients and found some who were willing to pay their long-overdue bills by bringing me evergreen trees, roots and all. For the next month, when I came home in the evenings, 12- to 15- foot spruce and balsam were in my drive-way. Planting them on our hillside was a chore that often ran well past midnight, but was a very pleasant one as I pictured the future – my own little forest and perhaps a trout stream.

OUR FRIEND JENNY

Jenny was strapped to the table and Peggy had started to drop ether. I prepped the abdomen and put on surgical gloves.

I had already opened the abdomen when I noted the ether was dropping too fast onto the gauze mask. Instead of reminding Peggy to slow down the drops, I said nothing. In moments Jenny stopped breathing.

Peggy looked at me and said, "Dr. Bauer, Dr. Bauer, Jenny isn't breathing." Tears rolled down her face as she realized that Jenny was gone. "What did I do wrong? Why didn't you say something?"

"Peggy, you were dropping the ether too fast," I started.

But Peggy broke in, "Why did you let me do it? You always told me before when I didn't do it right."

Jenny was a much-loved, gentle rabbit with unusually long ears. She was one of a half dozen rabbits I used for pregnancy tests. Instead of killing the rabbits, I put them to sleep and reused them on a rotating basis. I had also removed Jenny's appendix, a section of her intestines and a goiter for surgical experience. During these operations Peggy had been the anesthetist. Jenny was understandably a very special animal.

"Peggy, you've given drop ether for over a year. You should know how. Suppose it had been a human instead of a rabbit? This should be a good lesson. You are a smart girl, but you must watch closely every second while giving ether."

I was about to say more, but Peggy interrupted in an outburst of dismay, "You let Jenny die," and then in anger, "You let me do this awful thing to our poor Jenny!"

It was a dismal, almost silent week that followed. The usual cheerful banter and exchange of ideas between us was absent. Any conversations initiated by me were met with stony silence. Peggy's resolve not to talk to me unless absolutely necessary persisted.

After a week of this miserably cold atmosphere, I confronted Peggy at the end of office hours. "What is the matter?" I asked. I was distressed and missed the cheerful atmosphere we had had.

"You know what is the matter. You let Jenny die."

"Yes, I admit it. I did. But suppose you had been giving the ether to a farm woman at a home delivery, what then?"

"I just won't do it anymore, that's all," Peggy responded, her eyes filled with anger and her face set with grim determination.

"That's your right," I said, "but you know, Peggy, how much you like to help. You enjoy being there when a woman delivers. Actually, you do an excellent job, but while giving the ether to Jenny, you let your mind wander. The ether almost poured rather than dropped on the mask. I am sure you will never forget this experience." I spoke with deliberate care, for I recognized that Peggy's 'hurt' was additional evidence of her caring nature, her deep sensitivity for all creatures.

Peggy swallowed hard; her face broke into a half smile, her brown eyes looked into mine with her usual warmth, and she said in a questioning tone, "Truce?"

With the return of communication came the return of empathy. Exchanges of understanding and humor once again led to a united spirit in the care of our patients.

CHAPTER 23

QUARANTINE ON THE FARM

"Dr. Bill, Mom won't let me go to the high school dance unless you say I can. I'm really not sick."

"Your mother phoned me, Mary, and said you have missed two days of school. If you are too sick to go to school, don't you think, you are too sick to go to the dance?"

"No, I'm much better now. My throat hardly aches at all."

Mary was 16 and a bright high school student who lived on a farm with her parents and three brothers and four sisters. She was the only one with a sore throat.

Except for a slightly elevated temperature and a grayish-colored membrane in her throat, her examination was normal. The grayish membrane made me suspicious of diphtheria, so I took a throat culture. It proved positive for diphtheria bacilli. Mary had diphtheria, the only case of diphtheria I saw during my years of practice. The following days and weeks were some of the most difficult of my medical career.

Our hospital had no contagion ward, so Mary had to be treated at home. The farm had to be quarantined and posted. No one could come to or leave the farm. Arrangements had to be made for staple foods to be brought in safely. The entire milk production of this dairy farm had to be dumped.

The consequences of eight lively youngsters cooped up in the same house was bedlam, and it was questionable how much bed rest Mary actually got. To end the quarantine it was necessary to obtain three consecutive negative throat cultures. Before the first week was up, the parents were ready to throw in the towel. The whole family resented the frequent throat cultures and the quarantine. Needless to say, breaches of that quarantine were difficult to monitor. During these hectic days, my practice at the office and hospital continued as usual.

Each was a red letter day, but the tenth day was the most vivid. Mary's mother called in the midst of my afternoon office hours. "Peter is writhing in pain. It's his belly and he is throwing up. Please come check him."

When I examined Peter, there was no doubt about his diagnosis. Peter had appendicitis. I called the hospital superintendent, who, quite properly, refused to expose the hospital patients to potential contamination. Peter could not be admitted for surgery. It would have to be done at home, at the farmhouse. I consulted with Sister Angela, who ran the surgical department. She offered to get together the requisite equipment, a spinal anesthesia pack, and a surgical pack. I called another physician, who agreed to assist at the operation.

Darkness comes early in February. I made my plans and hurriedly made the necessary preparations so that the operation could be completed before darkness set in. But nightfall drew its curtains long before preparations were complete.

A firm mattress was chosen and placed on Peter's bed. A piece of plywood supported the mattress. The bed was then raised upon three wooden sawhorses onto which two-by-fours had been placed lengthwise. Facilities for scrubbing were easily planned, but proper lighting remained a problem. Since a spinal anesthesia would be used, there would be no danger of fire or explosion, but the farm had no electricity and the kerosene lamps would be inadequate. Then it dawned on me. I had a powerful searchlight on my car which I used to identify areas in the dark, especially when seeking unknown homes. I brought my car as close to a window as possible, spotted the light on a large mirror hanging on the wall, and centered the reflected light on Peter's abdomen.

Peter's mother signed the operative consent. Peggy prepared to monitor Peter's blood pressure, respirations, and pulse. I scrubbed and donned sterile gloves. "Peter," I said, "sit up and bend over, pull in your belly, and bend over as far as you can. It will hurt, but only for a minute."

Peter made a few initial quivers, bent over, and remained perfectly still. The spinal needle went in readily. Peggy prepared and painted the abdomen and then opened the surgical pack on a small table, upon which we had placed a suitably sized piece of plywood. My colleague scrubbed and I rescrubbed. We put on sterile gowns and gloves and began the operation.

The appendectomy proceeded without difficulty. The appendix was acutely dilated with gangrenous changes, but had not ruptured. After the surgery was completed I remained with Peter for several hours, then went home, relieved that it was over.

Peter was up and about long before I knew about it. In another three weeks the diphtheria cultures were negative. The family shouted their joy of release. It was not till several months later that I learned that the quarantine signs had kept outsiders from coming in but had not kept the insiders from going out. Fortunately, no other cases of diphtheria developed.

MY HEART OVERCAME MY JUDGMENT

Grandma Sorenson trotted into my consultation room, dragging her 15 year old granddaughter behind her.

"Anita's gotta have her appendix out. It's bothered her for a week," Grandma spoke with authority. She was forthright and stern and she took no guff from young or old.

"Let's look her over and see," I suggested.

"Waste of time, Dr. Bill. I know she's got appendicitis. My sister died of it, and she and I slept in the same bed. So I know."

"Remember last year when you thought your grandson, Jimmie, had laryngitis and I found a toy whistle caught in his throat?" I asked, trying to sound casual.

Grandma fidgeted in response, "I know Anita's got appendicitis, but I suppose you doctors feel better if you find out for yourselves. So give a look, Doc, but I know what you'll find."

Having been long subdued by her grandma's dominating influence made Anita a difficult patient, but after I gained her confidence, she admitted she had skipped several menstrual periods but repeatedly denied sexual activity. She was reluctant to be examined until her grandma insisted.

"Might as well, Anita. The doc's gotta be sure."

After examining Anita, I was sure she was pregnant, but when I mentioned it Grandma became livid. Sitting bolt upright, she presented a defiant picture, her loosely fitting teeth clacking in protest, yet the lines in her face conveying deep concern. With her eyes blazing, head held high, and her arms gesturing emphasis, she minced no words.

"You mean to tell me this child is pregnant? Are you outta your mind, Dr. Bill? 'Sake's alive, she's only a baby herself. She's just getting over playing with dolls."

"It's true. She's pregnant, Mrs. Sorenson; you might as well accept it."

"Well, then, I guess you'd better do an abortion. The quicker the better. You know she's my responsibility. Her parents separated years ago and both have left for parts unknown. To bring up two generations of children is more than enough for an old sow like me. I can't take on a third generation. So let's get on with the abortion."

Grandma had brought up eleven children of her own and was now burdened with Anita and her two younger brothers.

"Mrs. Sorenson," I said softly, "you will have to go elsewhere. I'm not going to moralize on what is right or wrong, but I will not perform an abortion on Anita. Please know that I respect your right to choose. Please respect mine."

With obvious disappointment, she looked me up and down. "But where will we go? You are our doctor. We trust you."

For several seconds we sat in silence, looking at one another. Then I said," I can understand your frustration. It is blinding your judgment. There has to be a better way than abortion. Let's explore other possibilities."

Apparently moved by my firmness, she agreed to listen, but I felt like a swimmer seeking shore against a flood tide. I looked at Anita, who sat silently, her hands clasped tightly in her lap. She looked like a troubled child unable to defend herself. I resolved to make a final effort.

"Mrs. Sorenson, you have eleven children, now grown up. You have three grandchildren living with you. Close your eyes. Pretend all fourteen are now living with you. In your imagination, take all fourteen behind your house, carefully choose the one you like the least and cut off his or her head with an ax. If you can do this, I will see that Anita has an abortion."

"Oh Doctor, you know I couldn't and wouldn't do that, " she muttered.

"Nor could I do an abortion," I said. "Under certain circumstances, it might be right, but not in Anita's case and not by me."

I saw from the look on Grandma's face that I had made some headway. A plan was beginning to form in my mind, the seeds for which, I suspect, had been planted long before by the irony of some people who couldn't have children and the many parents who had pregnancies they didn't want. I thought of families who had more children than they could support, of unmarried teenage girls whom I had delivered, and of young women who had come to me with infections and damage to their reproductive organs from back-room abortions.

In particular I thought of Walt and Susan Raddatz, who desperately wanted children but through an ironic twist of fate, though ideally suited for parenthood were unsuited for reproduction. For several years they sought to adopt, but their efforts had been fruitless.

Mrs. Sorenson was studying me intently. I felt her gaze as my daring scheme flashed through my mind. Would I dare such a plan? Would Grandma accept my proposition? Would I, could I, risk the loss of my medical license? At that moment of rash altruism, my good judgment vanished.

"If Anita were my daughter, " I began, "I would place her in the care of a nurse that I know. She lives on a farm with her husband and children. Anita could do chores and feel she is paying her way. The nurse would contact me whenever she felt it necessary, and I would go regularly to the farm to check Anita. When it was time for the baby to come, I would make a home delivery."

I paused and Anita looked up. Grandma still eyed me with a combination of suspicion and impatience but Anita, very attentive now, spoke up, "I'd like that Grandma."

"We don't need any more kids," Mrs. Sorenson interjected.

Glancing up, I ignored her interruption and continued, "I know of a couple who have tried for more than ten years to adopt a child since they are unable to have their own child. They are good farmers with a good money making farm and would welcome a child with great love.

"Anita would not have the mental or emotional anguish of abortion. The child would have care and much love. There would be no expense for you, no hospital charge, and no doctor charge. There would be no adoption agency or public knowledge. Both you and Anita would have the comfort of knowing that the baby would be well cared for."

Grandma and Anita looked at each other. Anita was evidently appealing and Grandma was absorbing the appeal.

"Doing it this way makes me feel good." I found myself whispering and wondered why. It is highly moral but highly irregular. In fact, it is illegal. I could lose my medical license."

"We wouldn't want that, " Grandma interjected. "Why would you lose your license?"

"Legal adoptions are set up to avoid careless and monetary adoptions. The purpose is to safeguard both babies and mothers. Through adoption agencies, babies are more apt to receive parents capable of love and support. Such a law reduces the possibility of babies being bought and sold. For me to arrange an adoption without going through proper channels is in violation of the law." My voice had risen but was still muffled as the realization of what I contemplated struck me with full force.

I was flabbergasted when Grandma responded without hesitation, "You must be crazy, young man, but if you are willing to take such a risk, we are too. You arrange it."

I did. Anita lived with Barbara, a nurse, and her husband, Bill, who operated a large farm. The farm proved to be an ideal situation for Anita. Barbara and Bill had even temperaments. They were good parents to their own three children, who ranged in age from two to six. They easily extended their love to Anita and kept her happily occupied with farm chores, washing dishes and clothes, and baby-sitting.

Meanwhile, I drove to the Raddatz farm. Susan was in the kitchen when I arrived.

"You still want a baby, don't you?" I asked. "I think I have a plan that will bring you one."

"What is it? When? How soon? A boy or a girl? Will it really be ours? Are you sure? Wait till I tell Walt. Oh, Doctor, after all these years, to have my own baby. I can't believe it."

"Hold on, Susan, Yes, it's quite possible, but first you and Walt must agree to the plan. Where is he, anyway?"

"I'll call him. He's in the barn," she cried as she ran out the kitchen door to fetch him.

In seconds both ran in and I told them of my rash plan. "Of course we'll do it, won't we, Walt?" Susan exclaimed, her face flushed with excitement. "Anything, just tell us what to do."

As I looked at these two and absorbed their aura of delightful anticipation, my resolve to carry out the plan was reinforced.

In the days that followed, Susan started the art of pregnancy deception, gradually enlarging her abdomen behind actual maternity garments. As Anita's abdomen increased, eighteen miles away Susan's abdomen increased. Susan visited the office regularly in her camouflaged state and I visited Anita regularly on the farm, following the same standards of pregnancy care as I followed in my office.

Months passed. During these months, Anita and Susan glowed. Anita glowed with the sense of peace and contentment she enjoyed on the farm. Susan glowed with the euphoria of expectation.

Meanwhile, my feelings ran hot and cold. Fearful of the potentially dire consequences of my involvement, I stewed. Happy with the apparent joy that had blossomed in these two, I too felt joy. But my apprehension never dispelled completely.

Taking my office nurse, Peggy, into my confidence, I told her of my imprudent decision to spare Anita from a likely abortion and to fulfill the maternal instincts of a deserving woman. Peggy worried and empathized with me. Somehow, sharing my dilemma with Peggy afforded me some relief. It was akin to exposing a white lie to an understanding friend. In truth, that is what this office nurse had been and continued to be for more than 30 years — an understanding friend.

The climactic moment was nearing. Anita was bursting with exuberance. Expectancy was at the threshold for all three of us — Anita, Susan, and me: Anita to be lightened of her pregnant burden, Susan to be released from her happy deception, and I to be relieved of my uneasiness about that deception.

The weight of my imprudence hovered over me. It was too late to retreat, I thought, for how could I go back on my word to either of them? I had no real choice but to see the pretense through.

In spite of my fears the entire act was a success. Each player performed her part with skill. Anita followed the labor instructions we had repeatedly practiced with unusual proficiency for one of her age, and at 2:00 A.M. on a clear night ablaze with a full moon, a seven-pound baby girl was delivered without complications.

A call alerted Susan who, having convinced her relatives that she was on the brink of having her first child, waited for me to deliver to her — her baby. Within an hour of birth, the newcomer was in the loving arms of her always-to-be mother and under the gaze of her always-to-be father.

Anita returned to live with Grandma. After graduating from high school, she went to beauty culture school and married a serviceman, moved out West and had a family. Then I lost contact with her.

Susan's love for her baby girl grew as the child grew. Each phase of the little girl's development was cradled with consummate care and concern guided by Susan's instinctive serenity, for she was a natural mother. Sharon, the baby, was all that Walt and Susan had hoped for. They often said, "She is the answer to our prayers."

Sharon grew up a happy girl and went to college. She later started a career in Minneapolis, after which I heard no more from her.

Two years after Sharon's birth, Grandma fell and broke her pelvis. I treated her at home with a sling made of materials from her barn. During frequent visits, we had much time to reflect on the deception we had perpetrated. Grandma often confided that, as stubborn as she had been, she was glad that Anita had not been aborted. Eleven years later, Grandma died, after a stubborn fight against cancer.

There was one more person in this deceptive act to account for — myself. Yes, the outcome was a very satisfactory one, but I still wavered between my gratification with the outcome and my nightmares with what might have been.

The emotions I had experienced were distinctly imprinted on my memory. Central to my thoughts was the resolve never again to permit my heart to overcome my judgment. With that, I made a silent convenant with God, thanking Him for my good fortune in not being discovered and promising never again to place myself in such a predicament. But I also expressed my gratitude that my illegal act had created such peace and joy in the others.

WHOSE FACE WAS RED?

Although it was January and well below zero outdoors, I flushed with embarrassment and I felt hot. As I sat on a barstool sipping a drink, the tiny woman who had caused my heat of embarrassment suddenly appeared and sat beside me, all five feet of her.

She looked up at me and smiled, her face glowing with gratitude she placed her little hand on mine.

"Thank you, Dr. Bill. Thank you so much. Please let me buy you a drink." Moments before her face and neck had been purple as she choked on a chunk of meat.

Still red with embarrassment, I found it difficult to face her.

"Thank you," I mumbled, "I guess I can use another drink."

"Don't be upset," she said. "I'm not. What you did worked. That's all that matters."

She must have noticed how red I was. I could still feel my blush, but with great delicacy she was attempting to ease my embarrassment, and I was grateful.

This was a cotillion night. Each month the local Cotillion Club held a dance at the local Golf and Supper Club. Everyone was dressed appropriately — women in long gowns and men in tuxedos or "Sunday best". A central dance floor was surrounded by tables, each table seating four to six couples. Some 40 couples were crowded into a small area. During the evening the din of the orchestra and the steady hum of voices had increased in tempo.

My wife and I were sitting with two other couples, trying to talk above the party sounds. Despite the orchestral din and the voices of the crowd, a sudden gasping behind me drew my attention. I turned to see this delicate creature gasping for air. Impulsively, I rose from my chair and stepped toward her.

I had but a few seconds to make up my mind what I would do. The Heimlich maneuver, a subdiaphragmatic pressure made with arms from behind, had received acceptance for releasing a foreign body caught in the throat. Blows to the back or chest and abdominal pressure were approved by some physicians but not by others because of the danger of driving the foreign object into the lungs. This delicate woman was like a child in size and weight. On two prior occasions, I had held a child upside down with one hand and massaged the front of the child's neck with the other. This released the foreign object.

Having made up my mind, I quickly grasped this tiny woman by the ankles, turned her upside down and massaged her neck towards her chin. Abruptly, a large chunk of meat spewed forth.

While still holding this petite woman upside down, I suddenly realized she was completely exposed to the crowd. With her dress hanging about her chest and overlapping my arms, she was dangling almost nude. With a quick move, I turned her back to her feet. In the same instant, I flushed with embarrassment and lit out of the room to the bar.

Sipping my second drink, I looked again at this fragile woman and noted her pale blue eyes and light blue evening gown. Her features were as delicate as her body. It had been an easy task to turn her upside down and massage her neck.

My thoughts raced back, reviewing past experiences with choking — .a four-year-old boy brought to my office with a toy whistle in his windpipe, a six-year-old girl with a peanut and chewing gum in her bronchial tube. Both were serious problems but neither was an emergency. Neither had demanded immediate action. But this one had.

During my college days I had taught swimming and lifesaving. Many times I had demonstrated artificial respiration: "Out goes the bad air, in comes the good air," I said as I applied pressure over the subdiaphragmatic area. But only once had I needed to use this method.

As an intern in Minneapolis, I had seen a doctor choke to death, a piece of meat in his throat. This event was particularly tragic because he was surrounded by doctors who thought he was having a heart attack.

"I am Nancy Hollis. Again, thank you" the voice sounded far away, but it was the tiny creature sitting beside me. Her voice startled me from my reverie.

"You are welcome," I said as I watched her slip from her barstool and reenter the ballroom.

CHAPTER 26

"LISTEN TO THE MOTHER, A GRANDMOTHER, OR A LOVING AUNT"

I bounced up the flight of stairs to my office, briskly opened the door, and shouted, "Good morning girls!"

"Good morning, Dr. Bauer!" both shouted in unison, and then Peggy added, "What's got into you?"

"It's such a splendid spring day," I said, beaming my broadest smile.

"Come on," Peggy persisted, her Irish eyes flashing disbelief. "Something good happened to you. It's more than spring fever's got you."

"Can't you tell what it is?" I asked, throwing out my chest.

"No, what? " Peggy asked.

"I became the father of a boy last night, and darned if my wife didn't insist that he have all five names."

"That's wonderful. We're happy for you, but it's a good thing that you're all keyed up, because you've a lot of house calls to make," said Ann, the newly hired receptionist.

And so began one of the most interesting days of my professional life, when I twice experienced the value of listening.

One of my pediatric professors had frequently said, "Listen to the mother, the grandmother, or a loving aunt. You will be astonished at what you learn." On this day I was made aware of what he meant.

My first call was to a farm, fifteen miles out of town, where I wrestled with a diagnosis for over an hour, making little headway. Calvin Foster, seventy years of age, lay doubled up in bed, groaning with upper abdominal pains. His pulse, blood pressure, and temperature were only slightly raised. His skin was clear and his lungs were normal. There was tenderness just above the naval but no rigidity, and neither his spleen nor his liver were enlarged.

I knew Calvin well and was familiar with his past history. He had no allergies, no diabetes, no qualitative food distress, no alcohol or drug problems.

Louisa, Calvin's wife, sat beside the bed, answering questions and occasionally offering information. We reviewed Calvin's symptoms. His bowels and urine were normal. He had eaten nothing unusual recently. He had not vomited.

"What's he got?" Louisa asked.

"Gosh, I don't know. I'm stumped. All I know is that he hurts and it's tender just above the naval."

"What can I do to make him comfortable?" Louisa asked.

"Keep a hot water bottle where it hurts and I'll be back this evening."

I got up to leave, and as Louisa walked me to the door, I said, "I haven't seen your daughter or her children for a long time. How are they?"

"Oh my daughter's fine. She and her husband just returned form a week's vacation. We took care of our two grandchildren while they were gone. The children just left here Sunday and now they're both sick. My daughter thinks they have the mumps and wants you to stop by on your way home, if you can."

As Louisa talked, everything fell into place. To Louisa's bewilderment, I turned and hurried back to Calvin's bedside. "Calvin, "I asked, about certain of the answer, "Have you ever had mumps?"

"Not that I know of," he answered.

"Well, you've got them now," I said. Sure enough, when I examined Calvin's scrotum it was decidedly tender, though not enlarged. The mumps virus had affected both his scrotum and his pancreas. Louisa had made the diagnosis for me.

My next call was at the home of the rotund widow, Florence Soper. At five-foot-two and one hundred eighty pounds, she looked like a bowling ball with a human head perched on top. Usually an incessant chatterbox, she seemed strangely quiet, except for her wheezing and the heaving of her generous chest. Florence had asthma and, as on two previous occasions, she was relieved by a "shot." Previously I had questioned her thoroughly about plants, animals, and the contents of her home. Since her answers had given no clue to the cause of her asthmatic episodes, I had suggested that we do skin tests, but she had decided not to have them.

Again I questioned her. She had no cats, no chickens, did not use feather pillows, had nothing new in the house. We went through a gamut of detailed questions. Again, I suggested skin tests. Florence said, "I'll think about it."

About this time, a figure only slightly less rotund than Florence's came through the kitchen door. It was Ruth, Florence's sister.

"I'm the one who called you, Dr. Bill. Those pills you gave Florence seem to help. She stays free of those asthma spells except on Thursdays. Why does she always get worse on Thursdays?"

It was an excellent question and also suggested an answer. "Where does Florence go on Thursdays? What does she do on Thursday?" I asked.

Ruth answered at once. "Every Thursday, Florence visits Mrs. Sears, who has been failing. She is an old friend."

"Has Mrs. Sears any animals in the house?" I asked.

"Oh yes, she has seven adorable cats," Florence said.

It seemed I had stumbled on the answer. "Perhaps you are allergic to cat fur," I suggested. "We could find out for certain if you agreed to taking the skin tests".

"I don't like shots. It's bad enough when I have to take one for my wheezing," Florence said, twisting her plump face into a distasteful look.

"Could you let Ruth take your place on Thursdays to visit Mrs. Sears?"

"Why? Why would that make a difference?" Ruth asked.

"If Florence is allergic to cat fur, she would no longer wheeze on Thursdays. Then we could be certain that she is allergic to cat fur and there would be no need for her to have skin tests."

With a little more persuasion both agreed. Florence became free of her asthma spells. Instead of visiting Mrs. Sears on Thursdays, Florence telephoned her every day.

Again I was impressed with the words of my pediatric professor:

"Listen to the mother, a grandmother, or a loving aunt."

CHAPTER 27

SUCCESS AND FAILURE

I had been in solo practice for only a year. My confidence and ability had increased, but more importantly I had learned there was no assurance that every diagnosis would be simple and every treatment successful.

In the midst of a busy afternoon, Hannah Robertson brought her four-month-old son to my office. He had suddenly developed periodic bouts of colic.

"He throws up after each feeding. He hurts, Dr. Bill, I can tell he hurts. He screws up his little face and then screams and I can hear loud rumblings from his stomach."

At the moment the little fellow appeared to be in no acute distress. His abdomen was soft and there was no mass. Hannah had been a patient of mine and I knew her to be reasonable and reliable. She was not the type to exaggerate or panic. The rumblings suggested intestinal obstruction, but examination revealed nothing.

I questioned Hannah in more detail. The infant had passed two semi-solid stools that day, which did not suggest obstruction. With intestinal obstruction, no stools are passed. Many diagnoses flashed through my mind, such as spasm or obstruction of the outlet of the stomach, but infants with these conditions have forceful, often projectile, vomiting but not intestinal rumblings.

Canceling the rest of my office schedule, I sat observing the infant for a long half-hour. There were no rumblings. An X-ray of his abdomen was not helpful. I obtained a urine specimen. It was negative. With blood taken from his heel, I made a blood smear and found the white cell count elevated.

I didn't know what to do. "When you don't know what to do, observe and do nothing." Although this advice came from my obstetrical professor, I discovered that it applied to most medical problems.

I arranged for mother and child to be hospitalized in a private room. In order that I might observe the infant first hand, a cot was placed in the room where I napped during the night.

At 3:00 A.M., Hannah awakened me. "My baby threw up all of his feeding. He was all right till the bottle was empty, then he threw it all up, every bit of it." She said, "What are we going to do?"

I needed to be sure of my next move.

Intussusception entered my mind as a possible diagnosis. This condition is a telescoping of the bowel, which creates an obstruction. But, if this were so, why had the infant passed two semi-solid stools? Mucous and blood are often passed, but not stools.

Hannah repeated her question. "Dr. Bill, what are we going to do? This is the way he was at home. I'm worried." Imploringly, her eyes met mine.

"We'll find an answer," I said with more confidence than I felt as I recalled a warning given by Dr. Bailey, a pediatric surgeon in Boston. I had read and reread it in his book: "Infants do not tolerate, for long, conditions that create intestinal obstruction. If surgery is needed, do it early."

I also recalled that, during my hospital training, I had observed five cases of intussusception. All had been treated conservatively. All had died. "If this is intussusception, I had better get with it," I said to myself, "but how can I be certain?"

My thoughts were suddenly interrupted by a shrill cry. I went to the crib and felt the infant's abdomen. There was resistance on the right side and a definite mass. Even without a stethoscope, loud rumblings were readily heard.

"Hannah," I said, almost shouting, "your baby has an obstruction of his large bowel, probably a telescoping of his small intestines into his colon. It will be necessary to operate at once."

"All right, Dr. Bill, do what you think is necessary." She seemed relieved that something was going to be done.

Within twenty minutes of alerting the operating room staff, the infant was anesthetized and we were ready to start the operation. Shortly into the operation, it became clear that extensive surgery would be required to remove the entire mass of telescoped bowel and rejoin the large and small intestines. I recalled another of Dr. Bailey's warnings: "Infants do not tolerate prolonged surgery of the intestines."

An idea came to me. Since intestinal motility passes feces down to and out of the rectum, why couldn't this same motility pass on this section of telescoped bowel, if I cut it loose? This could reduce the length and trauma of surgery. I sutured the small intestines to the colon, where it passed through the ileocecal valve, and then I cut the mass of telescoped bowel free. Miraculously, the mass then became completely free and I was able to remove it easily. After the caecum and abdomen were closed, the infant was returned to his crib.

Feeling tremendous relief from the uncertainty and responsibility of the last many hours, I went home to bed and instantly fell asleep.

A week later, I attended a clinico-pathological conference on intestinal obstruction in Minneapolis. During the conference, there was an exchange of experiences. My case on intussusception was well received, and I was encouraged to write it up for a medical journal.

I had never contemplated writing for a medical journal and was discouraged from doing so by the length of bibliographies I found at the end of most articles. Some years later, my brother, Dr. Donald Bauer, persuaded me to give it a serious try. After much stalling and rewriting, I submitted my article to the Wisconsin Medical Journal. It was published in their December 1950 issue.

I had enough sense to know that my article was actually the result of Dr. Bailey's sound advice, but when I saw the article in print, I was highly pleased. When I received a request for a reprint from a surgeon in Sweden, a feeling of accomplishment passed over me. But, as I was soon to be reminded, pride of accomplishment has no place in a country practice.

It was only a day after I received the request from Sweden for my surgical article when I had an urgent call from the emergency room.

"Hurry, Dr. Bauer, hurry. There's been a boiler explosion at the Marshall cheese factory. They are bringing in Gerhardt Juergens. He has been badly burned."

I arrived at the hospital only minutes before Gerhart was brought in. He was conscious but short of breath and spewing fluid from his mouth. Inhalation of the hot steam had severely burned the inner lining of his nose, mouth, throat, and lungs. He tried to talk but couldn't. His eyes communicated his pain.

Attempting to smile, he patiently lay on the hospital bed as I started intravenous serum replacement and applied Vaseline dressings to diminish blood serum loss from the third-degree burns on his hands, arms, neck, and face. Again he tried to speak but coughed and choked with each effort. I started suction of his mouth to keep up with the continuous secretion of plasma that threatened to suffocate him, but the plasma kept coming and Gerhart kept coughing and choking.

A sense of complete helplessness swept over me, for I realized that there was no way to stave off the continuous loss of serum oozing from the scorched lining of his nose, mouth, throat, and lungs. I could ease his pain with opiates. I could add serum to his system through his veins to replace what was being lost, but I could not stem the constant loss of serum. There was no way for me to put my finger in the dike.

Gerhart and his family were friends as well as patients. His children were about the same age as ours. His last name was Juergens, my mother's maiden name. He was a man endowed with a pleasing appearance and a likable personality. Under his management, the Marshall cheese factory had thrived.

As I sat by Gerhart's bed, watching him face a slow, agonizing death as he drowned in his own serum, I wondered whether we physicians ever get used to such tragedies. To the unnecessary deaths of young men and women, to the patients who are incurably ill, to the patients who die despite all we can do, to the babies born with severe birth defects.

My thoughts went back to the previous February. The roads were glutted with snow and visibility was markedly reduced when Betty was driving herself home from play practice at the high school. She missed a curve. Her car rolled over, then righted itself in the ditch. The driver of a passing car noticed the lights of

Betty's car shining into the woods. He notified the police and I was called.

When I arrived at the scene, Betty was gone. There were no bruises, no bumps, no scratches, and no lacerations. The chain she was wearing around her neck had caught on the gear shift and had strangled her.

Betty had been adopted by parents who wanted a large family. For seventeen years she had brought sunshine into their lives, even on the darkest days.

Betty's death had been so final. There was nothing I could do but pronounce her death. Gerhart was still alive, but I knew that nothing I could do would prevent him from drowning in his own serum. Again, I asked myself whether we physicians ever get used to such tragedies and their heartaches.

No, I don't think so.

CHAPTER 28

W.B.A.J.B.R.

William Bernhardt August Jurgens was a short man with a long name. He was my grandfather on my mother's side. My parents added my father's last name and gave the five names to me. One of my sons carries this name, which, in turn, he has given to one of his sons. This makes three of us.

Tina Rodalski entered the hospital with a temperature of 104 degrees and a pulse of 120. She was prostrate but conscious; her face was flushed, her skin dry, and her lips pale. Her swollen abdomen was tight and rigid, markedly painful and tender.

Tina was exceptionally attractive. Her pallor lent her an eerie sort of charm and was magnified by her contrasting inky-black, curly hair that framed her face. Although oriented, she was jittery and somehow I got the impression she was afraid.

Tina, who was 24, was born and reared in Poland. She lived there until she was captured by the Russians during the Second World War. The Russians found her to be a valuable asset and trained her for secretarial work. She spoke, could take dictation, and type in six languages — Estonian, Latvian, Polish, Russian, German, and English. Sometimes she had acted as a translator and sometimes as an interpretor.

Jerry, her husband, was 25. He was a local Polish-American, born and reared in Wisconsin. He was a farmer, a stocky six-footer, well-formed and ruggedly hand-some. At the end of the war, he met Tina in Europe. Within days of their initial encounter, they were married. Apparently, Tina had succumbed to Jerry's quick advances and physical charm.

This much I learned without too much trouble, but when I asked Tina about her illness, she hestitated as a look of fear washed over her face. Suddenly, with a gush of tears, came a flood of words: "Jerry and I met, married, and lived together for three months in an army camp, awaiting transportation to the States. When passage became available, I was pregnant. Jerry told me that an army official advised that an abortion be done to assure passage." Tina's speech faltered and then she whispered, " You know I'm Catholic, but I consented."

Tina wiped the tears from her face and then went on, "I had the abortion two weeks before we arrived in Wisconsin. When we got here, I developed a fever, was sick to my stomach, and had pains in my lower abdomen. It wasn't long after this that I vomited, had chills and a smelly discharge."

A decision had to be made regarding Tina's care. I explained that Tina had a pelvic abscess, requiring an operation. Her understanding of the situation was amazing. On the other hand, Jerry, who had never advanced beyond the fifth grade, became difficult.

"What do you mean she needs an operation?" She's not pregnant. She had an abortion in Frankfurt. She can't be infected. The doctors in Germany assured me she was all right. Just give her some pills"

And so it went. Even after demonstrating with drawings, I could not convince him that an operation was necessary. Tina settled the situation by signing an operative consent.

Before, during, and after the operation, Tina needed numerous transfusions. She had RH negative blood, so rare as to be present in only three to four percent of the population . In our rural area, this presented a problem, for blood banks were in their infancy. Fortunately, we had developed our own "walking blood bank." Many members of our community volunteered to be typed. They were listed by blood types along with their addresses and telephone numbers. When their blood types were needed, they were called. All told, Tina received 23 pints of this difficult-to-obtain blood. Another obstacle faced us. There were no antibiotics. Sulfa drugs were our only weapons to combat infection. Tina was given sulfdiazine around the clock. Her progress, though slow, was satisfactory.

Meanwhile, Jerry appeared at the hospital reeking of alcohol and the barn. He insulted the nurses and came at odd hours to visit Tina, often in the middle of the night. Covered with muck, unwashed, unshaven, he presented an obnoxious interruption to the nurses' routine. The nurses reported his actions and foul language to me and said they felt so threatened by him that they avoided him. "In fact, Dr. Bauer, he has often said he will kill you if his wife dies."

One Wednesday, my so-called day off, Jerry appeared while I was working in my trout hatchery. "How's Tina?" he asked.

"Pretty good," I answered.

Jerry raised his voice, "I want her to have specialists. Now! Right away! I want to take her to Minneapolis."

Before I answered, I thought of all the aggravations Jerry had put everyone through with his abusive manner. I thought of all that the hospital personnel had done for Tina and the many pints of blood given by strangers, some of whom had driven many miles.

"Jerry," I said as compassionately as I could, "your wife is getting everything she needs. There is nothing more anyone can do at present. You have no money, but even if you did, you could not get better medical care than she is getting right here. Moving her would be dangerous. But it is up to you. If you want to move her, go ahead."

"Are you sure she's all right?" he asked.

"Jerry, I'm not sure of anything. All I can tell you is that if this were my wife or daughter, I would sit tight. I would not move her."

Shaking his head up and down, Jerry disappeared out of the door of the trout hatchery. Ten minutes later, I had a phone call from one of my medical colleagues.

"Oh, Bill, then you are in town." he said. "There's a patient of yours here, Jerry Rodalski. He told me you are out of town. He wants me to get him a specialist for his wife."

Since I had previously consulted this physician concerning Tina's care, I asked what he thought and he agreed that moving her now would be unwise. He would tell Jerry so and send him back to my house.

I waited, sitting on the stone wall next to my hatchery. Within minutes, Jerry appeared. I urged him to sit down next to me on the wall. Then as we began to talk I stood up, frustration gushing from every pore. I was torn between anger and compassion. I was torn between shedding myself of further responsibility and saddling myself again with unappreciated efforts.

As I paced, I sized up Jerry anew. He was a well-built six feet of muscle. There was nothing fragile about him, save for his immature attitude. It was this attitude that I resented more than I was actually aware of, for suddenly, I found myself shaking him as one might a misbehaving child. No longer inhibited, my pent-up emotions were released in a full outburst of my accumulated resentments. Words I had often choked back now overflowed my lips.

"Jerry," I roared, "you are a first class S.O.B....." I shook him again and again. "Get your wife and get out of my sight. I don't ever want to see you again . I'll call the hospital and release her. Now, get the hell out of here!"

Immediately I was ashamed of what I had said and done, yet anger still welled up in me. "Jerry, you are an imbecile, " I said looking straight at him. "You are married to a fine, intelligent woman. She is twice the woman that you are a man. She doesn't complain. She had put up with so much from you. So have the nurses at the hospital. So have I."

All his belligerence was gone. Astonishment took its place. Perhaps he wondered how a physician had the nerve or the strength to shake him as I had. I wondered too.

But I wasn't finished. "Jerry, you are a stupid lout. You come to the hospital drunk. You are unwashed, uncombed, and stink of alcohol and the barn. You use language that should be reserved for men. You discredit all efforts made by nurses and doctors alike. On top of that, you have threatened that if you wife dies, you will kill me."

"I never said that.", Jerry muttered.

Anger recharged me. His threats had been made quite often. I was now really furious, charged up by his denial. "Get the hell out of here!" I said, and turned my back and started to walk away.

Jerry reached out his arm to touch me. His eyes filling with tears, he pleaded,

"Dr. Bauer, please take care of my wife."

I took his arm, sat down with him on the stone wall, and gazed at him intently. He looked so much like a little boy whom the teacher had caught throwing a spitball.

"Jerry, I might consider taking care of your wife again but only on four conditions. First, you must never again come to the hospital unless you are clean and properly dressed. Second, you must never be drunk or smelling of alcohol. Third, you must never use abusive language or criticize the nurses. If you don't like what is being done, come and tell me. The nurses will appreciate hearing good things. Do you understand?"

He nodded. But then I went on, "Jerry this is the fourth condition. Never again threaten to kill me if your wife dies. I didn't make your wife sick. I didn't abort her. I didn't have anything to do with it, and you know that. Is that understood?"

Gratefully, he agreed that he would live up to these four terms. And he did. It was an unbelievable metamorphosis. The nurses who had been timid in his presence, at best, did more than accept him— they showered him with attention. His wife, still weak from her infection, seemed to gain strength from this new husband. Unquestionably, her release from emotional tension helped her to get better.

The following week, Tina sat up for the first time. She sat by the open window. A soft whisper of wind played on her hair. The sun, following a week of intermittent spring showers, had drawn young leaves from their buds with the magic skill that only the artistry of God can perform. The same sun had unfolded Tina's spirit. She brightened daily. In fact, her spirit spread to other patients in her ward room, adding to their pleasure and hastening their recovery.

When Tina was well, she left the hospital. I recommended checkups for an indefinite time to assure she was completely free of infection. For three months she returned as directed. Then I saw her no more.

Two years later, Tina and Jerry came to the office again. Both looked happy and excited. Tina glowed. She had skipped three menstrual cycles. "Am I pregnant? Am I pregnant?" she asked.

She was, and her condition appeared to be satisfactory. Only minimal scar tissue remained from her infection. Six months later, Tina delivered an eight-pound, nine-ounce boy.

When it came time to sign the birth certificate, I was utterly surprised and profoundly moved. The infant's name on the birth certificate read, "William Bernhardt August Jurgens Bauer Rodalski." But more followed. Several weeks later, I was invited to attend the church baptism as the godfather of this youngster. Years passed, I no longer saw the parents or my godson.

One hot, humid, August day, 23 or 24 years later, a young man appeared in my office. He had specifically stated to the receptionist that he only came to greet me.

As he came through the door, I had a sense of recognition. He sat down beside my desk and offered me his hand. "I am Bill Rodalski, otherwise known as

William Bernhardt August Jurgens Bauer Rodalski."

Yes, something familiar about him had alerted me. Perhaps it was his chiseled features, his erect posture, or his solidly built frame. The more I looked , the more I realized he was a spittin' image of his father, a stocky six-footer, well-formed and ruggedly handsome. From him I learned that his parents had left the farm and moved to Chicago.

A few months before this visit, both of his parents had been killed in a car accident. He had always known why he had such a long name but he wanted to see 'the original," as he put it, for himself.

Head-On Collision

A large man-made muskie hung over the doorway of the tavern, an invitation to fishermen and hunters to stop for a drink and swap stories with the proprietor, Bob Holtman. Bob, a soft-spoken man, had a reputation as a good listener and a good storyteller. His brother, John, was the game warden. While John was busy in the woods listening to the pleas of sportsmen who had exceeded bag limits, Bob was busy in the tavern listening to the stories of sportsmen who were exceeding the limits of creditability.

It was Wednesday, my day off. Martin and I stopped at the tavern to have a beer. As we approached the bar, Bob greeted us, "Going trout fishing, eh? Yep, Grindstone Springs, I bet."

Martin laughed, "How did you ever guess that?" and then added, "How about a couple of beers?"

Bob sat on the barstool opposite us, his face grave. "Did you hear about Bruce's automobile accident?" he asked. "He left here at 2:00 p.m. He was going east on his way to Fifield and had a head-on collision with a car traveling west. The fellow in the other car was killed. No one saw the accident, but Bruce claims the other car was wandering all over the center strip."

"No, we didn't hear about it," Martin said.

"Well, Bruce is in a peck of trouble. He insists he was trying to avoid the other car. He braked, and then to avoid a collision, crossed the center strip to the other side. Just then the other car returned to its lane.

"How is Bruce?" I asked.

"He's OK," Bob said, "but of course he's worried. There are marks from his car showing that he was traveling on the wrong side of the road. This makes him legally responsible. The other car left no marks, so there's no proof it was ever on Bruce's side of the center lane.

"Poor Bruce," said Martin.

"Worse yet," Bob went on, "the police officer claims he smelled alcohol on

Bruce's breath. Bruce was in here just ten minutes before this happened, but he only had one beer. I'll swear to that."

Bruce was a rural mail carrier in the Radisson area, but he lived in Fifield, Wisconsin. He drove a Scout with the steering wheel on the right side to make delivery into mailboxes easier. Martin and I had met him at several trout streams. He seemed a very straightforward type and, according to Bob, Bruce wouldn't lie.

We were on our way to spend a day fishing, but the situation seemed so unfair that fishing lost its appeal. Bruce had taken only one beer, but the police officer smelled alcohol. No blood or breath tests had been taken. Bruce had crossed the center strip only to avoid the oncoming car, but was liable for traveling on the wrong side of the road. All of this flashed through my mind.

As I said, Bob was a good storyteller, but he was honest and sincere to the point that he watched his patrons closely and withheld drinks when one of them had had enough.

This set me to thinking. Something was wrong here, I decided. "What if the driver of the oncoming car had suffered an epileptic seizure or a fatal heart attack?" I asked aloud.

"What did you say?" Bob asked.

"I was really talking to myself, but what if the other driver had had an attack of some kind?"

"That makes sense," Bob said, "but what can we do?"

"We could talk to Bruce. Perhaps he could convince the Sawyer County Sheriff's Department to have an autopsy done. Bruce is your friend, Bob. You tell us what you want us to do."

Bob went to the telephone and called Bruce, but he wasn't home. Bob did talk to Kate, Bruce's wife, who asked if we would contact the sheriff's department. She would find her husband and meet us there.

About an hour later, we met — Bruce, Kate, Martin and I.

"Something is definitely wrong," I said, turning to Bruce. "The circumstances don't fit. Perhaps the driver of the other car had some sort of an attack. We have to convince the sheriff that an autopsy should be done. Then he will have to contact the dead man's family to see how they feel about it.

"But the law will have something to say about that," Kate said. "If there's a chance to prove Bruce wasn't responsible, we have to make them do it."

At this point, the sheriff came in and we explained our reason for being there. He was empathetic to our mission, but said if the dead man's family was unwilling it would be necessary to seek help from the state legal department.

The sheriff was clearly a man of experience and seemed to understand the situation. Realizing the need for urgency, I went further, "Trouble is, we must act at once. Would you be willing to call the undertaker and have him stall the embalming to prevent tissue changes that might disguise the cause of death?"

The sheriff went to the phone and talked to the undertaker who agreed to wait. Then the sheriff called the deceased man's wife, who willingly gave her consent. The autopsy was arranged and scheduled for 3:00 p.m. We were all in a state of nervous anticipation awaiting the results of the autopsy. Bruce sat with his face in his hands, then got up and paced back and forth. Putting her arm about Bruce's waist, Kate walked with him as he crossed and recrossed the small room. There was little for any of us to say, for our thoughts were all centered on what the autopsy would reveal.

Abruptly, Bruce stopped pacing. "I know I did the right thing. If I had it to do over again, I'd do it the same way. I was just trying to avoid him."

Kate put her arms around her husband and spoke softly, "Of course, Bruce, I know you did, and your friends do, too. That's why we're here."

There was nothing for the rest of us to say. We remained silent, realizing the situation was not of his own making, and we shared his anxiety to be proved innocent.

The phone rang. We all stood up as the sheriff answered. Our faces were all turned toward him. Bruce took two steps forward as if to get closer to the truth, his face marked with anxiety. Save for the slightly audible sounds at the other end of the phone, the room was hushed.

Abruptly, the sheriff hung up the phone, faced Bruce, now directly in front of him, and said, "The deceased man died of a heart attack. You were not at fault. I feel sure there will no further inquest."

CHAPTER 30

NO TIME FOR TESTS

Sweat rolled down my back. My shirt was soaked and my face dripped with each swing of the axe. My concentration was so complete I did not hear my wife call and was taken by surprise when she appeared beside me.

"There is a really urgent call," she stated simply.

Still relatively youthful and vigorous, I bounded up the hill to the house, ascended the stairs, and picked up the phone.

"My wife, my wife, she is unconscious. Come, Doctor, hurry."

"Tell me, when did she become unconscious?" I asked.

"Just a few minutes ago," he answered.

"How old is she?" I queried.

"Thirty-one," he said.

"Did she have any complaints before falling unconscious — headache, bellyache, chest pains?" I asked.

"She had a bellyache the last two hours, down low on the right side," he responded.

"Has she vomited, had a fever, been constipated, or missed a period? I hurriedly went through a short list of possible relevant symptoms.

"She missed her last two periods," he said. It's the first time she ever missed in our 13 years of marriage. We never had a baby.

At my request, he gave me his name — Tony Danvers. He lived south of Weyerhaeuser, 22 miles distant. Something had to be done to shorten the time-distance interval because I believed that his wife, Lois, might have a ruptured ectopic pregnancy. If so, she could rapidly bleed to death. At that time there was no ambulance service available.

"Can you lift your wife?" I asked.

"Sure, she's a little thing," he said.

"Pick her up, put her in the car, lay her on the back seat, and take her to the hospital. I'll meet you there. She will probably need an immediate operation.

Hurry! I said and hung up.

Before I showered, I called the hospital and briefed the operating room supervisor, asking her to have everything ready for an exploratory operation. I added that I suspected a ruptured ectopic pregnancy.

Within five minutes of my arrival at the hospital, Lois Danvers was in the operating room, still unconscious. She was in shock, her pulse feeble but regular. Her blood pressure was 60 over 0. Her color was actually as white as the sheet that covered her. Various signs suggested blood leakage into the abdomen.

The Sister anesthetist placed an ether cone over the patient's face and was about to start drop ether when I interrupted with, "Hold the ether. Give her oxygen instead. She's in absolute shock. She is almost gone. I doubt she'll feel anything. Let's see how she responds to the initial skin incision."

I made a midline skin incision. Lois did not stir. With urgent speed, I completed the opening and grasped the swollen fallopian tube while extracting massive dark blood clots. Between my left thumb and fingers I squeezed the ruptured artery and tied a stuture about it. Then with one snip of the scissors, I removed the tubal pregnancy and sutured the broad ligament over the raw stump. As I closed, I was told the patient had no blood pressure. Instead of closing each abdominal layer separately, I closed all abdominal layers together with a through and through suture of silk.

When I closed Lois's abdomen, it was less than 15 minutes since the operation began. Although there was no discernible blood pressure, we continued to give the patient oxygen, for she had respirations, rapid but shallow. She had barely stirred during the operation.

The patient's only chance depended on a blood transfusion, but so far no donor had been found. Just then Father Paul Parker appeared, called to give Mrs. Danvers the last rites.

I knew Father Paul well. "Father," I pleaded, "let me draw your blood for this lady."

"But we don't know if Father has the right type," Sister Mary intervened.

"She will die if she doesn't get blood," I exclaimed. "What difference would it make if she goes to heaven with the wrong blood or the right blood in her?"

Father Paul, bless him, acquiesced. He had large veins in his arm. As I entered the needle, I joshed, "Father, I expect to get Blatz beer out of you."

"Dr. Bauer, that's no way to talk at a moment like this. You should be ashamed," scolded the operating room supervisor.

Father Paul was an understanding soul. He appreciated that I was trying to relieve the severe tension that pervaded all of us. He responded spontaneously, "Yes, and I think you will get some Leinenkugels too."

Father's blood was drawn out of his veins in minutes and was soon seeping into Lois. Ten minutes later her blood pressure was perceptible but feeble. A half hour passed. Lois moved an arm, then opened her eyes, then closed them again.

All of us remained in the operating room. The tension had been broken, but our concern remained. Lois was still alive. She had undergone an operation without anesthesia and a blood transfusion without cross matching. We exchanged looks, silently aware that we were united in a special effort.

"Look," Sister Elizabeth whispered. "She moved again."

Her blood pressure is 60 over 0," the anesthetist said with a smile.

"Her color is better, whispered Father Paul. "My Irish blood must be good for her."

"God be praised," said the operating nurse.

Two hours passed as we watched and prayed. Lois muttered her first words as her blood pressure rose to 70 over 20. Meanwhile, two other pints of blood had been drawn, cross matched and started.

When her blood pressure rose to 80 over 40, Lois appeared to be in pain. A mild hypnotic was given and she was taken to a private room.

Lois Danvers lived and returned home. It was almost exactly a year later when Mr. Danvers called again.

"You remember my wife. She's got pains in her belly again and feels like she's going to pass out. She has skipped two monthlies. Should I bring her to the hospital?"

"By all means," I responded.

Lois had another ectopic pregnancy in the other tube. There was no special drama. This time she was not unconscious. She had anesthesia and required only one blood transfusion, which was cross matched.

Mr. and Mrs. Danvers lived on their farm for many years. They had always wanted children. Knowing with certainty that this was now impossible, they managed to adopt three and proved to be good parents.

No time for tests, but the Lord was with us.

CHAPTER 31

"THE LORD HELPS THOSE WHO HELP THEMSELVES"

After a good night's sleep, I felt vigorous and confident, ready to face whatever trials the day would bring. An unusually hearty breakfast fueled my energy. As I left the house for the hospital, I glanced at my assembled family with pride.

Even the miserably raw day did not deflate my spirits, nor did the usually down-in-the-mouth Nora Glidden in the business office at the hospital. Somehow I gave Mrs. Glidden my warmest smile as I passed, for I felt ready to challenge the world.

My patient, Esther Norton, a dear, sweet lady, was markedly jaundiced. Her x-rays had revealed nothing, but her history and physical exam strongly indicated blockage of her common duct with biliary gallstones. While scrubbing for the operation, my colleague and I rehashed other diagnostic possibilities such as cancer of the pancreas or of the common bile duct. However, we decided it was probably blockage by stones.

Soon after opening her abdomen, our diagnosis was confirmed. Mrs. Norton's common duct was loaded with stones, as were her hepatic ducts. I made an incision into the common duct, which was distended to four time its normal size. Many stones of varied sizes were removed but because of the presence of a thick, sticky bile muck, the stones emerged with great difficulty. Using a syringe, I proceeded to wash out the stones and muck with sterile water. The process reminded me of washing out a downspout matted down with needles and leaves.

Gradually more stones and muck reluctantly emerged, but despite repeated washings, the job appeared endless. The duct remained glutted with this sticky mass of stones and muck.

Twenty minutes passed. Frustration and a sensation of physical and emotional exhaustian gripped me. My high spirits abruptly left me and I felt powerless to combat an overwhelming feeling, not of ineptness, but of being ineffectual. A prayer, "God help me," came to my mind but not to my lips.

During that moment of frustration, vivid images flashed through my mind. Two years before, on the day before Christmas, I had been called to Esther's home. I saw again the marked neatness of the bare rooms with their uncarpeted floors. I saw again her husband's quiet concern and Esther's courage in the face of excruciating pain. I recalled her mulish refusal to go the hospital despite my earnest entreaties, her composure during the shot I gave her and the slumber she sank into before I left.

And then there flashed through my mind a day after Christmas, a year later, when I was again called to that bare but neat house. I recalled the same alarmed but quiet husband and the same stubborn but pain-filled wife. Again, she refused hospitalization and was relieved by the shot I gave her.

A year later, I saw her for the third time. It was the day after New Year's. Even in the dimly lit room, Effie's dark jaundice was readily discernible. The whites of her eyes were deep yellow but could not hide the intense pain she endured. Her liver was enlarged. Her urine was dark orange and her bowels clay-colored.

Although she remonstrated with me heatedly, I insisted on hospitalization, telling her she would have to get another doctor unless she promised to go, for her condition was life-threatening.

Only seconds passed during this reverie, but those memories reinforced my sense of urgency without easing my frustration. I looked over at the two doctors who were assisting, as if for help. I searched the eyes of the anesthetist. Not one of them seemed to share or even be aware of my frustration, but the answer to my silent prayer came almost instantly: "God helps those who help themselves."

As the truth of this struck me, new vitality, fresh enthusiasm and renewed assurance filled me and seemed to sharpen my imagination. Once again, the analogy of a downspout flashed before me, a spout impacted with wet decaying needles and leaves. This analogy suggested that Esther's glutted common duct could be better cleaned by flushing from both ends. I immediately made an incision in the duodenum into which the common duct emptied. This exposed the outlet of the common duct and made possible repeated washings through both openings. Soon the blockage was relieved. I inserted a T-tube into the common duct, sutured the duodenal incision and closed the abdominal wall. The operation was complete and the patient was returned to her room.

Esther's recovery was remarkably free of problems. Many stones of all sizes filled an olive jar at Esther's bedside, daily reminders of her pain and discomfort and of my struggles with frustration. Two weeks later, Esther went home, her T-tube still in place. A month later, it was removed.

Ten years after this operation, Esther's husband died of a heart attack. Esther continued well and spry until she was 78 when I had to remove her left breast because of a malignancy.

Another ten years went by. It was 1980 when Esther called again. My office had been closed for several years. I was seeing only former patients and only by appointment. Esther's voice was unmistakably clear in tone and as warm as usual, but with a touch of her old defiance as she insisted on an appointment I could not keep. We finally settled, however on a mutually agreeable time.

Now 88, Esther had unhesitatingly walked a mile to see me. Her bearing was erect and her gait that of a much younger woman. Her clothes still conveyed the combined impression of thrift, good taste, and personal care. Her hair, with only streaks of gray, was neatly combed. Esther smiled frequently as she spoke of her good health, her good luck and her work. She regularly mowed her own lawn and kept her small garden weeded. She had come to see me for a checkup.

I discovered a minor cardiac arrythmia, but saw no purpose in mentioning this to her. Other than this, Esther was in excellent condition.

"OH, YEAH? YOU SHOULD TRY IT SOME TIME!"

Statistics are usually dull and their reliability often questionable. Yet, consciously or unconsciously I was gathering data to discover, "How really painful is a woman's delivery of her baby?"

After delivering several hundred babies, my accumulated data appeared quite imposing to me: The first child is usually the most painful but the presentation (the particular position of the infant at the time of birth) makes a difference. For example, a breech (bottom end first) is usually more painful than head first. A large baby, a monstrosity, or twins can cause more pain.

As if to cast doubt on my personal research, I discovered some deliveries are almost completely without pain. In fact, one mother, whom I delivered of five children, insisted she never had any pain. For a time this brought my research to an abrupt halt, but then my curiosity got the best of me and I began to discover other facts — not earth-shaking, but valuable to me: Some women have a low threshhold for pain and accept pain with more difficulty. I also found that some women have a heightened sense of pain intensified by fear. Even if that fear is unwarranted, their fear will heighten their pain. Unthinking friends and neighbors may stimulate these fears by telling ghastly stories to the expectant mother. Unbelievably, even the mother of the expectant woman, is, at times, thoughtless enough to recite horror stories of her own labor experiences. Such stories are often exaggerated and dramatized by time or a hunger for attention.

These facts pointed out that my responsibilities were not all technical and mechanical. It was up to me to give the expectant mother assurances and reassurance during her prenatal care that would evolve into a confident communication between us at the time of delivery. When that time came, it was also important not to permit loud and unnecessary noises in the delivery room to disrupt that communication. On a few occasions, I found it necessary to banish noisy nurses.

My research, stimulated by my curiosity, had been beneficial but had not answered my original questions, "How really painful is a woman's delivery of her baby?"

One particularly memorable night, the answer came quite unexpectedly. A very blonde Swedish-American woman of 32 entered the hospital in labor. This was her fourth pregnancy. She had three living children, was in excellent condition, and was not at all apprehensive. She had experienced three normal pregnancies and three normal deliveries. This delivery promised to be normal as well. Her baby appeared to be about seven pounds, certainly not large. In fact, she previously delivered one baby weighing eight pounds.

Her labor contractions increased in severity and frequency as labor began in earnest. She responded perfectly to my requests to hold her breath and push with each pain. She relaxed when labor contractions ceased and pushed when labor contractions reoccurred. Our teamwork was accomplished with a certain finesse. Progress was definite.

The anesthetist was a Sister of the Servants of Mary, always reliable and definitely responsive to suggestion. Together, we made a good team and seemed to make the patient feel relaxed, confident and secure. But, in spite of this patient's feeling of security, she often cried out loudly. Sister consoled her with, "Now, now — it's all right. You'll be fine."

As labor progressed, the patient continued to react beautifully to instructions, although partially submerged by whiffs of ether. Her outcries, however, grew louder and more vehement and seemed stronger than her labor warranted. Again, Sister patting the patient's cheeks, attempted to soothe her with, "You'll soon be finished. The baby is almost here."

It was clear that the patient was in no difficulty. Labor was progressing normally. The patient continued to respond precisely to each suggestion. In fact, labor was almost complete. The baby's head was crowning — almost ready to emerge.

And then, like some shot-putters who let out a loud grunt with each superlative effort on heaving the shot, the expectant mother was punctuating each of her superlative efforts with a loud cry. To the Sister, the patient's protests seemed unnecessarily loud. With a slight but definite note of impatience, she said, "Oh, come now, it can't really be that bad!"

The woman rolled her sky-blue eyes upward and looked long and hard into the Sister's eyes. Then with remarkable composure, she answered, "Oh, yeah? You should try it sometime!"

My research had come to an end. Whatever the cause, however great or mild the pain — only the mother knows.

CHAPTER 33

THE INVINCIBLE MRS. DREW

Peggy ushered a well-dressed farm woman into the consultation room. Glancing up from my desk, I immediately recalled several previous encounters with her in my office, on her farm, and in the delivery room. She was a woman of solid proportions and firm ideas, accustomed to her own way and irreconcilable in defeat. "This could be no other than the incomparable and invincible Mrs. Drew," I said to myself, "so watch your P's and Q's ."

Mildred Drew wasted no time. While still in the act of sitting down, she asked, "How is Mrs. Stanton?"

"Fine, doing well," I answered.

"When will she be coming home?" Mrs. Drew asked. Then looking intently at me, she said, "You know, Denise and I are close friends. You can tell me anything."

Denise Stanton had been in the hospital for five days after undergoing a pan-hysterectomy, the removal of her uterus and both ovaries. Certainly it was not my place to share this information with others. That was her right, not mine.

"Tell me about Denise. What kind of operation did she have?" Mrs. Drew asked as candidly as if she were asking the time of day. "You know I'm only asking as a good neighbor."

"I'm sure you are," I answered, all the while wondering how I could end this personal inquisition.

"We've been neighbors about 20 years and we share a lot — about everything," Mrs. Drew continued.

Ostensibly, it seemed that Mrs. Drew sought information as a close friend, but it was obvious to me that she wanted to satisfy her insatiable curiosity. I decided to steer the conversation away from Denise and her operation.

"You look tops today, Mildred," I said. "Never saw you looking better. What brings you here today? What's your problem?"

I had caught her off-guard. For an instant she looked puzzled but she quickly recovered her self-possession. "Don't have none. Just came to see about Denise." Having regained her confidence, she went on, "I want to be ready to help her and need to know what's the matter so I can better take care of her."

Resting my head on my hand, I stared ahead as if in deep thought, "Mildred, I'm sure Denise will tell you all about it when she gets around to it."

Mrs. Drew's eyes narrowed. The loose folds of her plump face drew tight and she exploded. "What kind of a person do you think I am, anyhow? I can't ask her. You've got to tell me."

There was no doubt that Mildred Drew had made a trip specifically to learn all the details of her close neighbor's operation. I stood in the way of her obtaining the information she was so determined to get and she stood in the path of my busy office schedule. We were fencing with words and getting nowhere, and, obviously, she was not ready to give up.

I decided on a drastic maneuver. Assuming an attitude of great confidence, I leaned toward her and, in a semi-whispering voice, I asked, "Can you keep a secret?"

With a look of infinite delight, she leaned toward me to seize this prize, the exposure of her neighbor, the object of her visit. Trembling with a kind of joyous anticipation, she giggled, "Oh yes, Doctor."

With as much dignity as I could summon, I settled back in my desk chair and said, "So can I."

It was difficult not to smile, especially when I saw her face fall. She left as I entered an adjoining examining room. The receptionist later told me that Mrs. Drew stomped out of the office, muttering to herself, her face as red as a beet.

I can't deny that each time I recall the incident I enjoy it anew.

CHAPTER 34

HEARTACHE or HEART ATTACK?

"Lena is having a heart attack. Please come, Dr. Bill. She's holding her chest like she's in severe pain and she's breathing so fast. Hurry, Dr. Bill." It was Lena's father, who only one week before had buried his own father.

I hurried to the farm. On the way, I wondered what could cause an 11 year old girl to hold her chest as if in pain and breathe rapidly. Children with congenital heart problems or hearts damaged from rheumatic fever came to mind, but Lena's birth and childhood had been normal.

Lena was the Alton's only child. Doug and Melissa Alton had waited many long years for her arrival, and it was on their 15th wedding anniversary that she arrived. Only two weeks ago they had taken a trip to Michigan, their first separation from Lena, whom they left in the care of her grandparents.

The day after they left, Grandpa Alton had a severe heart attack, from which he died three days later. Lena was on the front porch of the farmhouse with her Grandpa when it happened. Shocked by what she saw, she ran into the garden, screaming for Grandma to come. When Grandma Alton came, she took in the situation with her accustomed calm, made Grandpa as comfortable as possible, then called me.

Meanwhile, "Lena sat watching, completely absorbed in her Grandpa's pain, twitching when he twitched and moaning when he moaned," Grandma Alton had explained, "This showed how much Lena loved her Grandpa."

When I arrived at the farmhouse, in answer to Mr. Alton's call, I found Lena lying quietly, eyes closed, face pale and expressionless.

"She's been quiet since I called you," her father said, "but I'm worried. Ever since Grandpa passed away, Lena won't eat and spends hours just staring into space."

Grandma interrupted. "We all miss Grandpa. He was so lovable."

Her eyes moistened and she swallowed hard. "But Lena misses him the most. She followed him around like she was his pet dog."

111

"Melissa even made Lena's favorite dessert, but she wouldn't touch it," Doug said. "What are we going to do, Dr. Bill?"

"Don't know. Let's look her over," I suggested as I put my stethoscope on Lena's chest. I found her heart and breath sounds to be perfectly normal. In the midst of my examination, Lena suddenly sat up in bed and started to grimace as if in pain, holding her chest with both hands. Her face was contorted and she moaned heavily. Then her breath came faster and faster and her face flushed red.

I sat on the edge of her bed and observed her closely. Her pulse was now rapid, and for the moment I was confounded. Then a bit of the truth came to me. Lena had always been an excellent mimic. She had frequently entertained the family with imitations of Uncle Harold's rolling walk, Aunt Mamie's wry face or cousin Gloria's high-pitched voice. Added to this much-practiced talent was the fact of Lena's intense horror at seeing her beloved Grandpa's initial heart attack.

My suspicions mounted as I noted Lena's deep, rapid breathing. She was hyperventilating, and it was certainly self-induced. I began to suspect that once again Lena was play-acting, but this time mimicking her Grandpa's heart attack.

For a long time I sat quietly on the bed, having motioned to her parents to remain silent also. Lena, exhausted from her efforts, seemed to fall asleep.

How do you tell parents that their child is faking a heart attack? That their child's facial contortions and moans are only a sham? It's hard, but somehow I did tell them, and somehow I made them understand that this was not the pretense of a malingerer or the pretense of a child to gain attention. To Lena, her 'heart attack' was real. To her it was not voluntary mimicry but an unconscious reaction to the loss of her grandpa. It was her way of expressing her sorrow and releasing it.

After our talk we looked in at Lena, who was still asleep. I left a mild sedative, suggesting it be used if Lena appeared to be greatly disturbed. The sedative was never needed, for the following day Lena became her old self again. She had finally accepted the loss of her grandpa and her parents accepted her reaction to that loss.

CHAPTER 35

THE LEGACY OF KARL'S MOST PRIZED POSSESSION

It was 1955 when Karl and Johanna first appeared in my office and, in time, they added a special flavor to my life. Both were typical Austrians, at least insofar as I pictured Austrians. Karl spoke in broken English with deep guttural tones from behind a sturdy white mustache, and wore loose knicker-like trousers. Johanna was soft-spoken. She had her hair wrapped about her head in a braid and was always clad in a generous apron. Their speech was a source of fascination, for they spoke as much with their eyes and hands as with their lips. Whether they smiled or grimaced, their eyes would light up and their hands would gesture with excitement.

Our first meeting occurred when Karl broke his left arm. Frustration marked his face. It took an hour of listening to appreciate the full measure of his distress. Karl gave violin lessons to supplement his meager savings. In his broken English he tried to convey how much he needed both arms, for his pupils learned as much from listening and observing him play as from his verbal instructions.

Soon after Karl's broken arm mended, Johanna contracted a viral pneumonia which lasted several weeks and required numerous calls to their home in the outlying Blue Hills. Each visit was a real treat for me.

These two elderly people were warm and charming. There was a comfortable relationship between them that did not exclude the visitor.

On one of these house calls, Karl was so intent on his violin playing that he did not notice my entrance. Twenty minutes passed. While he was absorbed in his playing, I was mesmerized. Confidently, his horsehair bow crossed back and forth over the violin strings. The violin, tucked under his chin, seemed to be a part of Karl himself.

This elderly couple continued to enchant me. There were times when I was drawn to their home for the sheer joy of conversing with them and listening to

Karl play music that only Fritz Kreisler or Jascha Heifeitz could have duplicated.

As the years passed and our friendship ripened, Karl exposed me to many violin pieces. He would tell with pride that he had played the solo parts of some concertos before large audiences in Austria. When Karl first mentioned Austria in my presence, he bit his lip, his eyes moistened and he turned away.

On one occasion, while we drank coffee, I explained how I came to practice medicine in northern Wisconsin. As though in exchange for this information, Karl related that he had come to the United States from his homeland, Austria, but gave few details and spoke with hesitation, as if confiding in me. It was during World War II. Passage to the United States had been difficult to obtain, so he had taken Johanna and a lad named Hans to Finland.

A few years later, all three embarked for the United States. They settled in Germantown, close to Philadelphia, so that he could be near a center of musical culture. Because of a chance meeting with a member of the Philharmonic, Karl was given an audition, followed by a regular position in the violin section. This lasted only a couple of years, for Karl tired easily and traveling back and forth to Philadelphia bore heavily on him. "Mostly," he whispered, "I was unhappy to be away from my beloved Johanna."

Months passed before I learned more of Karl and Johanna's background. Meanwhile, I was exposed to beautiful music, made exquisite by this master violinist. Karl played the most complicated pieces from memory, pieces such as Saint-Saens 'Introduction and Rondo Capricioso,' which required magnificent finger dexterity. As this elderly man's nimble fingers danced over the strings, the music sprang from his heart like water gushing from a spring.

It was late October. An early snow brightened the earth. The dreary-looking landscape of late fall had changed overnight with this fresh, white carpet of snow. Karl telephoned that Johanna had fallen in the garden. When I arrived, I learned that Johanna had been putting her garden to bed for the winter. Johanna was badly bruised, but she had no broken bones. We chatted for a spell, then Karl reached for his violin. He placed it under his chin and played a few notes.

"This is 'Finlandia,'" he said, "the national anthem of Finland. It was composed by Sibelius. I learned great respect for Sibelius when we were in Finland." Then he plucked and bowed the vibrant strains of 'Finlandia'.

When he finished playing, Karl looked at me and said, "Sibelius was a man of imagination and sentiment. He wrote a deeply emotional composition. It portrays a dying woman, bed-bound for weeks, who rises from her bed to dance with her husband[1]. In ecstasy, she whirls round and round in his arms — the final fulfillment of her long-sought desires. She then drops dead[1]. It is called 'Valse Triste.' I will play it for you."

After completing the music, Karl sat down. "You know," he said, "you have been a true friend. I must tell you more about us. We left Austria because we were frightened by the changes created by the war. We were glad to get to Finland but

---

[1] This was Karl's interpretation. The actual interpretation is that she dances with the devil.

felt safer when we arrived in the United States. Hans, who came with us, was a well-trained engineer. He is now in Oregon, where he has a good job."

Added to the beauty of Karl's music was the mystique of nostalgia. One of my earliest memories is of my father playing the violin. I often crawled out of bed and down the long staircase to hide behind a portierre to listen to him. Though not an expert like Karl, my father enjoyed playing and had some talent. The deep yearning to play the violin never left me but has been partially satisfied by the pleasures of listening.

When I first encountered Karl and Johanna, both were in their late 70's. Ten or 12 years had passed. Time was running out for Karl, it seemed. He had developed a rapidly invasive cancer. Resistant to all known treatment, it spread rapidly, leaving Karl gaunt, listless, and weak. He seldom played his violin. His will to live and remain at home were the only remaining signs of Karl's indomitable spirit. He refused hospitalization. "I need my Johanna."

One day Karl pleaded with me to send for Hans. It was obvious that Karl wanted to see Hans before he died, though he never said why.

Johanna and I consulted. Hans had not written for several years, but searching through old correspondence, Johanna found an address. With the cooperation of telephone operators and after a dozen or so calls, we managed to contact Hans. Hans agreed to come and flew from Portland to Minneapolis, where I picked him up.

When I left to get Hans, I feared Karl would be gone before we returned. Upon our return from Minneapolis, Johanna met us at the door. "I'm afraid he has gone." she said, her eyes wet with tears.

Karl lay on his bed, his eyes closed, his thin lips nearly as pale as his skin. I grasped one of his frail wrists but could find no pulse. Placing my stethoscope on his chest, I noted feeble heart sounds. My touch aroused him. His eyes opened and his gaze wandered about the room. He saw Hans standing at the foot of the bed. His eyes brightened and he managed to smile. He tried to raise himself but he could not. Pointing to the closet, he whispered, "Violin."

Johanna brought it — his cased violin. Somehow she knew what Karl wanted to do. She opened the case and placed the violin into Karl's shaking hands. Karl's eyes looked at his violin as one would look at a beloved child — with great tenderness. "Here, my grandson, this is for you. I would entrust it to no other." With that, Karl crumpled back and was gone.

Tears flooded Han's face. Sobbing quietly, Johanna leaned over Karl and kissed him repeatedly. Though heavy with sadness, the moment was charged with happy memories. There was a solemn stillness broken only by the sobbing.

Perhaps it was the serenity of the moment that held me. Tears moistened my eyes and a special piece of Sibelius' music seemed to fill the room. I heard the plaintive tones of 'Valse Triste' and pictured the dying woman in bed. Abruptly, the music rose in a burst of exultation and the women rose from her bed to dance with her husband — a final fulfillment of her long-sought desire. Like the dying woman, fulfilling her wish, Karl had fulfilled his wish to place his precious violin into Han's keeping.

Karl had said, "Grandson," so I inferred that Hans was Karl's grandson.

Karl had said, "I would entrust my violin to no other." This was Karl's most prized possession.

It was hardly a time to ask questions, but I didn't have to. Johanna and Hans filled in the details of their story. Yes, Hans was Karl and Johanna's grandson. Their daughter and son-in-law had been exterminated at Aushwitz by the Nazis, but Karl, Johanna, and Hans had escaped to Finland. They were Austrian Jews.

After the war they had emigrated to a suburb of Philadelphia. At the time they were unaware that it was named 'Germantown.' When they realized it, the connotation frightened them. By this time, Karl had his job in the violin section of the Philharmonic, so he and Johanna remained, but they sent Hans as far away as possible — to Oregon.

The people of Germantown never bothered them, but the fear instilled by Auschwitz hung over them. It was only when Karl played his music that they felt moments of freedom from their constant fear.

When Karl retired from his job at the Philharmonic, they decided to look for a farm. Both had been brought up on farms in Austria. A Mennonite whom they had met in Germantown knew of a farm for sale in Wisconsin. They bought it and moved.

When Karl broke his arm, a friend had suggested me as a doctor. Not until I attended him did he realize my German name. It alarmed him and his wife then, and for at least a year afterward. But as we came to know one another, their fear lessened.

Karl had always hoped that his grandson, Hans, would carry on his great love for the violin. To that end, over the years from Hans' early childhood, Karl had invested hours, days, weeks, and months teaching his grandson. Karl believed Hans had the talent and self discipline to become a great artist. So Karl wanted Hans to have his violin, which I now learned was the ultimate in violins, a Stradivarius.

What had kept Karl alive? What had made him hang on? Was it his profound desire to present his most prized possession to his grandson, Hans?

The formidable power and inscrutable mystery of human emotions come even to the country doctor.

CHAPTER 36

A WORLD RECORD BABY

Each spring and summer my fly rod became a permanent resident of my car. Returning from a home-call, I knew there was always the remote possibility of crossing a trout stream at the bewitching hour of twilight, a delightful time when trout often stirred to feeding activity. The hope, of course, was greater than the reality; seldom were the circumstances just right.

Actually, it was several years before the first opportunity came. Meanwhile, however, I was gathering and storing valuable information on trout streams within a 25-mile radius of my home, my usual home-call circuit. Each time I crossed an unfamiliar stream, I would check the water temperature; if appropriate, I would roll up my trousers, remove my shoes and socks and examine the stream's contents — its grasses, mosses, and the natural trout foods they contained. Those streams with abundant food life for trout — such as fresh water shrimp — took priority in my visions of future twilight rendezvous. This was, indeed, a selective approach but it served me well, for such opportunities were rare.

During one of my scouting jaunts, I was startled to see two oversize trout in a pool close to the main highway. The pool had been enlarged by boys into a swimming hole with a little ingenious placement of rocks and logs. My curiosity aroused, I scouted the pool whenever possible. Sneaking behind a stand of alder-bush, I was occasionally rewarded with a glimpse of these two monster trout. Each seemed to be more than five pounds. Although the food supply was excellent, it seemed strange that these trout continued to haunt a pool that was frequented by young swimmers.

I gave other streams similar surveillance. One of these had two bridges, four miles apart. Under each bridge the water flowed through a narrow and deep channel gouged out by high spring floods. With large boulders walling each channel, a natural 'lie' for good-sized trout to rest and feed had been created. Although these two spots often came to mind, the swimming hole continued to intrigue me most.

It was the last Friday in June. I had been called from supper to deliver a baby in a small town 20 miles away. As I passed the 'swimming hole' at 6:30 p.m., I conjured up the oft repeated hope of casting a fly over those two monster trout that lurked in its waters. But there was no way to induce nature to hurry or slacken the pace of delivery so that my possible streamside arrival would take place at the bewitching hour of twilight. All I could do was hope.

Jane Wharton was in active labor when I arrived. Her previous delivery had been twin girls, each more than seven pounds. One had been a breech, bottom first, but the difficulty encountered had been only moderate. As I considered this, I was happy to note that the urgency of my desire to face the two monster trout had not completely eradicated my medical judgment. Yet I was equally quick to note that I had not forgotten the trout, either.

Two hours later a large baby boy appeared with a vigorous, eager cry. A small tear in the mother's perineum required several stitches, which took another 15 minutes.

In my anxiousness to leave, I was hastily stuffing my obstetrical materials back into my bag when Jane's husband, Darryl, said, "What's your hurry? Why not have a bite to eat and some coffee or a glass of milk?"

"No thanks, Darryl," I said and then hesitated, reluctant to tell him the truth — my quest to tangle with one of the trout in the swimming hole. "Well, all right, Darryl, but I must leave soon or it will be too late."

"Too late for what?" Darryl asked.

I hesitated again, somewhat abashed to confess my eagerness to get to the swimming hole at a time when Jane and Darryl were enthused about their new son. Then I reasoned that friends would understand, and we had been friends for several years. But still somewhat uneasy, I blurted out, "I've got an appointment with a trout in the old swimming hole where Highway 8 crosses Moose Ear Creek."

Darryl grinned, "You old 'son of a gun,' still a trout fisherman at heart. Well, go ahead, but at least have a quick bite."

Having missed supper, I was grateful for the sandwich and the glass of milk, but I gulped them down and left in haste.

Within minutes I pulled up next to the stream and my fly rod was ready for action. After a few false casts, I dropped a dry fly at the head of the pool. It floated happily for some dozen feet. As it rode near the left undercut bank, it disappeared with a slight sucking sound but hardly a dimple in the water's surface. Cocking my wrist, I set the hook. Then the quiet of the evening was broken with the thrashing of a trout, who leapt and cavorted to my great joy, but not his.

Perhaps it was a mere ten minutes, but it seemed more like 30 when a voice startled me. It was Darryl Wharton, the new father. "What are you doing here?" I called.

"You didn't weigh my son." he answered. "My wife wants to know his weight."

"Darryl, " I said without turning my head, "I don't carry a baby scale. When your wife comes to the office next week, I will weigh the baby. My guess is that your son is better than nine pounds." As Darryl watched from the bank, I continued to battle the trout, who, by now, was showing signs of fatigue. Finally, as the trout came close to the bank, Darryl netted it.

As I weighed it on my trout scales, Darryl spoke up. "Say, Doc, you may not have a baby scale, but why couldn't we weigh my son on your trout scales?"

"Oh, come on now, Darryl. You don't really want me to do that...?" I said.

"Sure, I do. C'mon Doc. Let's do it now," he said as he walked toward his car.

So we went back to his home. The new arrival was returned to his birthday suit and placed in a baby blanket fashioned like a sling. This was attached with a large safety pin to the hook on my trout scales.

The indicator rose abruptly, passed ten pounds, and then passed 20 pounds. It settled on 22 pounds.

Darryl looked at me in bewilderment. I looked at him with disbelief. For a moment we were silent and then burst into laughter.

His first words remain indelibly in my mind: "What did you say that trout weighed?"

Then he continued, "According to your scales, this is probably the largest baby ever born, probably a world record."

To this day, the sequel to this incident remains a continuous razzing about the size of the trout I catch. Darryl's son weighed nine pounds at my office a week later. The weight of the monster trout I caught can never be revealed.

(Note: This chapter was published as a story in Fly Fishing, Feb. 1991)

CHAPTER 37

HOW I LEARNED TO HANDLE SEX PROBLEMS

When I attended medical school, there were no courses to teach sex. As my patients' confidence in me grew, questions concerning sex were asked more often. At first these questions dealt with the less personal aspects, such as: When should one discuss sex with children? What should you tell them? Should children of both sexes bathe together? Use the bathroom together? Up to what age? How much should parents expose themselves to their children? Is it all right for Bobby and Mary to crawl into bed with us? At what age should a child have his or her own room? What do you tell a girl about menses? At what age?

These questions were posed to me increasingly. I sought out information in textbooks and periodicals. With a developing background of ideas and some answers, I faced questions on sex with more confidence. But as my confidence improved, so also the questions became more personal and more difficult. While I ceased to blush outwardly, I continued to feel flushed inwardly. Men and women sought sound contraceptive advice. This was before the dawn of the Pill. Diaphragms, condoms and contraceptive jellies were considered the safest. Respectable people did not talk about these things, except to their physicians. Words like contraception, syphilis, gonorrhea, venereal disease and herpes were not used in ordinary conversation. Sanitary pads were not advertised. Abortions were illegal and performed under cover, with many untoward results, and gave much substance for gossip.

Realizing my incredible lack of knowledge to adequately sustain credibility, I added *Human Sexuality*, a medical monthly, to my reading list. Because of its openness and utter freedom of explanation, I devoured its contents. The magazine, however, was always kept recessed or hidden; I feared its open presence might embarrass my office girls or patients. How strangely naive this was in the light of pornographic periodicals now sprinkled liberally in barbershops and drugstores. But things were different then. There was no television bringing lingerie, pills for menstrual cramps, sanitary pads, and hemorrhoidal preparations into our living rooms. Even newspaper ads were restrictive.

I am not assuming the responsibility of saying that the gradual freedom of expression has been all bad or all good. Without doubt, some aspects of this freedom have added to the overpermissiveness of today. But this same freedom has reduced venereal disease and covert abortions. Fewer people have developed the severe complications of venereal disease and have been exposed to the hazards of septic abortion. Frankness brings welcome lucidity, like a breath of fresh air. On the other hand, completely unrestricted candidness can leave us naked, not only of proprieties but of morals as well.

With time, study, and experience, my approach became more sophisticated. At least I felt more comfortable dealing with sex problems, knowing I was more knowledgeable. Questions about masturbation, abortion, and contraception were answered with a measure of dignified assurance.

Still, I was haunted with a host of unanswered questions about myself, questions that deserved answers to satisfy my inner man. Should I accept the growing freedom of discarding all morals and all restraints, promulgated as the "new morality." I pondered on this time and again while driving on calls into the country. Permissiveness had erupted, and Dr. Benjamin Spock's book for parents may have been a catalyst. Permissiveness created a fertile soil for shaking loose all responsibility for our own behavior. The Pill was planted in this fertile soil, from which the "new morality" grew and prospered.

Sexual freedom advanced with this decline in the need for moral restraint. Responsibility for sexual behavior appeared unnecessary with the wide margin of safety from pregnancy that the Pill offered. Besides, psychologists advocated that we should all "do our own thing" and added that guilt feelings are bad. These strong influences on our society were abetted by the very real hazards of affluence. Family life was being eroded. Family communication was being undermined.

The results of these influences on our society and to family life were devastating and widespread. With the strong influence to shed responsibility, sexual permissiveness flourished. Divorce rates soared as extramarital sex increased. Teenage pregnancies soared as premarital sex increased. As by-products, abortions became common. Clinics offered contraceptive advice to minors without parental consent.

In the midst of these waves of change and the resulting flood of irresponsible sexual behavior, I felt I had to take a stand. Many women sought abortions. Following rape or incest, abortion appeared justified. Abortion on demand seemed intolerable. I took a stand, concluding that women had a right to make their own decisions. They should be advised by experienced counselors but must not be forced to accept that advice. By the same token, I felt no physician should be forced to do an abortion against his will, regardless of the circumstances. Thus, I reasoned, the decision to do or not to do an abortion must remain my prerogative. But I also felt I must not turn away a woman seeking an abortion, for this would imply turning away someone seeking and needing medical help. After all, I could reveal empathy for her situation and counsel her. Still, no matter how sympathetic I felt, something inside of me resisted doing an abortion. I might have changed my mind had I been faced with an incestuous or rape pregnancy, but I never was.

But I still had a personal problem to contend with. Where would a woman patient of mine go who insisted on an abortion after counseling, and if I refused to perform an abortion. The answer I so desperately sought came to me one night in a dream. It really was simple. While capable of doing much surgery, there was much I felt could be better performed by some specialist elsewhere. Using a similar explanation, I offered women the services of a clinic, licensed by the state, that specialized in dealing with women seeking abortions. It added to my inner comfort knowing that this clinic was serviced by social workers who managed to convince many women desiring abortions to carry their pregnancies to term.

Offering contraceptive advice to teenagers without parental consent still rankled me. Teenage girls often approached me for such advice. A pattern developed that proved sound. We held long conversations, during which I revealed interest and empathy. I listened attentively to their problems and extracted information about their family life, their boyfriends, school, and outside activities. Sufficient confidence was acquired so that most teenage girls returned for further sessions and many brought their boyfriends.

To this day, I am concerned with the problem and am convinced that parents should not abdicate their authority to the government, nor to reproductive health services, nor the medical profession. It is ironic that in some states parental consent must be given to pierce ears but not to provide contraceptive advice. Children are the responsibility of their parents. By taking away parental consent, we are further emasculating the role of parents and fostering irresponsibility. Family life needs strengthening, not weakening. One of the roles of the physician is to reinforce the family by reinforcing communication, not severing it, by supporting parental authority, not destroying it.

Experiences continued to accrue. My ability to respond to sexual queries became more skillful without being evasive. There were no simplistic answers, but questions about masturbation, sexual identity, and oral sex were best answered with complete candor. What harm can come from masturbation? What should I tell my son? How can I get my child to stop masturbating? These questions were often asked.

With marked embarrassment, a father blurted out, "Tom is 11; he likes to dress up in his sister's clothes. What can we do?" A mother was in obvious distress: "My husband doesn't seem to know, but our 15-year-old son dresses in his sister's clothes. If Dad ever finds out, he'll skin him alive."

Markedly upset, parents of a 16-year-old athlete announced that their son had dressed as a girl since five years of age. He had done it openly at home for the last four years. Someone had told them that he would grow out of it. Others assured them that, unless permitted, the boy would turn to drugs or become an alcoholic, so they permitted it. At this point, Carol, the daughter who had come with them, said rather bitterly, "My brother has more dresses, slips, and bras than I have. When I need something, I borrow it."

A pathetic case with a sad ending comes to mind. A 19-year-old boy consulted me about multiple raised spots on his lips and genitals. Questioning appeared pointless till I told him firmly that he had venereal herpes. He then poured out his story, admitting to having experienced oral sex. His mother was an alcoholic. He had slept with her regularly, starting when he was a youngster. Their relationship was incestuous. His marks previously in high school and then in college were top-notch. He had homosexual tendencies but, in reality, wanted to have a sex change. In time, I referred him to the University of Minnesota Hospital, where sex change operations were being performed. He was undergoing psychological and hormonal treatments when his impatience overcame his good sense. One evening he cut off his penis with a sharp knife. Bleeding profusely, he was taken to the hospital. Soon thereafter, his sex-change operation was completed. Several months passed. He/she met and married a sailor. Two years later he/she died of an overdose of drugs.

Yes, I was getting a liberal education on sex attitudes in all its various forms. Some were revolting. A young man, to be married in three days, had urinary burning and a creamy discharge. He had had intercourse with a prostitute recently while "in the city." His bride-to-be was one of my 'babies.' It was difficult to remain objective. Though I tried not to show it, I resented him. Holding back my rising animosity, I made a smear of his discharge, which was positive for gonorrhea. My hostility almost reached the breaking point when he refused to postpone the wedding date. Pleading was useless. Finally, I threatened to tell his bride-to-be or her family, whom I had known for 20 years. He threatened legal reprisal for breaching confidential information. When I alerted him to the legal requirement that his gonorrhea must be reported, he finally agreed to put off the wedding.

Over a period of weeks, a half-dozen couples assailed me with a common complaint. While attending premarital classes at their church, the young minister had embarrassed them. As much as they liked their new young minister and his sincere approach, they thought it was out-of-place for him to discuss the various positions of sexual intercourse. They were especially embarrassed when he diagrammed these positions. Would I talk to him? I did, although it was a might awkward.

Another delicate situation occurred that I am sure I would have bungled had it occurred at an earlier year in my practice. Called to a hotel at the early hours of the morning, I was suddenly confronted with a situation for which I was unprepared by experience or reading. A young man met me in the lobby and led me to an upstairs room. When my eyes became adjusted to the dim light, I noted there were four human forms surrounding the bed. Stretched out on the bed was a girl, covered with a bedspread. It was soon obvious that the group was made up of three young couples, all of whom had imbibed an excess of beer.

The young man who had led me from the lobby appeared to be the least intoxicated and the most concerned. Those surrounding the bed scattered as we approached. Slowly, the young man withdrew the bedspread. There lay a young woman, without clothes and with a beer bottle in her vagina. Held by a vacuum, the bottle could not be removed. For a moment, sheer embarrassment held me in its grip, intensified by a devastating awareness that I didn't know what to do. Somehow I mustered my resources and looked about. What I needed was something solid and heavy. There on the mantel was a metal figurine. At my request, a large Turkish towel was brought from the bathroom. I wrapped this about the bottle. With an attitude of confidence not shared by my inner man, I grasped the figurine in my right hand while holding the towel-wrapped bottle in my left. With a sudden blow, I smashed the bottle. The neck of the bottle was readily removed. I quickly covered the girl with the bedspread and as quickly retreated from the room, never requesting a fee for my call.

Yes, handling sexual problems became a requisite part of my practice. How astounding it was to learn the countless facets of sexual activity and its unending problems! Even more amazing was the sheer sexual ignorance of the general population. I found it easier, however, to be tolerant of this ignorance when I considered how long it had taken me to appreciate the many ramifications of sex and ferret out appropriate measures to handle them.

Being a physician, though a grave responsibility, can offer a fascinating education.

CHAPTER 38

AT THE END OF HIS ROPE

All was quiet. The sun burned with intensity, even at its low arc. Perhaps because of the heat, the usual shouts and taunts of children were absent. Only an occasional car could be heard. The railroad switchyard close by seemed abandoned. The day had been a difficult one, but now it was evening and I was enjoying it, seated on the north terrace of our home overlooking a trout pool. The beauty of the twilight and the hush of the evening brought to mind the opening lines of Thomas Gray's 'Elegy Written in a Country Churchyard.'

> *"Now fades the glimmering landscape on the sight,*
> *and all the air a solemn stillness holds,*
> *Save where the beetle wheels his droning flight,*
> *And drowsy tinklings lull the distant folds."*

The phone rang; its tone seemed unduly harsh. After running up two flights of stairs, I lifted the phone and heard a familiar woman's voice shout, "Come, Doctor, come. Billy has hung himself!"

In seconds, I was on the way to the Masterson farm, wondering why Billy, a 16 year-old youth, would hang himself. Billy had been named after me. He was the Masterson's second child. He had never been coddled and was an excellent student and a good athlete. Billy had been voted most popular in his class.

In 20 minutes I had covered the 18 miles to the farm. Those 20 minutes were occupied with my pondering on what had made Billy give up his life. His parents were easygoing. They did not scold harshly. Their punishments were never severe nor reckless. They were proud of their two sons and often told them so. Why then, I wondered. What had made Billy take his life? Why Billy? Why not his brother, Fred?

Then another question surfaced. Why was I rushing to the farm? With certainty, Billy would be gone. What could I do?

From somewhere in my past, I was reminded that, early in my life, I had placed no value on funerals. In my own immature way, I had misinterpreted the Bible. "Let the dead take care of the dead and the living of the living" had meant to me that the dead are gone and we can do nothing for them. As a physician, I soon realized that funerals are not for the dead, but are for the living, that those left behind need the cushioning solace of relatives and friends. So here, speeding along toward the farm, I knew that I could no longer do anything for Billy, but I should do something for the family.

Upon my arrival, I was immediately taken to the barn where Billy had hung himself from a hay rope. He had been lowered and released but was already black and stiff.

"What did we do wrong?" Mrs. Masterson asked. "Why did he do it? We loved him so. He was such a good boy." Wringing her hands, she looked up at me for answers.

"He always did his chores when he came home from school. He never missed going to church on Sunday. We thought we were good parents, but we must have done something wrong, Dr. Bill. Tell us," Mr. Masterson said, his eyes pleading to know.

After 20 years in practice, I knew there were no easy answers, if any. The family needed to express and sort out their own mixed-up emotions — their feelings of guilt, of shame, of resentment, and of remorse.

"Billy was a good boy," I said with firmness. "I know you were proud of him and I'm sure he loved both of you. Sometimes there are no answers. Things happen that we just don't understand." I was aware that the Mastersons needed to voice their own thoughts, not listen to my advice. I suggested we go into the house, where I listened to them for some time. Before I left, I gave a mild sedative to both parents.

As I drove slowly homeward, I thought of the vacuum Billy's death would leave. Though the Mastersons still had one son, that vacuum would always remain. Once again, verses of Gray's 'Elegy' came to mind:

> "For them no more the blazing hearth shall burn,
> Or busy housewife ply her evening care;
> No children run to lisp their sire's return,
> Or climb his knees the envied kiss to share."

And once again, I wondered why Billy had left the living on his own. Perhaps too much was expected of him or perhaps he expected too much of himself. He was bright, resourceful, and handsome. Honors were heaped on him. Perhaps he could not face the fact that he could not measure up to the person he was expected to be. In a real sense, Billy had come to "the end of his rope."

CHAPTER 39

"WHAT! AT THIS HOUR OF THE MORNING?"

I have laughed about this incident since, but it wasn't funny at the time. It depends, I guess, on your point-of-view.

"Doctor, this is Ethel Rawley. Come, please come. My husband, Randy, is bleeding," pleaded a female voice over the phone. It was 2:00 A.M. on a bitter, cold, February night. I had returned from a hospital delivery an hour earlier and had just gone to sleep.

"Where is the bleeding?" I asked sleepily.

"From the mouth," was the response.

"What happened? Did he fall?"

"No, the dentist pulled ten teeth yesterday," she answered with impatience.

"Did you call the dentist?"

"What! At this hour of the morning?"

Disturbed at this lack of concern for doctors, I hesitated, almost yielding to the temptation to chide her severely. But I overcame this temptation and directed her to place a washcloth, doubly folded and soaked in ice water, into her husband's mouth, then have him bite down on the cloth. I promised I would come at once.

When I arrived, I found Randy was no longer bleeding. I replaced the washcloth and tied an old scarf under his chin and over his head to maintain some pressure should he fall asleep. Although Randy had been alarmed and his wife concerned, they had cooperated completely. The Rawleys had been my patients for almost 20 years and they trusted me.

But I still felt abused and resentful that my dental brethren were not expected to rise from their warm beds in the middle of the night. I trudged to my car with a sense of self pity, drove home and returned to my own bed.

Again, deep in slumber, I dreamed church bells were summoning me to rise and attend church. It seemed the bells were demanding my presence with marked impatience. The repeated ringing finally alerted me to the telephone clanging beside my bed.

Sitting on the edge of the bed, I could see the clock. It was 4:00 A.M. I grasped the phone and gave my usual "Hello," yawning as I said it.

"Doc, this is Albert."

"Albert who?" I asked.

"Albert Monroe, you know, in Chetek."

"Yes?" I said pointedly.

"Doc, what time is my appointment tomorrow?" farmer Albert asked with the calm assurance of one making a request at midday.

At this point I was fit to be tied. I wanted to bellow a thousand invectives. My blood pressure was probably higher than it had ever been. I felt steam must be coming from my ears.

"Albert, I'm an early riser, but this is too early for me. Please call the office after nine o' clock." With that I hung up, pleased with myself that I had not expressed the actual thoughts that were running through my mind.

With my head back on my pillow I longed desperately for sleep, but the events of the night kept popping into my mind.

Actually, I was not angry, but I did feel abused and was too exhausted to just dismiss those unkind thoughts. So I rose, showered, and dressed.

Rancor is a poor companion with which to begin a new day. Yet a residual bitterness pursued me. Was this to be that kind of day? Even though the sky remained cloudless, clouds of resentment seemed to surround me.

My first appointment was to be at eight o' clock. I had scheduled a biopsy of a patient's tongue. The woman had a small growth on the tip of her tongue. Since she was a smoker, it seemed best to be certain it was not malignant. Besides, its presence bothered her speech and her eating. So I had decided to remove it and do a biopsy.

At 7:00 A.M. the phone rang. It was Sabrina, the patient with the growth on her tongue. "Dr. Bauer, please cancel my autopsy," she said. "I decided not to have it done. But thanks, anyway."

Despite my built-up frustrations and the bitterness simmering within me, an uncontrollable smile came to my lips. Then I howled with deeply satisfying laughter. My wife came running, "What is the matter? Are you sick?'

"No, not sick. Tired? Yes. But this last telephone call saved my day. I was to do a biopsy of a lady's tongue, but she just canceled it. Her words were, 'Please cancel my autopsy.' Perhaps you don't see the humor as I do, but apparently she has confused the terms autopsy and biopsy."

The children were up by then. The house buzzed with voices and trembled with running footsteps. A piano and a foot-pumped organ voiced their complaints. Soon a saxophone and the brassy sound of a cornet joined the musical fracas. As the din peaked, a pet rooster crowed in exultation from the cellar.

No longer able to contain my amusement, I roared with laughter. For the second time, Gussie came running.

"What is the matter with you this morning?" she asked, looking at me, her blue eyes serious.

"Sit down," I said, "and enjoy the show and humorous irony of the moment."

"Some years ago, in our courting days, I insisted that there would never be all that musical practice ruckus in our house. Do you remember? Just listen to it. It's awful, but isn't it wonderful?"

Rancor from the night's experiences was gone. In its place was a quiet amusement to brighten my day.

CASH ON DELIVERY

It was cold. Bitterly cold. The Flambeau River moaned, its aching back heavy with ice. The snow squeaked underfoot. Blasts from the north stung my exposed face and gnawed at my thin-gloved fingers. Not adept with snowshoes, I often floundered. With persistence, I reached my destination — an isolated cabin, its northeastern side concealed by a huge snowdrift.

The heavy door opened at my approach. A huge hand seized my obstetrical bag; another hand swallowed up my numb right hand, by way of greeting. The man's gentle voice belied his burly hulk. "So glad you made it, doctor. Come in."

A large bed filled the farthest corner of the room. The bed, like the cabin, was fashioned of hand-hewn logs. A woman with brown hair that hung to her waist sat on the bed, intermittently and quietly moaning. Her long, old-fashioned nightgown accentuated her small size, adding to her pixie-like appearance. She glanced up at me and spoke softly. "Glad you came."

A single stove, fabricated from a large oil drum, its belly filled with 16 inch logs, warmed the cabin. A ladder, braced against the lip of an opening above, led to the only other room, the attic.

The cabin had sparse furnishings: the one bed, two chests of drawers, and four chairs. A sink, overly large in the close quarters, was supplied with water by an inside hand pump. Clothes were neatly hung from wooden pegs. On the floor, close to the woman's dangling feet, was a homemade crib. Two kerosene lamps, their chimneys stained with carbon, flickered softly.

My rapid survey noted the presence of water, warmth, and light. It also noted the absence of stirrups to hold the knees, the need for better light and the necessity to use local anesthesia, if required, for the hazards of ether in such a place were obvious.

Having been awakened from my sleep by a phone call at 2:00 A.M., and having left a warm bed on such a cold night, I was unprepared for the terse greeting and the lack of adequate conditions for delivering a baby. But as my hands and face began to glow in the warmth of the room, an awareness of what these two had accomplished kindled an inner glow. They had done so much with so little. Besides, I mused, my isolated hosts were unaccustomed to guests and I was as strange to them as they were to me; this was our first meeting.

Recalling my college days, amusement overcame my annoyance. How frequently I had 'felt out' my wrestling opponent in the initial encounter. These two were 'feeling me out.' In the light of these thoughts, I warmed up to my task and these new friends-to-be.

While opening my bag and arranging my obstetrical pack, I questioned them. Laura and Jacob Carter had built this cabin and a barn during the summer, having left Chicago when Jacob lost his job as a law clerk. Since they had no phone, I was curious to learn how they had arranged to reach me in the dead of night with the temperature below zero.

Jacob's explanation was simple. Arrangements had been made with a neighbor who lived directly across the river. When Jacob swung a kerosene lantern back and forth, that would be the signal for the neighbor to call me.

After examining Laura's heart, lungs, and blood pressure, I checked the fetal heartbeat and position of the baby. Then I timed Laura's contractions. Since this was her first pregnancy, I estimated we would still have time for preparation. At my bidding, Jacob went out to the barn and returned with two large screw eyes, some rope, and leather straps. The large-eyed screws were fastened into overhead logs. Rope was tied to these screws. At the proper level, the leather straps were fashioned into supports for Laura's flexed knees.

Much needed to be done. Fortunately, the Crandons had a mirror. I hung it in a tilted position about six feet above the floor and then asked Jacob to clean the chimney of the kerosene lamp. By trial and error, we discovered the proper spot to place it so that the mirror would reflect the light onto the foot of the bed.

Laura seemed such a little sprite, yet appeared confident. She listened carefully as I discussed the mechanism of labor pains. "Pain," I suggested, "will be markedly reduced by cooperation. I will tell you when to push and when to pant."

Laura's contractions became more frequent and her pains more severe. She pushed with the pains and panted softly in between. "Just relax when there are no pains," I suggested.

But the time had come. I placed Laura's legs in the leather supports we had fashioned, swabbed her, and scrubbed my hands and arms in water Jacob had heated. Then I put on my own gown and mask and finally my sterile gloves.

Jacob sat on the side of the bed. During labor contractions, he placed Laura's hands on ropes we had tied to the sideboards of the bed. "Pull on these," he would say. During remissions, he would grasp both of her hands. "That was fine, Laura," he would approve with enthusiasm.

Injecting novocaine to reduce her pain gave me a little time to clearly note their responses to one another, but I felt reassured by his loving sounds of encouragement and her cooperative pushing.

As the stretching continued, I decided an incision of the perineum was necessary to prevent undue tearing. This was her first baby and a large one, at that.

That grand moment of a new arrival was at hand. As so often in the past, I was gripped with a sensation of reverence. As always, it seemed a special privilege to witness the start of new life. I contemplated its mysterious origins, its unique genetic influence, and wondered what lay ahead for this newcomer. Outwardly, I was flushed with excitement.

The male infant was large, perhaps nine pounds. Wrapping him in a large bath towel, I placed him in Laura's eagerly outstretched arms. Lonnie trembled as she clutched her baby and nestled him beside her.

Jacob stared at her and the infant in disbelief. When his astonishment wore off, he asked what he could do. I had him readjust the light. In spite of Laura's excellent cooperation and the incision I had made, a large tear had occurred. Repair consumed a good hour. Meanwhile, Jacob had placed the baby in the homemade crib.

Every so often Laura would turn her head and peek at the newcomer. "Freddy," she would whisper, her grave voice tender with emotion. Soon, however, Laura fell into a deep sleep.

As I completed the repair, Jacob made a pot of coffee. We sat drinking it and nibbling at a prune cake Laura had made. For some time we chatted, for I was curious to learn why two graduates from the University of Chicago had chosen to live here in the wilderness. There was insufficient time to really find out, but Jacob made it clear that they were both glad to escape the jungle of Chicago.

I rose to leave for home. Jacob approached Laura's bed, nudged her gently and said, "The doctor is leaving."

Laura opened her eyes and glanced at me. "Good-bye, doctor, thanks so much." With that, she reached under the mattress with her left hand, bringing out a handful of bills and then asked, "How much do we owe you?"

Immersed in conflicting emotions, I hesitated for a brief moment. Then I said, "$25."

She counted out the bills and handed them to me. Certainly, this is what C.O.D. means: Cash on Delivery!

CHAPTER 41

THE START OF MY ANNUAL PILGRIMAGE

It was my first evening at a surgical symposium in Chicago. At dinner I was seated opposite Dr. Sterling Bunnell, a renowned hand surgeon. We fell into an interesting conversation and though he was twenty years my senior, we seemed to hit it off. As dessert was served, he said, "Why don't you visit me in San Francisco sometime?"

"Sure will," I replied and let it go at that. I still retained a strong dislike for large cities like New York, Boston, and Chicago. The notion that San Francisco might be equally offensive occurred to me; during the next half hour the thought of visiting Dr. Bunnell ran repeatedly through my mind. There were many hand injuries in the Ladysmith area, for lumbering was a major industry. Additional hand injuries occurred in the paper mill and the dry milk plant.

"Wonder if he really meant his invitation?" I asked myself. "No, he was just being friendly," I reasoned. "A man with his reputation wouldn't bother with a small town doctor like me. This man is Dr. Sterling Bunnell, the world's foremost hand surgeon." His complete name had gone throughout my mind over and over, accentuating his importance.

Just then I noticed Dr. Bunnell across the room, sipping coffee. I hurried over and, with a feeling that my mouth was full of cotton, I asked, "When would you like me to come?"

"Oh, let me see, Bill," he said, eyeing me carefully. "How about January? No use coming this month; with the Christmas holidays, people won't want to have elective surgery. But, in January, there will be ample material to demonstrate."

"Great!" I exploded with enthusiasm as disbelief in my good fortune overwhelmed me. "I'll send you a letter telling you when you can expect me."

Billy and Christi, our two oldest, were in elementary school. Mark was a toddler and Tim a baby. On January 1st, I started for San Francisco by car, taking Billy and Christi with me. My wife, Gussie, stayed home with Mark and Tim. When I arrived in San Francisco, I rented a small apartment and arranged for the children to attend pubic school. I was ready to work and to learn and was excited to start.

It was a marvelous month. Dr. Bunnell was an adept surgeon and an excellent teacher with a profound knowledge of anatomy. He was a man respected by his colleagues and patients alike. One morning, for example, he took the place of a surgeon just starting a deep neck operation, perhaps the most complicated part of all human anatomy. The surgeon had suffered a heart attack. After the operation was completed, I learned that Dr. Bunnell having limited his practice to hand surgery, had not performed any surgery of the neck for 25 years, yet I overheard the assisting surgeons praising his skill.

The month's experience benefited me in many ways. My ability to treat wounds of the upper extremities improved and I soon found I was better able to treat all cases of trauma. In addition, I had picked up tidbits of wisdom from Dr. Bunnell. He explained that tendons exposed to radiation often developed chronic tendonitis and radiation to the face and neck often caused thyroid cancer.

"Don't permit a dermatologist to give your patients radiation for acne of the face and neck or radiation of the hands and arms for dermatitis," he warned.

On my first day home, I was tested. George Putnam's right hand had been caught in a motorized press at the paper mill. The space between the rollers that crushed George's hand was less than one-quarter inch. The bones were broken and tendons torn. The hand was a bloody mess and there was marked danger of infection. Before my session with Dr. Bunnell, amputation would have seemed advisable, but now I was prepared to attempt the tedious but possible route of repair. I took pictures of the hand before surgery with the intention of sending them to my tutor and hoped the results would warrant taking more pictures after surgery.

Months later, when the insurance company refused to pay the $150.00 I charged for several operations, numerous casts, and months of dressings, I was glad that I had taken the pictures both before and after. The adjuster for the insurance company hadn't believed that the hand had been so badly maimed to begin with.

The state Board of Review checked the patient's hand, studied the X-rays and pictures, and examined the hospital and office records.

Turning to the insurance company's representative, the chairman of the Board of Review noted, "Not a bad job, probably would have cost your company thousands of dollars in the city. I suggest you settle with the doctor not for $150.00 but for $200.00."

The San Francisco trip taught me to recognize and accept opportunities that came my way. Dr. Bunnell was a leader in his field, yet he had taken me, a country doctor, into his office, hospital, and home. He had permitted me to scrub and operate with him. This was far better than taking a refresher course. The next time a doctor said, "Come and see me sometime," I immediately answered, "When?"

Thus came about my annual pilgrimage to increase my medical knowledge: to Chicago for orthopedics, to Madison for thyroid surgery, to Salt Lake City for gallbladder surgery, and others. Dr. Bunnell's surgical facility and his clear anatomical knowledge underlined the importance of anatomy. Dr. Arnold Jackson's incomparable local anesthesia for thyroid surgery made a general anesthesia unnecessary. Dr. N.F. Hicken's insistence on X-ray of the biliary system during surgery helped me to foresee possible anatomical abnormalities. Because others in the medical profession had taken the time to share their knowledge freely, both in person and in writing, I knew I was a better doctor.

CHAPTER 42

A TRACTOR PULL SQUARED THE BILL

With only 25 miles of blacktop roads in Rusk County in the '40's, sinkholes, plain mud, frost heaves, and snowdrifts often assailed me. Therefore, an extra supply of warm clothes, a shovel, a swede saw, an axe, snowshoes, and several jacks were necessary equipment. Despite my plans to be prepared, however, there were times when my efforts to cope with the elements proved futile. Such was the case one early spring night when my car slithered into a sinkhole. I cut down several poplars and cut them into suitable sections to form a base for jacking up my car. I used another poplar as a lever, but the car not only refused to budge, it also sank deeper into the hole. Both wheels were mired up to the middle of the hubcaps.

Although concern for Anna Maples, over whose home the stork was hovering, fueled my efforts, the situation remained hopeless; in fact, it was growing worse. A cold wind had chilled my sweat; my clothes were matted with a sticky clay; my coat and trousers were ripped. In my exhausted state, my imagination conjured up mischievous gremlins scampering about in elfish delight, mocking me and my entrenched car.

Even after putting on a woolen overjacket, I still shivered but sat for a few minutes to regroup my thoughts. I decided to walk for help. I knew it was two miles to a farm where there was a large tractor.

When I set out, all the candles in the sky were out. Inky blackness made progress slow and difficult. I had not covered 50 yards before I plopped into another sinkhole. Up to my knees in mud, ice, and water, I struggled to release my feet from the clay ooze that gripped me. It seemed a losing battle. Finally, my feet came loose but my shoes remained in the mucky ooze and were not retrieved.

My wet socks were poor insulation from the cold and provided no padding or protection from stones, ice, or snow. In short order, my feet were sore, numb, and swollen, but I plodded on with the dim hope that the stork had also been mired in mud.

When at last I reached the farm, exhausted and shivering, my banging on the door brought Marvin, a 16-year-old youth clad in his pajamas. His intense gaze absorbed my outer appearance, but with slow recognition. With a sweep of his arm, he ushered in this ghostly, tattered apparition that had wandered to his door.

"What are you doing out at this hour of the night?" he began. Then with a half-hearted attempt at humor, he ventured, "Taking a mud bath?"

About this time, Bessie Barton, the young man's mother, stumbled into the poorly lit room. She took one look at me and exclaimed, "God, you look awful. Come here by the fire. I'll get you some coffee. Marvin, go get the doctor a pair of dry trousers and a dry shirt."

In a matter of minutes I was warmed, renewed in spirit by my two hospitable friends, and had explained my presence as well as my urgent need to reach the Maples' farmhouse before the stork.

Marvin got out the farm tractor. Together we rode it back to my car and without much difficulty, pulled it out. Then he advised me on how to reroute my approach to the Maple's farm by a road free of sinkholes.

Twenty minutes later I was at Mrs. Maple's bedside. An hour passed. Her labor pains became stronger. As the sun's rays leapt over the horizon and peeped through the curtains that draped her window, the new arrival bellowed its first protest at entering this world.

Somehow, I felt my struggle to get to the delivery had taken more effort than had Mrs. Maple's effort to have the baby, but I was wise enough not to say so.

There was an interesting sequel to this sinkhole experience. About a year before, Bessie Barton had given birth to a baby at her home. The afterbirth had stubbornly refused to deliver. After four long hours of waiting, I manually removed it, using up-to-the-elbow sterile gloves. At the time I was paid my usual fee for a delivery — $25. I was not paid the extra $10 for removal of the afterbirth. Peggy sent Mrs. Barton a bill a month later to remind her, but payment was never received.

Two days after Marvin Barton pulled me out of the sinkhole with the tractor, the original bill for extracting the afterbirth the previous year came back to my office. On it was written in large letters, "Paid in full for pulling your car out of the mud — signed, Bessie Barton."

CHAPTER 43

IF NOTHING ELSE, THEIR ACTIONS WERE HUMAN

The cost of medical care in Rusk County was low. The physicians' fees were low and the Servite Sisters kept their hospital rates low. Many patients did not understand what it took to tend the sick with quality care at minimal cost. Only the Sisters' dedication made it possible. Sisters carried bedpans, bathed and fed patients, cooked meals, and farmed. Yet the Sisters' farm could not produce enough food to support the Sisterhood and the hospital. Some food had to be bought and some was given to them. One Friday, the entire hospital was fed by a large catfish I had caught.

Some of the food needed was begged for. Imagine, if you will, the potential indignities of begging for food and trying to explain the necessity for so doing. Most of the time these Sisters managed to humble themselves for the task.

In June 1947, I was called to the Frank farm. "Grandpa is off his feed. He's got quite a cough and sweats like hell. Sure would appreciate it if you'd come to see him," Martha Frank said.

"Could it wait a bit?" I asked. "I'm pretty well loaded today."

"Sure, Dr. Bill. He's been off his feed all winter and has had night sweats for a year. How about tomorrow?"

"Fine, I'll be there in the morning."

The Franks, through much physical exertion and thrift, had developed a dairy farm that supported them on a marginal level. Their modest means were balanced with modest wants. Both were redheaded, could flare up at a moment's notice, and were mulish. Yet both were kind, thoughtful, and understanding. They had a boy and a girl who also sported red hair.

As I pulled into the farm, a black labrador ran to greet me, snarling as I opened the car door. He soon recognized me as a friend and followed me into the house, where my two redheaded hosts were finishing their midmorning coffee.

"Sit down," Martha said, "and have a cup. Would you like a piece of pie?"

"No, thanks. I'll sit with you a spell and sip some coffee, but I'd better get on with looking at Grandpa. Tell me about him."

"Not much to tell," Todd said. "He's coughed so long we got used to it, but I think it's worse these last few weeks. He spits up some greenish stuff and he hardly eats anymore. Martha thinks he's thinner, and I guess he is."

"How are the children? Do they cough? What about you two, do you cough?" I asked.

"No, we're fine, but Grandma has coughed some," Todd said. "You can look at her, too, if you've a mind to."

When we entered their room, Grandpa was asleep on a rocker and Grandma was napping on a divan. They were in their 70's and appeared pale and thin, but did not seem acutely ill. Martha awakened them gently. "The doctor is here," she said. "He wants to check you."

Both sat up and coughed at once with deep, productive parozyms. Examination of their chests strongly suggested tuberculosis.

"I hate to mention it, but it sounds like they could have tuberculosis," I said. "I'll make some smears and it will be best if each one of you has a tuberculin test and a chest X-ray."

At mention of X-rays, Martha flew into a rage. "X-rays for all six of us? You mean at the hospital? Will the Sisters demand a down payment again? When our son broke his leg, they wanted money before they would X-ray him. Our record was always good. We always paid every cent, not on time, mind you, but as soon as we could." Color mounted in her cheeks and her red hair was flying as she tossed her head from side to side.

"I know how you feel," I said, "but we must take some X-rays. It's important."

"No, you don't know how I feel," Martha shouted, emphasizing the word 'don't'. "Those darn Sisters; no, those damn Sisters! They don't know what it's like to sweat it out here on the farm, to get up early and strip the cows, feed them and clean up their muck, to cut and bring in hay. They have it easy with their fancy buildings and everything laid out for them." Martha presented a fiery picture of indignation.

I was about to tell her some of the problems the Sisters had, how they had to beg for food and how they ran a farm, cooked, bathed patients, and yet needed to take in enough money to run the hospital. It was just as well that I hesitated, for at that very moment, the tight, angry lines on Martha's face relaxed.

"Want to hear something funny?" she asked. "You should have been here last week, you would have laughed yourself sick." She smiled and went on. "A station wagon full of Sisters came here. They asked if we could spare some chickens for the hospital. When I thought of how they insisted on a down payment when our son broke his leg, I was about to say 'No,' but I got an idea. My chickens run free, so I told them if they could catch six, they could have them."

Martha laughed loudly. Her contagious laugh and her red hair conspired to magnify her mischievous look as she continued. "You should have seen them Sisters with their long skirts sweeping the dust, chasing them hens. We set by the window and watched. It was a sight to see."

Obviously, it had been an amusing and satisfying occasion for the Franks, but it must have been an agonizing and frustrating experience for the Sisters, who went away without catching a single chicken.

Martha's description of the chase was undeniably amusing. Torn though I was between empathy for the Franks and sympathy for the Sisters, I was not kept from joining in their laughter. It seemed to me that both parties had some justification for their actions, which were, if nothing else, human.

CHAPTER 44

A LONG TWENTY SECONDS

"This is Mrs. March, Sam's wife. I'm the new president of the Parent-Teacher Association (PTA). I need a favor of you."

I knew the voice well. Two years before I had removed her spleen ruptured in a car accident. "Yes, April, I'm listening. What can I do for you?"

"When the new grade school is completed, we want you to be our speaker. Will you do it?"

"When will that be and what do you want me to talk about?" I asked.

"Can't tell when the school will be finished, maybe by May — but we want you to suggest some ideas on how to handle children. Would you do that for me?"

With increasing frequency, I had been requested to give short talks on subjects related to my profession and had accepted the invitations as a civic responsibility. These experiences soon impressed me with the truth of Abraham Lincoln's observation that the shorter the speech, the longer the time needed for preparation.

"By the way, how long do you want me to talk?" I asked.

"About 10 to 15 minutes. Would that be OK?"

I wasn't overjoyed with the idea, but I said,"I guess I can do that , but be sure to call me at least a month ahead of time, if you can."

In the months that followed, April's request was completely forgotten. One evening, out of the blue, Gussie remarked, "Your talk to the PTA is next Monday."

"It is? When did you hear about it?" I asked.

"April called this morning to remind you, and I saw it in the paper."

"She wants me to talk about handling children. Gosh, she hasn't given me much time to think about it."

"I'm afraid you have the wrong idea, Bill. She wants you to talk on how to raise young children."

"That can't be," I interrupted. "You've got it all wrong."

"Oh, no, I haven't. Look here at the announcement in the paper."

What I saw was immediately upsetting: "Dr. William Bauer will talk Monday night at the new grade school's first PTA meeting. His subject is "How to Raise Young Children."

"I can't do it. No way will I do it. How can I tell our neighbors and friends how they should raise their children? Imagine how we could feel in the next few years if our own became problems?"

Of course I had to fulfill my obligation, though I winced many times in the next few days thinking about it. I thought of my own five children. I was proud of them and realized how much they had taught me. As a matter of fact, they were bringing me up rather well. I was a better father because of them, but I didn't want to talk as a parent but as a doctor. By dealing with the familiar aspects of my profession, I could direct my attention to my audience without the need to look at notes. Long drives into the country for home calls gave me time to think about my subject, to practice talking out loud and generally piece together my speech.

But how could I escape the stigma of the announcement, "How to Raise Young Children?" It troubled me until I thought of three-year-old Tommy and his mother. This robust lad had been running her ragged. She had often consulted me about his lack of toilet training. He would drop his shorts and let go anywhere, except in his potty. Her frustration reached its peak the day he brought his potty containing a large bowel movement into the living room where she was entertaining four ladies. Very humiliated, she spanked him, put him to bed and called me. It was difficult to reason with her, but I finally calmed her down, explaining, "Tommy brought the potty into the living room to show he had accomplished what you wanted. He was trying to please you and he felt good about it."

Other encounters with children came to mind, and I realized these experiences as a physician — but not as a father — should be the substance of my talk. Sharing such experiences with my audience might even relieve me of the stigma of the announcement, "How to Raise Young Children."

The day came. I fumed and I fussed. Actually, I felt confident about the talk. Rehearsing it several times, I felt it seemed relevant, the length was proper at ten minutes, and my familiarity with the subject made notes superfluous. But I continued to worry. I could not think of how to begin such a speech, "How to Raise Young Children."

The day wore on. Evening came at last. Still upset, I could not eat supper. At 8:00 P.M., I entered the school's multi-purpose room. Only about 200 people were present, but they seemed more like thousands. As I walked to the front of the room, suddenly there was complete silence. April, the PTA president, introduced me. Her words were so generous that I should have been relieved of my distress, but I still floundered for the proper words with which to begin. All week I had searched and finally found a way to avoid telling my neighbors and friends how to raise young children, but I didn't know how to begin. The silence continued. My face flushed and I could feel its heat.

Seeking help, I asked God to give me the right words.

Instantly, the words came clearly: "How fortunate you people are to have a speaker who has learned so much about young children."

The realization of what I had said raced through my mind. The urge to dash from the room, to escape, was unbearable. The silence became utterly painful. There was no question that I had the complete attention of my audience. I could feel their eyes, all 200 pairs needling my skin.

Another 20 seconds of silence were suddenly broken by a voice, — my voice, I was surprised to find out: "Oh, if I had only known when my children were younger what I know now. And if I only knew today what I hope to learn in the next ten years about raising older children."

My flushing ceased, my pulse slowed, my heart returned to my chest and ceased thumping. The audience responded with delightful appreciation. Somehow, they seemed to have understood my predicament and smilingly accepted my unaffected explanation. This set me at ease to share some of my fascinating encounters with children.

This experience taught me a lesson, useful to me as a country doctor — the importance of being straightforward, not fearing to be myself. It also taught me not to be too easily pressured into accepting invitations to speak.

MARIE WAS A CHARACTER
or
ENTERTAINMENT IN THE OPERATING ROOM

When Marie first entered my office, she was in her late 60's. Her muddy gray hair, deeply furrowed face, large ears, and bulbous nose gave her a strangely elfish appearance. Actually, she was ugly — not repulsive, just plain ugly. Her ugliness struck me when I first entered the room and stayed with me till Marie spoke. Then abruptly, her ugly mask disintegrated as furrows changed into pleasing lines and her lively blue eyes captured mine. She spoke clearly, her words falling from her mouth with a light, swinging lilt. Held by her merry patter, I could not recall at what point her bulbous nose and oversized ears seemed to have vanished.

"I came here to be near my cousin, Esther. She is my only living relative, but I'm out to find a doctor who is not an old grouch. I've got high blood pressure and a poor heart. My doctor says it filbrillates or something. Anyhow, it's irregular. I can hear irregular beating when I lie down."

I was fascinated by her lighthearted air. She spoke as if telling a humorous anecdote. Then her tone suddenly changed. "I'm really worried. Out of the blue, I started to throw up black stuff. It happens quite often."

"When did this start?" I asked.

"Just before I left Minneapolis. By the way, I'm also a diabetic and take 45 units of insulin every day."

After chatting for a few minutes, I stood up and looked at this woman who intrigued me with her warm, open manner. "If you don't find me too much of an old grouch," I said, "why don't you make an appointment for next week? Meanwhile, stay on the same diet and insulin and whatever pills your Minneapolis doctor prescribed."

Marie returned the following week. Urine and blood tests demonstrated that her diabetes was under control. Her blood pressure was high, suggesting the need to increase her medication, but her filbrillating heart appeared relatively stable. X-rays of her upper gastrointestinal tract revealed that the source of her bleeding was in the duodenum. Medications to soothe and quiet the bleeding were prescribed.

For several months Marie did well, but then the bleeding became more severe and Marie became a frequent visitor to my office and a frequent hospital guest. Transfusions became necessary to overcome the loss of blood.

One day Marie asked with a sly smile, "Why don't you put me under the knife?" and when I said nothing, she went on. "It would save us both a lot of messing around."

"It might at that, Marie, but I don't think it's wise. Because of your diabetes, high blood pressure, and filbrillating heart, I think its best to keep messing around with medications and transfusions."

"Sometimes it scares me when I throw up big chunks of black stuff." Marie scowled and then winked at me.

"Well, Marie, there's only one other possibility I can suggest — that is to send you to a large medical center. Perhaps with the added skills of both anesthesia and surgery, doctors there might venture to operate."

Marie agreed, and I arranged an appointment. When she returned from the medical center, she gave me one of her impish looks. "It's no use. The doctors said it would be too dangerous. So, what are we gonna do?"

A letter from the medical center verified Marie's statement. Surgery was considered too hazardous because of her poor general condition.

We established an almost regular routine. When the bleeding was severe, an outpatient transfusion or two was given, following which Marie rested for two hours at the hospital. When the bleeding was not severe, Marie appeared at my office every two weeks to have her blood pressure, heart, and diabetes checked.

An interesting side of this regime developed and became an accepted part of each visit to the hospital or my office. Consistently, Marie would pose the same question: "I know you are busy, but do you have time for a story?" When assured that I would take the time, she would relate a spicy tale. Her obvious pleasure in telling a joke persuaded me to enlarge her audience. Thus, when possible, I included the office girls.

Her good humor, high spirits, and storytelling carried Marie through many months in spite of her multiple aggravations. They also made a delightful intermission to many an office hour. Despite her ugly appearance and her difficult medical problems, this engaging woman was a real delight and inspiration to all of us.

Two years passed, during which time office and hospital sessions continued basically unchanged. I continued to anticipate Marie's visits with pleasure, but a new difficulty arose. Marie had a lump in her left breast. "I've had it for several months, and it's getting larger," she said. "Maybe you had better take a look."

It was easily identified. "Marie, it's cancerous." I said. "You should have shown me this sooner."

"Didn't think it amounted to anything. It didn't hurt, and people my age get spots and lumps everywhere." Marie looked at me with a 'now-don't-you-dare-scold-me' look and then asked, "What are you gonna do about it?"

"It should be removed, Marie; the sooner, the better."

"But you said I couldn't undergo surgery and so did the clinic you sent me to," Marie said matter-of-factly.

"This surgery will not have the same risk to your heart and blood pressure as surgery to your intestines would. Your breast can be removed under local anesthesia. You can remain awake."

"OK," Marie said. "Let's get on with it."

"Better think on it, Marie. You let me know."

It was a Monday that I will always remember. Though Marie appeared well composed, I gave her a mild hypnotic injection. In spite of it, she chatted contentedly with the anesthetist as she was being wheeled into the operating room. Still talking, she was lifted onto the operating table. The wire screen separating the head and neck from the chest was put in place, and the area of the left breast was painted and draped. The anesthetist arranged her equipment and the scrub nurse arranged the surgical instruments. A colleague, who had agreed to assist me, stepped up to the patient's right side as I approached the left. Marie was still talking.

"Better rest a bit," the Sister-anesthetist said as she ran her long fingers gently over the patient's cheeks. "The doctor will want you quiet."

I began the operation. Marie was quiet. After a while, Marie spoke up with merriment in her voice: "Do you think they are old enough?"

Accustomed as I was to her stories, I knew what was coming. I looked about. The scrub nurse was a sophisticated person. The head nurse and the anesthetist were Catholic Sisters. Both were accustomed to the many unorthodox words that were sometimes expressed by patients undergoing general anesthesia. In spite of this, knowing Marie and her stories, I feared what might follow. Nevertheless, I leaned over the partition that separated Marie's head from the operative area and said, "Sure, Marie, they are old enough." As I spoke, I winked knowingly, with the hope that she would not deliver one of her spiciest tales.

Marie began at once: "There were an engaging young man who became a priest. He was born, attended grammar school and high school in the same parish in Idaho. Even the seminary he attended was situated in the same parish. When he graduated, a church opening was available, also in the same parish.

"For ten years, the young priest made an indelible impression on his congregation. His even disposition and his excellent sermons were much appreciated. On the tenth anniversary of his priestly duties, the head deacon spoke at the completion of the morning service. Standing beside the priest, he said, 'Here is a check for $1,000, and here is the key to a new Chevrolet parked out in front. We want you to go to San Francisco and have a good time for two weeks. We know you have never stepped out of the county and hope this trip will demonstrate how much we have esteemed you as our priest.'

"The untraveled and unworldly priest reached San Francisco, parked his car, and noted a strange tubular device with a small head fastened to the curb. He asked a passerby what it was for. With a note of sarcasm, the passing stranger said, 'That's a parking meter. Better put a nickel in it or the police will tow your car away!'

"Looking about, the priest entered the nearest business place, seeking change for the meter. It proved to be a topless-waitress restaurant. Waiting beside the cash register, the bug-eyed priest watched uncomfortably as a waitress approached. 'What can I do for you?' the girl asked.

"'Ca-ca-ca could you gi-gi-gi-give me t-t-t-two ni-ni-nipples for a dime?' the embarrassed priest stuttered."

Subdued laughter was followed by a moment of embarrassed silence. Then a nurse gallantly spoke up, "What courage it must have taken her to tell a story while losing her breast!"

The operation was completed. Marie left the hospital and continued to brighten many a day for me and others. Marie was a real character — a beautiful character.

CHAPTER 46

A MOMENT OF SELF-PITY

It was early afternoon. The waiting room was stuffed with people. A staccato of sounds — the whimpering of babies, the cries of children, and the tumult of adult voices — were all thrown together like a multi-vegetable stew. Adding to this tempest of human sound was the incessant ringing of the phone, like a bell-buoy's constant warning of a nearby reef.

Peggy suddenly broke into the consultation room. "There's an emergency at the hospital; a hand was caught in a paper press." As I hurried out the back door into subzero weather, she shouted after me, "A woman has been rushed to the delivery room. When will you be back? What should I tell all these patients?"

Twice during the previous night I had delivered a baby, one in a farmhouse a few miles out in the country, and one in the hospital. An early morning call from a patient had particularly irritated me because of its demanding tones. A mid-morning operation had been unduly delayed for 15 minutes because a preoperative hypo had been forgotten. As I drove to the hospital, my inner calm was disturbed and my outer feathers were ruffled. The short mile to the hospital gave me little time to soothe my mind or smooth my feathers.

Poking my head into the emergency room, I advised scrubbing and cleansing the badly lacerated hand. But I did so with more than necessary emphasis. There was an impatience to my words that seemed to follow me into the elevator on my way up to the delivery room. I flushed with recognition of my own annoyance and inwardly vowed to exercise more self-restraint.

The seven-pound baby was a breech (bottom first), requiring time and patience, both of which were in short supply. Everything came out well, but the procedure exacted an immeasurable toll on my composure.

I rushed downstairs and into the emergency room. When I saw the patient's lacerated hand, I gasped at the abbreviated cleansing that had been done. Dirt and oil were evident among the torn tissues. Recalling my vow of self-control, I said nothing and cleansed the hand myself, but I am sure my annoyance was clearly visible. I managed to call upon my reserves but, in truth, they were nearly exhausted. An hour later the torn tendons were intact, the skin sutured, and the hand dressed and splinted.

I phoned the office and told Peggy I would be there in ten or 15 minutes. I noted her sigh of relief over and above the medley of voices in the packed waiting room. Then I went to the doctors room and just sat, drinking a glass of orange juice. It was a judicious decision, ten minutes of "catching my breath." Many thoughts flowed through my mind, some good, some bad, some positive, some negative. I asked questions of myself and tried to find answers.

Why had I come to this far, out-of-the-way community, to this poor county that vied with Florence County as the poorest in the state? Why? Why, when I could spend so little time with my growing family? We now had four children, but how often did I really share time with them? Only last week, Billy had asked, "You're coming to our school program tonight, aren't you, Dad?"

"I sure am," I had responded, but I did not get there in time to hear Billy say his piece, for Fanny Bliven's eight-month-old baby had gotten a safety pin caught in his throat.

Thanksgiving Day also came to mind. Christi had come to my desk, where I was busily reading. "The turkey will be ready for our Thanksgiving dinner in half an hour, Dad. Mom says we should all be ready. "She wants us to look really nice."

I went upstairs, showered, and dressed. We assembled at the table, said Grace, and I stood up to carve the Thanksgiving bird. The phone rang and I was off to the hospital. Marly Danson's baby chose to come a week early.

My thoughts continued to tumble. The day's sub-zero temperature made me think of the severe winters and unpaved roads we 'enjoyed.' Roads were often blocked with snow, glared with ice, or made impassable by mud. I had learned to carry three car jacks, an axe, a band saw, extra clothes, and snowshoes. In spite of these precautions, getting pulled out of drifts or mud holes by farmers with their tractors was not unusual.

Suddenly, there flashed through my thoughts a horse-drawn cutter, winding its way 20-odd miles through a blinding snowstorm. The driver, a physician, on reaching the farmhouse found an 80-year-old man with anuria. Unable to pass his urine, his abdomen was painfully distended, sticking out like a seventh-month pregnancy in a frail woman. To his dismay, the doctor found he had no catheter, no sterile tube to pass into the bladder through the urethra, which was obstructed by an enlarged prostate. The doctor had to return to Ladysmith and then back to the farm, another 40-mile trip. All told, he traveled more than 80 miles with a horse-drawn cutter in blinding snow. He charged $8, in lieu of which, several months later, he was presented with two old hens. This incident occurred before I arrived in Ladysmith. It was an actual experience of one of my predecessors, a remarkable man and a remarkable doctor.

My daydreams came to an abrupt halt as Sister Theresa asked if I wanted another glass of orange juice. "No thanks," I said and stood up. My 10 or 15 minutes of "catching my breath" was over. No longer filled with self-pity, I hurried back to the office. I was now ready to face my responsibilities with renewed vigor and enthusiasm and to accept the disadvantages that go along with the advantages of living in this northern, out of the way place. In no way could I compare my discomforts with those of the physicians who had preceded me and blazed the trail that made my life so rewarding.

CHAPTER 47

A SURPRISING REQUEST

For several years, Mennonites trickled into my office with increasing frequency, and more and more Mennonite women sought my obstetrical services. I was at a loss to explain this, because my first run-in with a Mennonite had not been auspicious. That run-in took place after my second winter in Wisconsin, a winter heavy with snow and harsh with cold.

It was an early spring morning. There had been little thawing and most thoroughfares were still bordered with snowpiles higher than the vehicles that traveled between them. The rising arc of the March sun had taken only small bites from the northwestern snowbanks, but melting trails of water slid down the southeastern highway slopes. There, hidden from the sun by the high snowbanks, the trails of water quickly refroze, glazing the road. These intermittent patches of ice necessitated caution and slow speed, but I was totally unprepared for the situation that was to confront me.

As I neared my destination, the road became more tortuous and hilly. When I reached the top of a rise, I saw below me a horse-drawn wagon facing west, with two women on the seat. In the other lane, beside the farm wagon but facing east, sat a farm truck completely blocking the road. A woman in the truck was busily chatting with the two sitting on the wagon. One hundred fifty feet of glare ice stretched downhill from me to them. Almost instinctively, I turned the steering wheel toward the right snowbank but my car proceeded forward. Then I turned toward the left snowbank. My car continued unwaveringly toward the farm wagon, hit its rear with a noisy wallop, and startled the pair of horses . They broke loose and ran down the road.

The entire episode took less than a minute. The two Mennonite women, a mother and her daughter, remained sitting in the wagon. In the farm truck sat the third woman. The mother on the farm wagon was bleeding briskly from a cut on her face and lip. Together, we entered a nearby farmhouse, where I sutured her cuts and checked all three women for other possible injuries. I found none, but advised them to check with their physicians and then went on to complete my house call.

After this inauspicious incident, it seemed odd that so many Mennonite families sought my services. For years I mused about it, often recalling that moment when my car slid into the farm wagon.

"Hurry, Doctor, Mrs. Cummings needs you. Drive south on the Ingram road about three miles. There will be several lights on the right side." The phone clicked as the person hung up.

The voice was unfamiliar. The name, Mrs. Cummings, was also unfamiliar, but I knew the area was populated by several Mennonite families. I had also learned that Mennonites often called when a mother was in labor, even when there had been no prenatal care. So, I took my obstetrical bag along.

Within 30 minutes, I turned into the farm driveway. As my headlights lit the yard, I noted several large tents, a half-dozen tables, two cooking fires, and about 30 people. All the women had on their distinctive white caps and most wore generous white aprons. As I opened the car door, a pleasant babble of voices and the enticing odors of cooking hit at the same moment.

There was no time for further appraisal, for I was ushered into the farmhouse with haste. The delivery of a boy took place within the hour. After the baby and new mother were checked, I packed my bag. Prepared to leave, I gave last-minute instructions. At this point, three elderly Mennonite men approached me. "Wouldn't you like some food? Perhaps some coffee and pie?"

Another spoke. "This is a special celebration for us." He explained why, but I never did understand. Perhaps it was the birth of a long-hoped-for firstborn. The third gentleman, who resembled a Norman Rockwell portrait of a much-beloved grandfather, was obviously the eldest man in the group. He took me aside and requested that I join the three of them in the biggest tent after I finished eating. I did not become uneasy, for I was accustomed to many surprises in this north country. But my curiosity was intense.

By now, in my late 30's, I had been matured by many unexpected experiences. I was ready to be paid my $25 fee, and ready to chat with these Mennonites, some whom I knew and others whom I had never met. But I was not ready for what took place.

As soon as I stepped into the tent, the three elders approached me. They invited me to sit down with them on canvas camp chairs around a wooden table. Immediately, other men in the tent withdrew. The eldest addressed me. "We have a favor to ask of you. Please listen. It means a great deal to us." He hesitated.

Another continued, "We have held you up as an example to our young people as a fine young man."

The third went on, "About seven or eight years ago, through no fault of your own, you smashed into the farm wagon of one of our members that was blocking the road. You never asked for recompense."

The eldest now rose and stood looking down at me. "Dr. Bauer, as an example to our youth, we want you to quit smoking. We have become fond of you. We'd like you to do this for us."

The impact of this request was more than surprising. It was shocking. Of course, I was pleased by the compliment. The whole subject was delivered with such intensity that I could not mistake it for flattery. Their request was not something I could take lightly, for these three were acting with marked respect. Though I was flustered, I tried to conceal it and resolved to respond honestly.

"I'll give your request much thought, but I won't promise." I said, extending both of my hands to these three elders. "But I want you to know that I appreciate your kind thoughts."

Actually, it took another six or seven years before I determined to give up tobacco, but in respect for their request, I no longer smoked in my office or in the homes I entered as a physician.

Being a country doctor is full of surprises

JOHNNIE and the HORSE DOCTOR

I was called to the emergency room. It was 1:00 in the morning. A 15-year-old boy lay on the examining table, streaming blood from multiple lacerations on his face. He reeked of alcohol and was swearing at the Sister-nurse cleaning his wounds. His father, who stood over him, was frozen with anxiety and too numb to speak. Since his presence was obviously of no advantage, I asked him to wait in the hall.

The youth, who continued to explode four-letter words upon seeing me, shouted, "Get that g...d...horse doctor out of here." After listening to his curses for five minutes while I was examining his wounds, I turned him over and gave him three or four lusty whacks on his bare bottom and told him he could get another doctor.

Hearing the ruckus, the boy's father burst through the door. I was sure he would rush to his son's defense, but instead he said, "Good for you, Dr. Bill. I should have done that a long time ago."

Possibly I could have handled the situation more skillfully, but at the moment I thought the boy needed to be shaken up. He had been driving without a license, was drinking though underage, and was abusive to those trying to help him. Even though he was loaded with beer and had called me a horse doctor, I should not have been so readily miffed. I was ashamed of my own behavior, but persuaded by Johnnie's father, I completed the suturing of Johnnie's lacerations.

In my unsettled state, physically exhausted and emotionally upset, I went to my office. It was now 3:00. Why couldn't I have found another way to get to Johnnie? How could I have been so stupid as to spank this 15-year-old boy? Perhaps he deserved it, but this was not a proper method for a doctor who prided himself on his ability to treat children.

I had always loved children, had taught many how to swim and play tennis, had tutored teenagers in high school subjects, and had read books on child psychology. During the past ten years of my practice, I thought I had learned a great deal about handling children. I had resolved to treat them not only as children but also as little people, little individuals, each with personalities strictly their own. Tonight, I had violated my resolve. Certainly, I should have found a better approach than to spank Johnnie.

Thoroughly disgusted with myself, I sat and stewed. With fondness I remembered Elsie, a five-year-old Mennonite girl who had come to my office holding a blood-soaked washcloth tightly against her cheek. She looked up at me with large unblinking blue eyes as her mother explained, "Elsie has a large, gaping wound below her right eye, and she's scared to death."

I remembered picking her up and setting her on the examining table.

"Do you have a pet at home?" I asked. "A dog, a cat, a rabbit, or maybe a favorite cow?" I spoke soothingly in much the same tone as I talked to farm dogs that growled at my approach. Elsie looked at me warily.

"How many sisters do you have?" I asked. Elsie opened her mouth but, still on her guard, said nothing.

I remembered leaning over her, patting her right hand, then taking it and rubbing it gently across the fine stubble of my hastily shaven face. Our eyes met. That I gained her confidence was evident as she offered the suggestions of a smile and words poured from her mouth.

"I've got a pony, Dr. Bill," she said. "He's all mine. Uncle Amos gave him to me last week. I've ridden him twice and he's real cute."

I responded, "I'm sure he is and I'll have to come out to your farm and see him. Would you let me do that?"

"Oh, you bet," she answered as I removed her left hand from her face, still holding the blood-stained cloth.

"We had better look at your cut," I suggested, removing the makeshift bandage. "How did it happen?"

"I fell off the pony. I guess I have a lot to learn about riding."

"I'm sure you'll learn. When you and the pony get to know each other, you will find riding can be great fun," I said.

Then looking at the gaping wound, I added, "You are a pretty girl. We must close that cut so you won't have a nasty scar."

"All right," she answered, "but will it hurt?"

"It will hurt some, but not as much as when you fell of your pony. I'll go ever so slowly. You can squeeze my arm when it hurts and then I'll wait until you are ready again," I explained.

As the fine needle punctured her skin, her eyes sought mine. When her hand squeezed my left arm, I hesitated, and when her hold on my arm relaxed, I placed the second suture. And so we continued until the wound was closed. Amazingly, Elsie never whimpered. When I completed the dressing, she sat up and gave me a full payment for my patience —- a hug and a kiss — and then asked, "Will I still be pretty?"

With pride, I recalled that seldom afterwards did I need to use a local anesthetic to sew up cuts in children, but the thought of how I had treated Johnnie soon dispelled my pride.

Half asleep with exhaustion and half awake with guilt, past images and events continued to sweep before me. I had learned that children readily mimic others and had used this to advantage. Instead of using a tongue blade to look at a child's throat, I would open my own mouth and suck in air to demonstrate what I wanted the child to do. In most cases, it worked and avoided gagging the child.

I smiled to myself when I thought about Carol, a four-year-old. She had come into the office with a high fever and sore throat, her eyes brimming with tears. When I opened my mouth and sucked in air, her bright eyes followed my movements with avid interest. When I closed my mouth, she looked directly into my eyes and with a straight face, said, "My doctor, what a big mouth you have!"

I fell asleep sitting there in my office, still uneasy about spanking Johnnie. It wasn't until morning, when I went home to clean up and have breakfast, that my mind was put to rest. I resolved to get to know this young man and try to gain his confidence.

Being called 'horse doctor' had riled me at the time, but my getting upset led not only to some good changes in Johnnie but also in me. Johnnie became more respectful of others and he and I became good friends, good enough friends so that he brought some of his buddies to see me. From our talks, I learned a great deal more about teenagers than I had absorbed from books, especially their manners and their activities, which too often include smoking, using alcohol, and even using drugs. How most boys and girls undergo insecurity that becomes cloaked in shyness or camouflaged in bragging. How in these muddled-up teenage years, young people feel sandwiched between opposing forces. On the one hand, they are pressured by the mores of church, school, and home, and on the other hand by the current opinions of peers and their awakening drives of maturity. How maturity then becomes a rending process as the teenager attempts to separate himself from these powerful, contradictory forces.

It was from these talks that I also learned what troubled most teenagers. They are full of questions they are unprepared to answer and which, in turn, frustrate them. Where am I going? What am I doing here? What is life all about? What am I going to do with my life?

Insights gained indirectly from my spanking incident with Johnnie added new meaning to my counseling of youngsters.

Shortly after getting to know Johnnie, Mr. and Mrs. John Reynolds came to my office with their daughters, Daisy and Trisha, who were 13 and 14. Both girls were exceptionally pretty and looked very grownup for their ages, but it soon became apparent that they were surly, belligerent, and disrespectful. Their parents had brought them in to me, hoping I could help straighten them out.

The insights I had gained from my experience with Johnnie gave me the courage to try, but the girls seemed unreachable. The atmosphere was charged with animosity as all four of them talked heatedly at the same time, so I arranged to talk to the girls and their parents separately. The parents were especially distressed about the kind of friends the girls had and the late hours they kept. The girls felt they were being treated like babies and that their parents were old fashioned. "They are squares," each girl said, more than once.

I listened to both sides and suggested a few compromises. I tried to get the parents to recall their own teenage years and how they had felt. I tried to get the girls to appreciate some of the dangers of peer dependency. The discussion seemed to get nowhere. The girls thought I, too, was a 'square,' and I felt hopeless to do more.

Two weeks later, Daisy, the younger of the two, phoned to ask me to come out to the farm. Her Irish setter had torn his belly open jumping a barbed-wire fence.

My first reaction was to send her to a 'vet' but something held me back. Her Irish setter meant a great deal to her. Perhaps more than anything else, it tied her to the farm. Although Daisy helped milk cows and helped in other ways, she did her chores under great protest. But she treasured her dog and had voluntarily sought my help, even though two weeks before I had vigorously protested her peer dependence. Perhaps she was revealing faith in me, even though I was a 'square.' "Please, Dr. Bill," she pleaded, "I love him so. He is my best friend."

I went to the farm, prepared to use drop ether, but even though his wounds were severe and his abdominal organs protruded, an anesthetic was unnecessary, for the dog responded to my initial overtures with apparent confidence.

While I shaved the dog's abdomen, he merely whimpered. When I sutured his wounds, I sutured a single stitch, hesitated, and then sutured again, just as I did when suturing children. Each time I stopped, I would talk to the dog and look into his eyes before starting again. While I was working on the dog, his head lay in Daisy's lap as she whispered soothingly to him.

In a week the Irish setter was back on duty, a solace to Daisy and a help to the farm, for he aided in bringing the cows from pasture.

During the following ten years, both Daisy and her sister, Trisha, like Johnnie, became my friends. Each of them brought other teenagers to see me. It seemed they no longer frowned on me as a 'square.' Both married and moved to California and, occasionally, they write or phone for personal advice.

Yes, teenagers, beset with their problems of growing up, were a frequent challenge that often taxed all my resources. But, hearing Daisy plead, "Please, Dr. Bill, he is my best friend," suggested a confidence in me that swelled my ego; and having Johnnie as a friend, after being riled by his calling me 'a g..d... horse doctor," warmed my heart.

THE CASE OF THE RED SUSPENDERS

Promise of a good deer season was in the air. It was snowing, and on the morrow the season would begin. Butch, a 50-year-old auto mechanic, had once again offered the use of his cabin, set deep in the woods of the Nail Creek area. Marty, a school bus driver, and Tony, a school teacher, both in their late 40's, had already left to prepare the cabin — to cut wood for the potbellied heating stove and to clean out the old bugs and spider webs.

There was more than the prospect of tracking a deer that drew the four of us to this remote spot. There was a beauty in each tree, each bush, and even in each withered fern wrapped in ermine. There was also the special beauty of past memories that each of us carried within and the special beauty of anticipation of five days together.

Rather late that night, the Friday before opening day of the season, Butch and I set out for the cabin. As we turned east down an old logging road, the snow made the going rough. Balsam and spruce, heavy with snow, bowed their heads in mute acknowledgment of our passage. Another deer season was at hand.

As we approached the cabin, its windows flickered with the light of the kerosene lamps within and splashed reflections on the snow already ten inches deep. Butch and I trudged through heavy drifts and entered the cabin. Huddled over a cribbage board, Marty and Tony shouted a greeting but did not get up. The odor of mildew combined with the sweet scent of burning pine, assailed us. The potbellied stove, fashioned from an old oil drum, its maw recently filled with split logs, literally danced a jig on the wooden floor. A bottle of Old Crow, already sampled, and a half pack of Old Milwaukee beer, with two cans missing, sat invitingly on the large wooden table that was centered in the room.

We carried our gear to one of the two bunkbeds that covered the east wall and sat down, gazing about the room as if for the first time, but actually assimilating past experiences into the framework of the present moment.

A large, old-fashioned sink, bought for $1.00 at a garage sale, and a long counter with cupboards above, handtooled by Butch, covered the west wall. Beneath the counter were three large coolers to keep fresh our five-day supply of fruits, vegetables, and meats, and on the counter sat a three-burner Coleman stove. As I looked about and opened a can of beer, the thought occurred to me that the cabin was crude, but it had the essentials of warmth, a place to sleep, food to eat, and would once again be the center for camaraderie.

Early the following morning, I was up making breakfast. The fragrance of coffee, pancakes, bacon, and sausages soon overwhelmed the lingering pungency of the mildew that had gathered since the preceding deer season. Warmed by the potbellied stove that once again cavorted with its belly full of fresh logs and brightened by the sun piercing its first light through the two east windows, the cabin bustled with the cheerful jibes of four men long known to each other.

"Time to go," said Tony, rising from his chair. "Got my belly full in spite of you fellows tryin' to hog it all."

"I'd never worry about you gettin' your share," Marty said. "Your hands are quick as lightning."

We set out. More than a foot of snow made progress slow. The wind had curled drifts into eerie shapes that sparkled in the rays of the rising sun. The sky was blue; our hearts were light. For us, the deer season, with all its trials, hazards, and joys, had truly begun.

For two days, we skirted ridges, pushed through snowdrifts, and took positions in likely spots near deer trails, but we saw no deer. Late each afternoon we tramped back to our cabin to replenish our energies with a savory meal and a long night's rest. On the third day, Martin shot a five-point buck within a hundred yards of the cabin and, on the fourth day, Tony shot an eight-pointer that we had to drag a mile.

Although no deer were killed on the fifth day, our last one, it remains unforgettable. Having shot their deer, Martin and Tony volunteered to make a drive around a large ridge. Butch and I would take a stand at the west end of a hillside, where a draw was formed between two ridges, making an exquisite vantage point. Not only was it a good plan but it should also have worked. Three deer came through the draw, all three of them bucks. Butch and I both took shots, but both shots missed. The startled deer dashed off through the heavy snow with uncanny ease. In sharp contrast, Martin and Tony, who soon appeared, lumbered through the snow with great effort. After some scathing insults regarding our marksmanship, we all returned to the cabin for a rest. After lunch, Martin and Tony generously offered to make another drive through a larger draw a mile or so to the east.

Butch and I accepted the offer and settled in the lee of a large white pine to shelter us from the bitter north wind that had sprung up. Three hours passed. In spite of the partial protection from the wind, we became chilled. The sun was now behind the southern tip of the ridge and the wind had whipped up.

"I'm freezing," Butch said. "How are you doing?"

"I'm frozen, too. The fellows should have been here by now. I'm getting worried."

"Dusk is startin' to settle in. I wonder what happened to them?" Butch asked. "I don't think there are any other hunters in this neck of the woods. We've seen no tracks other than our own, so we don't have to worry about a stray bullet."

"Why don't you stay here, Butch? I'll top the ridge and look for them. If I find any trouble, I'll fire two shots in quick succession. If I don't see them, I'll start back to the cabin from the other end of this ridge."

"OK, Bill," Butch said, "but I'd like another shot at a deer. See you at the cabin soon. I'll wait just a little longer. Maybe a deer will still come through this draw."

I searched the full length of the ravine, concerned for Marty and Tony. The snow was deep at the northeastern edge of the ridge. It had started to snow again and visibility was poor. I stumbled several times, meanwhile getting increasingly anxious for Marty and Tony. Then I started to worry about Butch. He had said he wanted another shot at a deer. Butch was a fellow who never gave up. He always completed the job at hand and was more than likely to hang on 'til the last moment for that one more shot.

It was dusk. I stopped to concentrate on finding several familiar landmarks, and when certain of my direction, headed for the cabin. Now I was worried about all three companions. In a matter of moments I found the main trail, soon saw the light of the kerosene lamps winking at me through the cabin windows, and burst happily into the cabin. Marty greeted me with,"Where's Butch?"

"He's either still lookin' for you or draggin' a deer. We never saw you fellas and started to get worried. But you know Butch. He probably stayed on that ridge hoping for a shot 'til the last light of the sun faded."

"We had a problem," Tony said. "Sorry, but we never did make that drive. I had 'the runs,' and after going several times it seemed I'd better come back to the cabin."

Marty broke in. "Yeah, Tony sure was busy for a spell. He had to stop four times on the way back."

"What will we do about Butch?" I asked.

"I wouldn't worry about Butch," Tony said. "He's a regular woodchuck. He can find his way in the dark."

"I guess you're right, but I'm going to turn on the headlights of my car. It's getting awful dark out there with the snow falling again."

When I came back in, I looked at Tony and asked, "Are you feeling rotten, Tony? I could make you some tea and toast and I have some medicine in my bag, if you'd like some."

"No, I'm feelin' better, but I sure left my mark there in the woods before we got back here, if you know what I mean."

"Yeah, I've been through it. Are you sure you wouldn't like some tea?"

"No, I'll eat what you fellows eat, but I'll go light," Tony said. "You don't have to doctor me, Doc, you're on vacation."

Half an hour went by. Supper was ready. No Butch. "What do you fellows think we should do?" I asked.

"Let's wait another half hour. That Butch couldn't get lost if he tried. Besides, this is his cabin and he knows this territory well," Tony said.

"Let's eat. I'm starved," Marty said. "Butch can eat when he comes."

The cabin had warmed up and the chill had left our bones, so we pulled the table a short distance from the roaring fire and sat down, leaving the side closest to the fire for Butch.

"Wonder if he got a deer," said Tony. "It wouldn't surprise me none if he tried draggin' it all the way here in the dark. He's the muliest man I know."

We were soon busy devouring "Dr. Bill's Mulligan Stew" — a concoction of boiled potatoes, carrots, and onions, to which is added two cans of chunky soup and a can of tomato soup. Ten minutes passed, then suddenly the door burst open and the snow-draped figure of Butch appeared. "You sons of bitches," he gasped. "Couldn't you wait for me to get back ? Been lookin' all over for you. Where in hell have you been?"

Martin shot back at him, "Sorry, Butch, I can't swallow that. I know you too well. You've been lookin' for that last shot, I know. Well? Tell us, did you get one? Have you dragged in a deer?"

"Simmer down," Tony said, "Come on, we got some of Dr. Bill's stew waiting for you."

Butch took off his outer jacket, shook off the remnants of snow and hung it on the back of his chair. Then he warmed himself by the potbellied stove and paced the floor as if in deep thought, but he said nothing and finally sat down. For a few minutes only the sounds of four hungry men slurping soup and the crackling of the fire could be heard. Suddenly Marty stopped eating, put his hand to his nose, looked at each of us suspiciously and then pushed back his chair.

"Somethin's rotten in Denmark," he said. "Tony, you havin' trouble again?"

"No, everything's fine," Tony said.

I pushed back my chair and got up. An unpleasant odor was getting stronger by the minute. Continuing to eat was out of the question. As I retreated from the table, Marty and Tony got up and joined me. Butch sat alone, leaning heavily on the back of his chair on which hung his bright red hunting jacket. He didn't seem the least perturbed.

"Butch," Marty yelled, "did you shit?"

Butch shook his head, then he turned to Marty and said, "No, of course not. What's the matter with you fellas? You pickin' on me just 'cause I'm late?" Then he screwed up his face into one of Butch's very special grins and continued, "Oh, I meant to tell you. I made a great find today. Someone left their brand-new suspenders out there in the woods. I saw the red color peekin' through the new snow on an old white pine stump. They were stiff like they were frozen. I crumpled them up and put them in my pocket." With that, he reached into the right-hand pocket of his jacket hanging on the back of his chair and extracted a pair of bright red suspenders. As the suspenders appeared, dripping with moisture, the nauseating smell became so intense that Tony opened the cabin door and the three of us leapt outside.

I looked at Martin and then at Tony. I knew something was up. Both of them were snickering. Something was going on that I knew nothing about.

Tony stuck his head in the doorway. "Butch," he shouted. "For a smart automobile mechanic you sure can be stupid. Martin and I never did get to make that drive, 'cause I had the runs. The first time it came so fast I barely had time to drop my pants and underwear, and in my hurry I forgot to pull my suspenders out of the way, so I left them there on the stump. Those are my suspenders you picked up, but you can have them."

Tony started to laugh, and Martin and I joined in. The more we thought about it, the more hilarious it got.

"Butch, open one of the windows and throw out those stinking suspenders and hunting jacket so we can come in. It's cold out here," Martin pleaded.

We watched as Butch rose slowly, held the dripping suspenders in his right hand, and pulled his hunting jacket off the back of his chair with his left. He seemed mesmerized as he advanced slowly to the door, measured step by measured step. The silly grin on his face started us laughing again. As Butch reached the door, he heaved out the suspenders, then stepped into the snow. Very deliberately, he hung his jacket on a six-foot balsam fir with the same meticulous care as one would hang a newly pressed dinner jacket.

The three of us scrambled back inside, opened two windows and stood with our backs to the stove. In moments, Butch came back in with the same silly grin on his face, but said not a word.

"Don't feel badly," Martin said. "Tony doesn't want the suspenders back. He said you can keep them."

CHAPTER 50

"I'M GOING HOME"

"Good morning, Dr. Bill," spoke a most pleasant voice. "Can you stop to see Herman? His face and neck are all speckled. I think he has measles."

"Sure can" I replied. "Be there in about an hour."

Sandra Gessup had seven children, each of whom she had delivered with difficulty but without complaint. She was 29 and her children, three boys and four girls, ranged in ages from two to nine years.

I enjoyed going to the Gessup home. In spite of its bare walls and bare floors, it radiated a comfortable warmth. Even the sounds and smells of this house were appealing. Though the nine-member family was crowded into a kitchen-dining room, a bath, and three bedrooms, I never felt a sense of congestion. The children's clothes, though generously patched, were always clean and tidy. In the many visits I made to this home, all nine occupants were kempt and well-mannered. Smiles and laughter were characteristic in the midst of scarcity. This house was truly a home.

When I arrived, I noted Herman's barking cough, his red eyes, and the typical confluent measles rash. After I wrote out a prescription and made some suggestions for his care, I turned to Sandra's husband, Mike. "Have you noticed how pale Sandra is?"

"No, I haven't," he answered.

Then I turned to Sandra. "You seem unsteady on your feet and your abdomen bulges. Are you pregnant again?"

"No, I'm sure I'm not, but I have felt kind of weak, and you're right — I do sort of stagger sometimes."

"Mike, can you bring Sandra to the office this afternoon? I'd like to check her over."

As the receptionist brought Sandra into the examining room, her pallor, accentuated by her dark hair and brown eyes, again struck me. Examination revealed an enlarged liver, ascites (abdominal fluid), and a pelvic mass associat-

163

ed with the left ovary and tube. A blood test verified that her paleness was due to a marked anemia. Cancer of the left ovary with metastases to the liver was the logical diagnosis, but I hesitated to say so. It seemed that Sandra interpreted my hesitation. She spoke calmly. "I'm not afraid, Dr. Bill. Tell us the truth."

I did. Sandra's eyes revealed her deep concern. For a moment, no one spoke, then Sandra asked, "How long would I have to live? Who would take care of my children?"

In 40+ years, I have not indulged in estimating the time that might be allotted till death intervenes with life. Nor did I then. Her candid approach made further hesitation inappropriate. Convinced by the spongy feel of the mass, the irregularity of the liver enlargement, the ascites and the anemia, I advised an abdominal tap. This could relieve abdominal pressure and possibly assure a clarification of the diagnosis. Moreover, a blood transfusion would give her renewed strength and vitality.

The following day, as an outpatient, she received a transfusion and underwent an abdominal tap using local anesthesia. Then she went home. A specimen of the cloudy fluid drawn from her abdomen was sent to a pathology laboratory for analysis.

A phone call from the lab two days later confirmed the diagnosis of ovarian cancer and the type-pseudomucinous cystic adenocarcinoma. It was a type unresponsive to all known methods of treatment and was already too widely spread to consider any form of treatment. This was discussed with Sandra and Mike.

For two months I tapped Sandra's abdomen at intervals of seven to ten days. Gradually, she required more frequent relief as fluid filled her abdomen more rapidly and interfered with the movement of her diaphragm, making her very short of breath. Transfusions also became necessary more frequently.

One day Mike called, rambling excitedly. "There's a place in Texas that has a new treatment. They have cured people with cancer. Our neighbor knows someone who has been cured. What do you think, Dr. Bill?"

"Let's talk about it. I'll drop by after office hours, Mike," I answered, realizing at once that I would be faced with a most difficult task.

When I arrived, Sandra and Mike were bursting with optimism. Both talked at once. One neighbor had implored them to go to Texas, another to go to Mexico. Familiarity with both suggested establishments and their pseudo-medical successes made my position of counseling touchy. At the moment, it seemed cruel to bring them back to reality. Yet I fully appreciated what I had perceived so often before — the clutching of a straw by a drowning person. The devastating nature of Sandra's cancer was well known to me. With how much responsibility should I charge myself to prevent Sandra and Mike from getting further in debt unnecessarily? And most important, how could I prevent their wasting precious moments of Sandra's remaining days, searching for a curative pot of gold at the end of an illusive rainbow?

"Sandra," I began, "laetrile is supposedly the newest treatment for cancer. Unfortunately, in the hands of the medical profession, it has not proved beneficial. In fact, it has sometimes proved harmful. The treatment centers you mentioned use laetrile and claim great success. If laetrile were as good as they claim, don't you think the medical profession would be using it?"

"Then you don't believe we should go?" Mike asked with a look of disappointment.

"No, I don't, Mike, but I have an idea. Would you have faith in the opinion of a doctor at the Mayo Clinic?"

Both Sandra and Mike nodded their heads and I went on. "You would only have to travel one hundred miles or so, rather than two thousand. One of my medical friends is a gynecologist, a specialist in diseases of female organs, at the clinic. I'll call him and make an appointment."

Bob agreed to see them the next day. I sent along Sandra's complete medical history. Bob called me the following evening. Reluctantly he had verified the diagnosis, spent two hours with the Gessup's and made no charge. "As kindly but as firmly as possible, I assured them that laetrile could not benefit Sandra," he said, "but I had nothing to offer. I only hope they are convinced not to make that trip to Texas or Mexico."

The Gessups called me later that same evening. "Your friend, Dr. Wallace, was real nice to us. We decided not to go south for the treatments. We're going to stay home."

Downhill changes in Sandra developed rapidly. Weakness and inability to get about tortured her. She remained overnight in the hospital following each of her abdominal taps, which were now done twice weekly.

Her wan appearance and her withered skin were in deep contrast to her agile smile and the sparkle that remained in her dark brown eyes. Her gentle words belied the struggle that went on within her. Her few requests and her consummate patience contradicted the little time remaining for her.

Then came the day of her last paracentesis (abdominal tap), though I knew it not. Sandra entered the hospital on a Friday. When I entered her room, she made one of her few requests. "Would you remove Enid's tonsils while I am here? Could she stay here in my room?"

This meant some definite changes in hospital routine and some questionable infringements on regulations. But it was a special request from a special person under special circumstances. So, it was accomplished. Sandra had her abdominal tap and her daughter had her tonsils removed. The daughter's crib was placed in her mother's room.

The following morning, both were ready to go home. Mike entered the room at 8:00 A.M., took his daughter out of the crib, and carried her to his car. Shortly he returned.

The nurse brought in a wheelchair for Sandra. We stood watching Sandra rise slowly from the bed. With her dark brown eyes now deeply set from her emaciation, she looked directly at me. She hovered over the wheelchair for an instant. Then she smiled and clearly spoke three words: "I'm going home."

With that, she dropped into the wheelchair and she was gone. She had gone to her rightful place — home to heaven:

On Mother's Day, I was moved to send the following letter:

Dear Mike and dear children:

Dads can be special, but mothers are very, very special. Your mother was very, very special.

Even to me she was special. Her light footsteps as she bounced down the hall still echo in my mind. I see her pallid cheeks, her gentle smile, how she emphasized her words with a firm look and her constant habit of pointing.

Her love for all was incomparable. Somehow, she was always involved, giving of herself, often to exhaustion. She went to bat for you children, but also for the neighborhood, even the dogs. She patched, darned and mended your hearts as well as your clothes. She washed, starched, and ironed your souls, as well as your dresses and shirts.

After school she was always available, attentive to your accomplishments and your woes. She 'taxied' you to movies, to Scouts and to parties. She scolded, chided, admonished and pleaded. She fed you when hungry. She nursed you when sick. She helped you with homework. She tucked you in bed. Your needs were her needs.

In brief — she was a bundle of joy, a package of comfort and a world of love.

I, too, miss her on this Mother's Day. But I know that if she were here, she would bounce down the hall, point her finger with a firm look, smile gently, then scold, chide, admonish and plead, "Carry on!"

Dr. Bill

CHAPTER 5

THE IMPORTANCE OF KEEPING YOUR HOUSE IN ORDER

It was Sunday. I had promised myself and my wife that I would go to church. I felt an immense need to go, especially since for three Sundays I had made excuses not to go, excuses that seemed somewhat inadequate, even to me.

It was an exquisite July morning, the sky brushed clear by a gentle breeze, the air crisp, and the sun piercing that crispness with a warmth that made my skin surface respond with a special delight, a delight that penetrated my whole being. The joy of being alive coursed through my vessels.

It seemed a shame to leave this outdoors to attend church indoors. It occurred to me that Jesus spoke outdoors. He had no church, no temple. But in I went.

Following the first hymn, a hand pressed my arm and I was told there was a telephone call for me in the minister's study. "It's an emergency," the usher said.

When I answered the phone, a woman's voice plaintively spoke. "Dr. Bauer, this is Hannah Hopkins. I need you. I'm in real trouble. Please, please come right away!"

As I hung up the phone, my mind filled with ambivalent thoughts. Here was an excuse to get outdoors, but a home call would not be outdoors. Like anyone else, I needed what the church could give, but someone needed what I had to give. Torn by such antithetical thoughts, I hurried to the Hopkins home with my car windows wide open, absorbing the magnanimous offerings of the outdoors.

Within seconds of my knocking, Hannah answered her door. She was dressed only in a slip and house slippers, and her hair was uncombed. Taken by surprise, I covered my embarrassment by asking to see the sick person.

"I'm the one who needs you," she answered. "Come, I must talk to you."

As Hannah led me through the back hallway, I could not help noticing the mess. Boxes and newspapers were piled in disarray. Actually, we had to climb over some of them to get to the living room.

The living room was as disheveled as any I had ever seen. Clothes were strewn on chairs and the floor like confetti. Grime and smudges were on the walls and grime and plain dirt were on the rugs. No civilized person could spend a peaceful moment in such a place.

"The children, all five of them, are at Sunday school," Hannah said, picking up a muddle of soiled clothes and throwing them on the floor so I could sit down.

I swallowed this excuse for drawing me from the church service with little sympathy, feeling that at least she could have been properly dressed, and wondering what cyclone could have dismantled this house without removing the roof. Since my wife and I also have five children, I knew they could create havoc in a short time, but the spectacle that faced me was beyond description.

Hannah sat on the edge of a straight chair with a half-empty cereal box on it and began to talk. At first I listened with reservation, but soon found myself attending every word. The mess in the house retreated from my thoughts as my sympathy for this mother of five grew.

A year before, Hannah's husband, Harold, had taken an office job in Eau Claire, Wisconsin, 60 miles away. He left home at 7:00 A.M. and returned at 7:00 P.M., five days a week. Eight months before, Harold had started to stay out until 10:00 P.M., twice a week. As the months went by, this tardiness increased to midnight, and on some nights, he did not come home at all. Then finally he failed to return home even for the weekends.

In spite of her appearance, Hannah could be a rational and attractive woman. Having seen her through five pregnancies, I knew her rather well. Her husband was a man of 40, two years older than Hannah. He would never set the world on fire, but he was prudent, honest, and hard-working. It seemed a mystery that he would avoid coming home, where he was so much needed.

Hannah continued, her eyes brimming with tears and her voice heavy with emotion. "Harold hasn't been home for a week. Yesterday I got a letter. He wants a divorce; he wants to marry his secretary. Doctor, we've been married 11 years and have five children. I don't understand it. What can I do?"

Looking around the room, I was struck again by the overwhelming confusion. Through an open doorway I could see the kitchen was as chaotic as the room we were in. I said, "Hannah, how long has your house looked like this?"

"What do you mean, Doctor?"

I stood up and, motioning with my hands, said, "Come on, Hannah, look for yourself. Nothing is in its place. Apparently, nothing has a place. When did you last clean your house?"

"Not for quite a while, I guess," she answered.

"Now Hannah, when your husband comes home from Eau Claire, do you look like you do now?"

"No, not exactly."

"I mean do you dress up, try to look nice, when he comes home?"

"No, I don't have time. I am too busy. I have five children, Doctor; besides, it doesn't matter to him. He doesn't care how I look."

Now the answer to Hannah's problem seemed clear to me. I sat down and faced her. "Hannah, you are one damn fool. For an intelligent woman, I can't understand how blind you have become. You don't realize it, but you have been getting unfair competition. The secretary in your husband's office is always dressed and clean. Harold doesn't see her when she is not at her best. To make the competition even more unfair, the only time he sees you is when you are at your worst."

"I never thought of that," she said, looking down at herself.

"Oh Hannah, it isn't a question, on this beautiful Sunday, of religion or morals. It is a question of facing facts, plain facts. If you want to hold your husband, win him back. Give him something to come back to, to come home to. Clean this house, scrub it; restore order to chaos. Fix yourself up; dress the way you used to when you dated him. You are an attractive woman when you want to be."

Hannah looked up at me and I saw tears streaming down her face. She opened her mouth as though to speak, but no words came. For several moments her chest heaved quietly as she wept.

I stood up and looked down at her. At the moment Hannah gave the appearance of a little girl whose doll had been lost. I wanted to put my arms about her to reassure and comfort her, but her state of undress made this seem inappropriate.

Hannah stood up, wiped her tears with a towel that had been draped over a nearby chair, and then pleaded, "Please Dr. Bill, will you leave a sedative for me?"

Feeling she needed to recoup her self-possession on solid terms, I quietly refused. "Hannah, I know you can handle the situation if you make up your mind to. You don't need a sedative; you need only the desire to win Harold back."

She thanked me as I lingered at the door. A strange pair we made — me in my Sunday best and she in her slippers and slip.

A month later, she invited me to her home for lunch. A metamorphosis had taken place — a miracle of soap and water, elbow grease, and determination. Hannah wore a becoming dress of pastel blue. Her hair was neat and well-styled. Hannah, like the house, had made a complete transformation.

"My Harold gave up his position in Eau Claire. He has a job at the local lumberyard. I don't know how to thank you, Dr. Bill."

"You already have," I said.

Today, Harold and Hannah still live in the same house, grandparents many times.

HOW MY INDIAN FRIEND PAID HIS BILL

His black hair swung over his broad shoulders as he hobbled into my examining room. His dark eyes stared at me, sizing me up and down. I had never seen him before, but it was obvious from the red cast to his skin and his high cheekbones that he was an Indian.

"Me, John. My leg need help. You help me?"

"Sure, John," I said. "Lie down on my examining table and we'll take a look." I removed a rag that was wrapped about his left leg from knee to ankle. Two-thirds of his tibia was exposed and the long gash also revealed a torn calf muscle plastered with leaves.

"What are the leaves for?" I asked.

"My daughter put them on. Stop bleeding and good for healing."

As I removed the leaves, a greenish discharge with a putrid odor oozed out of the wound.

"When did this happen?" I asked.

"Week ago. Logging hook tore my leg."

I cut away the dead tissue and liberally washed the wound, syringing among torn muscles. Following this, I put drains in place and dressed the wound with a large cushion of gauze to allow for further drainage.

"John, I'm going to give you a shot to prevent lockjaw and gangrene. Do you know what that means?"

John nodded his head. "I know," was all he said.

"I want you to take two of these pills every four hours, all night and all day. The pills are sulfadiazine to stop the infection. Come back in three days. Come back if the dressing becomes dirty."

"OK, I do. Thanks," and he hobbled out.

The following day, John was back. His dressing looked clean. There was a little drainage. I replaced the dressings with a fresh one and then turned to John and asked, "Why did you come back today? Everything looks good."

"Need more medicine, Doctor," he answered.

"But I gave you more than enough for three days," I said.

"Took it all," he said, gesturing with both hands.

"But why?" I asked.

"If a little good, more better," was his brief reply.

A month passed before John's wound healed and another month before he was ready to return to the logging team where he worked to support his wife and daughter. The large overdose of sulfadiazine John had taken apparently had not affected him adversely.

The following February, John again appeared at my office. I thought he had come to make arrangements to pay his bill.

"I hear you like to fish," he said.

"Yes, I do."

"I take you fishing. When can you go?'

We made arrangements to go the next Wednesday. I was to meet him not later than 12 o'clock on the Couderay River. But John said nothing about making arrangements to pay his medical bill.

That Wednesday proved a memorable one and an instructive one. At noon we entered a canvas shanty on the frozen river. Through a hole we chiseled in the ice, John dangled a frog-like contraption he had whittled out of cedar, to which he had attached rubber from an old innertube and a small piece of lead to weigh it down. John bobbed it up and down through the hole, giving the frog good action, which attracted several muskies. Though John missed three times, he did catch two muskies, each about three feet long, with his three-pronged spear.

At one o'clock, John announced, "No use to try longer now. We try for wall-eye later."

It became apparent that John had a rationale for his fishing. He was convinced the noon hour was best for spearing muskies. An hour before sunset was best for minnow-fishing for walleyes.

While John and I ate sandwiches together at a small restaurant nearby, he asked me if I could stop to see his wife. "She sick for long time. No money for doctors or hospitals."

His home was truly a hovel. It was built of hand-hewn logs and caulked with some filler that I could not discern. Once within, I noted a bunkbed made of cedar that stood in one corner. On its lower tier lay an elderly looking woman. A square table and three chairs, also of cedar were centered in the single room. Clothes hung from pegs. A wood-burning stove was used for both heating and cooking. Three shelves above the stove held a cluster of pots and pans; others hung from nails closeby.

Turning my head, I viewed the area half hidden by a blanket that draped a log running across the east side of the room. Behind the blanket sat as winsome and exquisite a woman as I had ever seen. She was rocking gently back and forth in another chair of cedar. Behind her was another bed. Other details escaped me, for at my approach the young woman rose and greeted me.

With her dark brown eyes flashing and her easy smile, she said," I am John's daughter. My father has talked much of you."

I found it difficult to keep my eyes off her. The young woman was 18 and had infinite charm as well as beauty. Her coal-black hair hung a full 30 inches from the top of her head. Her stunning appearance at once reminded me of Captain John Smith's description of Pocahontas.

Like her father, she wasted no words. "You have come to see Ma. Father said he would bring his doctor friend here." With that, she led me to the bed where her mother was stretched out.

The sick woman proved to be only 38 but looked at least 70. She was darker than her husband and daughter and, as she opened her eyes, I knew why. The whites of her eyes were a deep orange. Her urine was the color of oranges. She had no strength to walk. She ate only a mouthful or two at a time and lived mostly on water and tea. I urged her to lie back again so I could examine her. Feeling her abdomen left little doubt in my mind that John's wife had cancer of the liver, for the liver was firm and knobby.

To be certain of my diagnosis , I went to my car and returned with my stethoscope. Both lungs gave clear evidence of metastatic lesions, positive evidence of the spread of cancer.

John and I conferred. My suggestion of hospitalization was met with complete refusal. It was obvious that little could be done and we all knew that. Months had passed without medical help and now all three of them accepted the imminence of death.

Why had John asked me to see his wife? Why were all three so accepting of death? Why had he taken me fishing?

Perhaps John wanted outside assurance that nothing could be done for his wife. Perhaps all three in their closeness felt secure in their faith, though nothing was said about it. I still did not know why John had taken me fishing, however, unless it was his way to have me see his wife.

At three o'clock, John announced we would go fishing. We left his wife and daughter and started for the Chippewa Flowage, a part called Chief Lake. We needed time to chisel holes through 20 inches of ice. On the frozen lake, I noted many holes with a thin skin of ice over them.

"Why can't we use some of these holes that are already made?" I asked.

"They belong to Indian friends," John said.

Many of these holes had lines fastened to sticks. John tested them. On some there were hooked fish. John knew which hole belonged to which Indian and carried the fish up to the homes that rose along the high bank of the lake.

I was amazed and moved by the simple honesty of my guide. And so we chiseled our own holes through 20 inches of ice.

It was an hour before sunset when our holes were ready. The walleyes, John assured me, would soon be approaching the shallow water along the shore to feed. I had two holes and John had two. Our minnows were impaled on hooks. We were ready.

Abruptly, I heard a whistle, not unlike that of a bobwhite. Then another and another and more followed, each louder than the one before, as the whistles seemed to approach us.

Quietly, John pulled up my lines, stuck my short ice fishing poles under the snow, and then said, "The game warden will be here in a moment."

I was bewildered, for I had a license to fish, but I said nothing. Soon the game warden appeared, spoke to John, greeted me with, "Nice day," and departed.

My curiosity was soon answered. "This lake, in winter, for Indians only. White man not allowed to fish here." John stated.

"What was the whistling about?" I asked.

"Friends warn game warden coming." he answered.

It was now obvious that John had planned my day well, even to being sure I would not be caught fishing in Chief Lake. He had arranged with his fellow Indians to alert him of the game warden's approach by the whistling signals.

When darkness fell, we had caught eight nice walleyes. John offered me four, which I accepted.

On the trip home I realized how much I had learned about my fellow humans. We all have a need to maintain self-respect, to have a pride in what we can do — be it little or much. And I knew, for sure, that John's taking me fishing was his payment for my care of his festered leg.

CHAPTER 53

HOSPITAL ROUNDS

One morning as I started rounds on the first floor of the hospital, I met Brian Macky, a 90-year-old man, taking his morning stroll. Though darkly jaundiced and suffering from cancer of the pancreas, he was nimble of mind as well as of foot. As we chatted, a young nurse passed, her cap perched jauntily on her head and her uniform smartly starched. Brian turned and eyed her up and down. As he turned back, he winked at me and said, "What a figure!"

"You sure gave her the once over," I said, with a knowing smile. "Aren't you getting a little old for that sort of thing?"

"Oh, no," he said. "You never get too old to look."

I had not always stopped to chat with the elderly. When short of time I found it easier to skip them, but I soon discovered that spending a few minutes with them was like a tonic for them, and I found it rewarding as well.

I had three patients in the large ward at the east end of the floor. Joe Meadows was one of them, a shy young man. Joe was a problem. Whether from shyness or fear, he refused to move. The nurses had tried to get him up, as we did most post-operative patients, but Joe refused. Three days earlier I had removed his appendix. Since then he had hardly stirred. Joe's abdomen was tense and highly distended with gas. Neither stoops nor a rectal tube had relieved him.

The nurse making rounds with me was both sophisticated and experienced. She approached the young man. "Joe, what are we going to do with you?" she said. "You haven't budged for three days. Your belly is still tight and full of gas. Dr. Bauer will think we haven't done our jobs."

Joe glanced at the nurse with the look of a ten-year-old boy not wishing to be scolded. The nurse grasped Joe's hand, demanding his full attention. "You're impossible," she said. "If you would only pass some gas, it would be a feather in my cap."

Joe looked at her with uncertainty. Then he stared at her cap, took a deep breath and said, "All right, Miss Thompson, stand at the foot of my bed and I'll make you an Indian chief."

The nurse gave me one of those knowing looks. It said, "Time to leave." As we walked up the hall, I assured her that I would return and extract the young man from his bed and walk him up the hall.

We moved on to another room. A 14-year-old boy named Tom Jefferson was sitting in a chair, his left leg elevated on another chair. The left leg was cast in plaster from toe to thigh and his right arm was cast from wrist to armpit.

Tom had osteomyelitis, a migratory infection that moves from bone to bone. He was being treated with the Orr method, encasing the affected limbs in plaster casts. Antibiotics were as yet unknown.

Tom had been a miserable patient to treat. Understandably depressed by his condition, with only a promise of respite but no promise of cure, he had been stubborn and uncooperative. Worse yet, he rarely responded to questions, refused to see visitors, and ate poorly.

Only a week before, I had entered Tom's room with the greeting, "Good morning, Mr. President. How is Thomas Jefferson?" Tom had smiled and before he had time to think about his malady, he replied, "Fine, John Hancock, let's get on with the constitutional papers." We had both laughed, and on subsequent visits I followed up this pleasantry, calling him Mr. President.

As the nurse and I entered his room I called out, "Mr. President, what will Congress do with the proposed bill?"

Tom raised his right arm, cast and all, screwed up his face into a resolute grimace and demanded, "Who goes there, friend or foe?"

It was time to change Tom's casts. Without present-day antibiotics, osteomyelitis was a nasty situation, with much foul-smelling discharge. Using hand cutters, the nurse and I removed the old casts with their strong odor, cleaned the drainage areas and put on fresh casts. Thomas Jefferson never flinched. As I worked I said, "You be sure to tell me if anything hurts, Mr. President."

"A president leads the nation with strength, not complaints," he countered.

When the nurse and I were leaving, Tom asked if I could have his school lessons and books sent to the hospital. This was the first time he had shown an interest in anything. It was a step forward in his mental attitude that boded well.

As the nurse and I entered a double room, we came upon a scene that will forever remain etched on my mind. White-headed Andrew Wells was on his knees, a straight-edged razor in his hand, and standing in front of him, completely naked, was his elderly roommate, George Pearson. Andrew's hospital gown hung loosely from his neck, held only by a single tie. George, without a stitch on, stood half bent over. As he talked about his coming operation, his handlebar mustache bobbed up and down. Obviously, neither gentleman was aware of our presence nor of the picture they presented.

"Good morning," I said, startling both of them.

Andrew, on his knees, razor in hand, turned his head and simply stated, "I'm getting him ready so you can cut him tomorrow. He's afraid to shave his own belly, so I'm doing it for him."

At that time, there were no orderlies in our hospital to shave male patients.

Before surgery each doctor shaved his own male patients or, at times, patients shaved themselves. I had removed Andrew's prostate three days before. He was shaving George, who was heading for the operating room the following day. The nurse and I just happened in at the right time to take in 'the show.'

When we completed rounds on the men's floor, we went up to the second floor, which was reserved for women. A women approached me as soon as we arrived. "Please, Dr. Bill, take some time with my daughter, Grace. She trusts you."

Grace was a new admission who had been sexually molested during the previous night. I had been called about 4:00 A.M. by Grace's father and met him in the emergency room, where his daughter lay screaming on the examining table. After giving Grace a 'hypo' to calm her, I consulted with her parents. A decision was made to counteract potential venereal infections and possible pregnancy.

When we entered Grace's room, I was troubled by her totally distraught state. Her usually neat appearance was replaced with uncombed hair, scratched face and neck, and a faraway look in her eyes. I sat down on the bed and touched her cold hand with mine. I spoke to her about her family and friends. At this point, the nurse, who had been accompanying me on rounds, discreetly left the room.

Grace, now a 17-year-old senior in high school, had an excellent reputation. She was a good student, had played on the girl's basketball and track teams, and was a member of the student council. She also sang in her church choir and was a Sunday school teacher. I thought of all this as I sat and watched her struggle with her inner torment. Her faraway look continued for a long time.

Suddenly her silence was broken by sobs and then a few hesitant sentences. "Dr. Bill, I feel so dirty . . . I can't wash it off . . . I'll kill him . . . I feel like killing myself."

As she talked, her face clearly expressed her contempt for her attacker, but then, characteristically, she softened her tone and said, "I wouldn't really kill him. I couldn't, but he doesn't deserve to live. What did I ever do to deserve this? He was like a wild animal."

Past experience had taught me the uselessness of words of solace, however well intended. I knew more could be gained by listening than by offering sympathy. Twenty minutes later, seemingly exhausted, Grace fell back on her pillow. I ordered a 'hypo' to ensure rest and then met her mother in the hall.

"Grace's world is shattered," I said. "I'm afraid she could destroy herself, and after what she has been through, one couldn't blame her. We must support her; have someone with her at all times ready to listen. I suggest a private nurse for those hours when she would be alone." I promised to come back later in the day.

Making hospital rounds offered me another dimension in which to communicate and commiserate with my patients, another opportunity to observe, talk, share, listen, and sometimes — to have a lot of fun.

CHAPTER 54

A DOCTOR'S FAMILY ALSO DESERVES HIS BEST

Ned was gone. The basket of the cherry picker holding Ned had collided with a power line and, with a loud crackling of sparks and flames, he had been electrocuted.

Ned's fellow workers and a small group of people who had gathered spoke in near whispers. I stood and stared down at the young man lying on the ground. It was hard to keep control; to swallow the enormous lump in my throat; to act the calm doctor who is supposed to reassure the sick, the wounded, and the bereaved. I shook with a combination of anger and frustration. I knew this young man — kind, gentle, and industrious — popular with adults and peers alike. His first real job had been this one with the power company. He was so young . . . his life had ended before it had barely begun.

The drawn faces of the people about me, people whom I knew, were indistinguishable; their voices babbled without meaning. There seemed no rhyme or reason to life if this lad could be snatched away so readily.

Then I asked myself, "How could his mother and father accept this loss if I found it so difficult?" I pondered on this, but no satisfactory answer crept into my thoughts.

I returned to my office and launched myself into the multiple tasks that confronted me, but Ned's lifeless figure could not be erased from my mind.

It was one of those sticky summer days. Many youngsters escaped the heat by spending the day in a river or lake, but in my hot office the young whimpered, the elderly groaned, and the phone rang incessantly.

I was about to incise a carbuncle when Peggy rushed in. "A young man has drowned in the Chippewa River. Here are the directions to get there." She handed me a slip of paper.

My arrival was much too late. Bob, a young redhead, had long since perished. This stocky 24-year-old had consumed more than six cans of beer. His friends had also imbibed heavily. Members of his group, three couples, had been swimming and drinking. The current at this spot of the river was not violent; it moved at about five to eight miles an hour. The depth of the water varied from three to five feet.

Suddenly, the group realized that Bob was missing. Alarmed, they scanned the river. A hundred yards down river Bob's body appeared, then disappeared, only to reappear moments later farther down the river; it was 20 minutes before they dragged him in.

I knelt beside Bob, who lay on a blanket. After observing the already darkened body and realizing that nothing could be done, I looked up at the solemn faces that surrounded me. I scrutinized each face. Their shared fear was obvious.

It was some time before I could speak and even then I mumbled, as if talking to myself. "Bob is gone."

I stood up from my kneeling position. Remaining silent, I looked straight ahead at nothing. I did not see or hear the river or the five young people waiting for me to say something. All I could see was Bob's purple face.

One of the young women stepped to my side and touched me. With pleading eyes and tears streaming down her cheeks, she said, "He is my husband. He can't be dead just like that. Isn't there anything you can do?"

I cleared my throat and hoped for the right words. "I wish there were, but it's too late. It has been more than an hour since Bob drowned."

Bob's wife (I never did learn her name) put her head on my shoulder and shook with sobs. "What will I do? What will I do? We left our two little ones with Grandma. What will I do?"

I tried to comfort her, but all I could think of was her return home and how desolate that homecoming would be.

Again I returned to the office but found it difficult to settle down to the routine of office practice. I incised the carbuncle, took histories, did physicals, and gave shots almost by rote; my heart wasn't in it. Trying to answer the problems of my patients could not blot out the images of Ned and Bob.

I was upset and edgy, yet realized I had to satisfy the patients who had waited so long to be taken care of. Finally, when the office was cleared of patients, I left for home, forgetting to thank Peggy for staying so late. It was about 8:00 P.M.

When I arrived home I flopped into my chair, thoroughly exhausted and still thinking of Ned's electrocution and Bob's drowning. My family was at the table, finishing supper. Our youngest, Cathi, came to my chair, crawled into my lap, and gave me a kiss. Then looking up at me with her hazel eyes, she asked, "Can I get you something to eat, Daddy?"

Although it was more than 35 years ago, it hurts even now to think of my response. In no way did I acknowledge her thoughtfulness. I merely murmured, "No, Cathi."

A few minutes later, Tim the second youngest, came to my chair, smiled at me and asked, "Would you like a drink?" Without looking at him and completely ignoring his strong desire to please me, I said, "No, thanks." There was nothing offensive in my words, but my attitude and my tone clearly said, "Leave me alone."

My wife, understanding my mood and my exhaustion, gently ushered the children out of the room and up to bed. My family had waited till after eight o'clock in order to eat with me, and I was incapable of responding to their thoughtfulness.

When Gussie came back from putting the children to bed, she sat beside me and said, "You must have had a really tough day. You look all worn out. I'll bring your supper here to your chair." She reached over and gave me a squeeze that said more than words, and went to warm my supper.

As I sat there relaxing, briefly relieved of all professional responsibility, I gradually became aware of what an old grouch I was. All day I had tried to give my best to my patients. Now that I was home with the most important people in my life, why wasn't I able to respond to them — to give them some of my best?

Abruptly, I rose from my chair and raced upstairs to the children's rooms. I hugged each one with unusual tenderness, well aware of my own need for their affection. One of the children, I can't recall which one, put a finger up to my eyes and asked, "Daddy, why are you crying?"

By now I was filled with emotion. Tears fell without restraint. As I sat with all five of them, I appreciated how much I had to be thankful for.

When I returned downstairs, I hugged my wife with a special fondness, grateful for her understanding and support. Gussie and I talked as I ate my supper. I shared my chargrin and vowed to try harder to save some of my best for my family.

Those days are now long gone, but the stark reality of that evening has never left me. On many later occasions, I recognized fatigue and tried to save some of my best for my own family. Unfortunately, this was not always possible.

CHAPTER 55

THE NEED TO EXPECT the UNEXPECTED

"The blood is too dark," I exclaimed, turning to the anesthetist. "What's the trouble?"

"There must be a blockage of her trachea," she answered, "or perhaps laryngospasm."

In seconds the blood looked even darker. "Get the tracheotomy set," I called out to the circulating nurse.

A long minute passed. The patient was not breathing. Her face was suffused with dark blood.

"I can't find the tracheotomy set." The circulating nurse spoke with anxiety. "Someone must have misplaced it."

The words of a Minneapolis surgeon came to mind: "Regardless of how complete your preparation or caution, unexpected situations arise and must be met without panic."

I reached over the shield that separated the operative field from the anesthetist and seized one of the plastic tubes used to intubate a patient. It wasn't sterile, but sterility was not of immediate concern; getting oxygen into the patient was. I cut a crosswise opening between two tracheal rings in her neck and inserted the unsterile tube. Then I hooked the tube to the oxygen machine. Almost at once, the patient started to breath. Then pink color slowly came back into her face and the blood lost its dark hue.

By using the unsterile tube, I had contaminated the operative field, the patient's neck —for I was removing her thyroid gland. But I had no choice. Without oxygen, she would not have survived. When her color, respirations, and pulse returned to normal, the field was repainted and redraped. I scrubbed again, put on a fresh gown and completed the operation.

Later in the doctor's room, I began to worry. There was a strong possibility that my patient's neck would become infected, but I had little time to fret about it for just then the circulating nurse poked her head in the door.

"Mr. Cooper is almost asleep. Time to scrub."

Amos Cooper had suffered countless gallbladder attacks. He had always resisted surgery, but during his last attack his gallbladder became so distended with pus that it finally ruptured. Amos was a very sick man.

Following weeks of hospitalization and treatments with antibiotics, Amos gradually improved but continued to be severely jaundiced. Stones blocked the passage of bile from the liver to the upper intestines. Finally, after tearful pleadings from his wife, Amos agreed to surgery.

Opening Amos's abdomen was no problem, for he was muscular and had no excess fat. Once inside, however, dissection was hampered by multiple adhesions. Pus from the ruptured gallbladder had spilled into the abdominal cavity of Amos's body. Numerous adhesions had formed that walled off some structures and displaced others. I was faced with a conglomerate of tissues that made identification exceedingly difficult. The sorting-out process required gentle pulling apart of adhesions and delicate touches with the scalpel.

After 20 minutes of dissecting the adhesions, anatomical structures were just beginning to be apparent. The common bile duct was partially visible. Suddenly, the operative area spurted blood like a geyser. I knew at once that I must have cut or nicked the large hepatic artery that feeds blood to the liver. Reaching down with my left hand, I grasped the spurting area between my thumb and forefinger and shut off the geyser. Using suction, my colleagues cleared the area of blood, exposing the rent in the hepatic artery. Gingerly, I released the artery from the enveloping adhesions and then sutured the rent in the artery with fine thread. With the unexpected emergency resolved, I was now able to complete the surgery by removing the stones and inserting a T-tube into the common duct to drain off the excess bile.

The unexpected had happened for the second time in one morning. Both times I had been supported by the wise words of the Minneapolis surgeon, "Unexpected situations arise and must be met without panic."

Late that evening, at about midnight, I wandered outdoors, seeking something I sorely needed but could not have put into words. I had been thinking about my morning experiences, grateful for those words, "The need to expect the unexpected." But I needed to be outdoors in my cathedral to thank God for those words.

I stood on the bridge that crossed our North Pool. Silently, a prayer reached my lips, a prayer I had often repeated: "Thanks, Father, for the special help this morning. Please help me to catch up on all my accumulated paper work. Permit me to be with my family for at least one meal each day, and give me the opportunity to catch up with myself so I can remain master of my own ship."

PART THREE

Part three marks a transition in the development of my practice. I had developed a certain self-confidence, probably because I now had a loyal following of two generation families and a few families of three generations.

More and more I was becoming aware that there was always much more to learn.

Perhaps, most of all, I was grateful for all my blessings, particularly my wife and children and the fact that we had settled in a country atmosphere rather than a stuffy urban one.

Table of Contents

Part Three

CHAPTER 56

GOD GAVE US "DOMINION OVER ALL THE EARTH"

The hearing room was filled to capacity with men and women, most of whom were passionate objectors to animal experimentation. The appeals of pro-vivisectionists were met with vehement protests, those of the anti-vivisectionists with loud acclaim.

During my hospital training, I had witnessed a mother and her five-year-old daughter slowly die of diphtheria, which gave me genuine respect for diphtheria's powerful toxin. It also gave me a profound appreciation of the value of vaccines, for this mother and child had not been vaccinated against diphtheria. It was the memory of this experience that had motivated me to defend animal experimentation at this legislative hearing in Madison, Wisconsin.

The leader of the Senate Committee called upon me to speak. An almost irresistible urge to escape from theses passionate objectors came over me, but my thoughts leapt back to the unvaccinated mother and child and the distress I had felt knowing that medical science was helpless to combat the diphtheria toxin that was slowly killing them.

When I entered the room, I had noted women with fox-, mink-, and squirrel-trimmed coats. I invited three of them to come to the dais. I asked if anyone had eaten lamb chops, beef or chicken for lunch. Several women raised their hands. I invited three of them to come up front.

Normally, I am direct. I call a spade a spade. I find the need for histrionics distasteful. But again the mother and her daughter flashed through my mind. Arranging the women in a line, I approached each with a question:

"What did you have for lunch?"

"What kind of fur is your collar made of?"

To my surprise, the women responded as I'd hoped.

"I had two delicious lamb chops."

185

"The chicken was southern fried, remarkably tender."

"The beef stroganoff was excellent — just the right amount of mushrooms."

"My collar is made of silver fox. I like it because when the wind blows, I can cuddle in it."

"Squirrel is all I can afford, but I like it."

"My husband gave me this mink-collared coat. Someday I hope to have a coat made entirely of mink."

The ladies returned to their seats, unaware of their contribution to my cause.

"Is there anyone in this room who has lost a child to cancer?" I asked.

A woman stood up and, with tears in her eyes, said, "My four-year-old daughter died of cancer only two weeks ago." Then a couple stood up, and the husband said they had lost their seven-year-old son to leukemia.

My moment of truth was at hand. Would I botch it? Would my audience listen to or boo me? I recalled that most of them were, in a real sense, adversaries. More than that, they were somewhat overzealous in their spirited anxiety to defend animals from maltreatment. How could I win them over? How could I let them know I agreed with their basic principles yet communicate my message?

Suddenly I realized that my sympathy for the dying woman and her daughter had clouded my thinking with excessive emotion, just as the anti-vivisectionists' concern for animals had clouded theirs. This realization made me decide to choose my words cautiously so as not to antagonize my audience.

"All animals should be treated with respect," I said with more calm than I felt. "Improper treatment of all animals should and must be abolished, whether in homes, farms, zoos or laboratories; whether dogs, cats, rats, mice, sheep, horses, cows, pigs, tigers, bears, or zebras.

I looked over my audience. They no longer seemed adversaries. The room was silent and they were listening. This gave me courage to continue.

"God gave man dominion over all the earth and the creatures on land, sea and air. God did not say, . . . use them for food, but not for dissection; use them for clothes, but not for experimentation; use them as pets, but not to make life safer for humans. God did not prescribe such choices nor make such exceptions, but we can be certain He did not want abuse.

The room was still hushed and I continued.

"We are led to believe that each life should serve a purpose. If a person can give up his life for another, so can an animal. Given dominion over all the earth, we should use that dominion wisely, with reverence for all.

"Our feelings, rather than reason, often rule us. All of us, including you and me, are too often governed by emotion. Consider how I have felt helplessly watching children die because of limited medical knowledge. Those parents who told us that their children died of leukemia and cancer can empathize with the intensity of my feelings. We need animal experimentation to reduce such tragedies, but if I come on too strongly, forgive me on the grounds that exposure to such tragedies I have seen as a doctor stirs my emotions and urges me to fight against this Senate bill. I can understand the strong feelings of those of you who are against animal dissection, however. You are equally moved and equally sincere."

I looked about, expecting a reaction, but none came so I went on. "For the moment, at least, let us try to come to terms. We know animals are slaughtered for food and for clothing. Many of us have trapped mice and rats to prevent our homes from being overrun with rodents. Animal dissection in laboratories is a means of improving health. All of us should be motivated by the same sincere purpose — to prevent animal abuse."

I hesitated, then went on. "Let's join forces. Let's make more rigid rules to prevent animal suffering under all conditions. Slaughterhouses, zoos, pets, homes, laboratories — all engaged in animal care or use — should be encouraged to treat animals with respect. More stringent rules and better enforcement should be required. But the value of animals for food, clothing, and improved health must not be curtailed. An all-inclusive adage should be, "Use animals, but do not abuse them."

A standing ovation did not follow, but there was a respectful silence, and the Senate bill opposing animal dissection did not pass. Animal usage for experimentation, however, remains a real problem because of human nature. Most of us exhibit irrational behavior when our emotions are stirred. At such times, black is black and white is white, and there is nothing in between.

CHAPTER 57

"THE THINGS I CANNOT CHANGE"

It all began with the sudden death of Anthony Abbitz at 1:30 in the morning. When I arrived at his home, I found he had already succumbed to a massive heart attack. According to his wife, he had keeled over as he rose from his bed to go to the bathroom.

Anthony was a kindly man, a massive six-foot giant, huge of chest and limb, but somewhat limited in intelligence. His large frame lay sprawled on the floor, surrounded by his weeping, panic-stricken family. What would this family do? Anthony left his wife and three teenage sons with little but the clothes on their backs and the memory of his ever-present kindness. Anthony was only 35. In my frustration, I could find little to comfort his family.

That afternoon Edna Manson entered the hospital with a threatened stillbirth at seven and one-half months of pregnancy. How much Edna wanted that child after 13 years of barrenness could not be exaggerated. She felt no fetal movements, and I could hear no fetal heart sounds. Even more discouraging, Edna had a foul, brownish-colored vaginal discharge, which also suggested that the fetus was dead. I consulted with my colleagues, who suggested that birth should be encouraged. Although I agreed, I could not bring myself to do so, hoping for Edna's sake that the infant was alive.

About three o'clock the following morning, I rushed to the hospital in answer to a parent's anxious call, but found there was nothing to be done. Four teenagers had been killed in a two-car accident. I had brought all four of them into the world and felt both frustrated and depressed. After trying to comfort the parents, I returned home but could not sleep. I thought of Anthony and his abrupt passing. Visions of the four teenagers repeatedly swept through my mind, along with incidents in their brief lives. I thought of Edna and her child she so much wanted but threatened to be stillborn. Unable to sleep, I rose and showered. As I dressed, I wondered if Edna's infant was still alive in spite of all signs and symptoms to the contrary.

Though it was only 6:00 A.M., I went to see Edna at the hospital. She was awake.

"Edna," I said, "I don't really know what to do. Your pulse, temperature, and respirations are all normal, and that's to the good. Your white blood cells have increased, but that's not necessarily a sign of infection. The white count is always elevated during pregnancy. On the other hand, I can't explain away the brownish vaginal discharge nor the lack of movement of the fetus. I am also concerned that I am unable to hear the infant's heart sounds. But the X-ray shows a skeleton of a seven- or eight-month fetus."

I hesitated, but Edna made no response. Then I continued. "Edna, the child within your womb, if dead, could be toxic to you and could endanger your life. My problem is that, while I know how much you want this child, I can't stand by and let it be a hazard to your life. On the other hand, I have read of similar cases where the child was still alive, even with a foul discharge. What should we do?"

"I'd like to wait," she said. "I want to talk to my husband and get his point of view."

At 1:00 P.M. I started office hours, tired and markedly frustrated. My first consultation was with Ronald Wallace, a 55-year-old man. He wanted me to check his father, who was 96 years old and was in Ronald's car behind the office.

Paul Wallace was in the back of the car, his legs spread apart in a most awkward position. He was partially sitting up and partially lying down, supported by pillows. He was squirming about, obviously in marked discomfort, with a mass about the size of a basketball between his thighs. Moans from the old man were almost constant as he writhed continuously. Paul had a scrotal hernia into which much of his abdominal contents had passed. Before I could offer a word of suggestion, Ronald spoke up. "I don't know what can be done for Dad, but I don't want you to operate. I hope you understand that. He's too old."

At that moment it seemed there was nothing to be said. Watching the old fellow writhe and hearing him moan reinforced my mounting belief that he deserved to be relieved of his suffering. Between moans, Paul informed me, "I can't sleep and I can't eat. I haven't moved my bowels for a week."

What do you do for a 96-year-old man whose son has sternly forbidden an operation? Do you put him to bed and submerge him with hypos? Once more I felt frustrated and defeated. While contemplating what I might suggest, I listened to Paul's heart, took his blood pressure and checked his lungs. I found all were unusually good for a man of 96.

Returning to my office, I had my nurse prepare an opiate and inject it into Paul's arm. Meanwhile, I talked to Ronald.

"What would you suggest we do for your father?" I began.

"Anything but operate," Ronald responded.

"Should we let him slowly starve and wear himself out in pain or keep him submerged in hypos?"

"You must know what to do. I don't, but I know he will never stand an operation," Ronald gulped.

"Suppose you couldn't lie down, sit or stand without pain. Suppose you couldn't eat or move your bowels. What would you want done?" I asked with a touch of impatience.

"I just don't know. Guess I'd like to be taken out of my misery," Ronald answered.

"Well, that's something we are not going to do, Ronald. Let's consider what might happen if he does have an operation. Your Dad has only one chance to live comfortably, and that is to have his hernia repaired, returning his intestines into his abdomen. Suppose he does die during or after the operation, what has he lost? If we don't operate, he will suffer terribly but will die anyway. Certainly he deserves the chance to live comfortably."

Richard listened but seemed unconvinced. I went on. "Last week I refused to do a simple operation to remove a patient's bladder stones. His grown children were insistent that I operate to prevent frequent need to change catheters. The man was 78 but had suffered several strokes. I felt he could get along without the hazard of an operation. Your Dad does not have this option."

Yes, the last two days had been frustrating and had left me with a sense of near defeat. Mentally, I reviewed those days: Anthony Abbitz's sudden death from a severe heart attack and his family left without support; the four teenagers killed in a head-on collision; Mrs. Manson, who desperately wanted a child, threatened with the loss of her only pregnancy; and now, a 96-year-old man for whom surgery offered the only relief.

Early the following morning, tornado winds whipped Ladysmith, tearing off roofs and felling trees. Cars were crushed. Homes were destroyed. Our neighborhood was completely blocked by fallen trees, and all power was shut down. Gussie and I made coffee over a fire in the fireplace and shared it with our neighbors. The conversation centered on the storm, the high winds and the damage. Then someone remarked, "But not a single injury has been reported." We toasted our good fortune, clicking our coffee cups together in unison. Then all walked to work.

As I walked the mile to the hospital, the devastation I passed made me wonder how Ladysmith escaped without human injury. "How fortunate," I thought out loud. "But why no injuries or deaths?" I stood for a long moment, contemplating, seeking an answer. The words of St. Francis of Assisi came to mind:

THE SERENITY PRAYER

God grant me the Serenity
to accept the things I cannot change . . .
Courage to change
the things I can . . .
and Wisdom to know the difference.

The true meaning of his words struck me and, with a more positive attitude, I continued to walk, once again aware of my human limitations.

It may have been this more positive attitude that made Ronald grant permission to operate on his father. He was on the hospital steps waiting for me. "Let's give it a try," he said." I think you're right. Dad deserves a chance. Go ahead and operate."

Later that morning, I operated on Paul, using a local anesthetic. It was a leisurely operation, lasting three-and-one-half hours. I recall using kangaroo tendons, which I had long before stored away for some such purpose as this, to help strengthen the elderly man's friable tissues. Paul returned home in ten days and, free of pain, lived until he was 101 years of age.

Edna was in the hospital for four weeks. In all that time, I was never able to hear a fetal heartbeat nor could two of my colleagues. She continued to have her foul brown vaginal discharge, but since there were no signs that Edna's health was in jeopardy, we continued to wait. At eight and one-half months, Edna delivered a normal seven pound female.

To this day, I credit the tornado for relieving me of my frustration and sense of defeat. The tornado left a path of havoc through our town and left me with the recognition of a power beyond my control. This, in turn, made me appreciate the wisdom of the words of St. Francis of Assisi.

CHAPTER 58

MOTHERS MAKE GOOD NURSES

Lance was 14. While bird-hunting with his Dad, Milton Brunner, he attempted to duck under a barbed wire fence with gun in hand. His .410-gauge shotgun went off, discharging pellets into and through his genitals. One testicle was completely destroyed; the other was more than two-thirds destroyed and the penis was riddled with holes.

It added to my concern that both parents were close friends of mine and the father was a fishing companion.

The extensive damage was an immediate problem with the risk of infection, but what worried me most was the probability of long-term urinary and sexual dysfunction.

What could I tell the parents? After estimating the damage, I felt the lad should be under the care of a urologist. I looked at the parents, who were not yet aware of the severity of the problem, but I knew they had to be told.

"Lance is young. Healing in the young proceeds at a fast pace, but this is a serious situation. I believe it would be best to place him in the hands of a urinary specialist. The shotgun wound could affect his whole life unless properly cared for."

"What do you mean, 'it will affect his whole life'?" Milton asked.

"I'm sure you don't realize how much damage has been done. Lance has only a small part of one testicle left. The rest has been destroyed. His penis has dozens of holes, and the urinary stream leaks through most of them. It will be a touchy problem and will take weeks and maybe months of care."

Lance's mother, Pat, started to cry. Then, wiping away her tears, she said, "If you show me what to do, I'll take care of him."

"I'm sure you can," I said, because I knew that with a little reassurance she would, but before I could say anything more, Milton said, "You know we can't afford a specialist and pay for a long stay in the hospital. We want the best for Lance, but can't you take care of him?"

I didn't want the full responsibility but could appreciate the parents' financial problem, yet I knew that whatever my decision would be, both parents would cooperate fully. "Let's keep him here in our hospital for two or three days and see how Lance gets along. Then we can decide what is best to do."

Both agreed. My first task was to place a retention catheter through the riddled penis into the bladder to prevent urine from by-passing the urethral channel and seeping out through the multiple holes. Then I irrigated the numerous wounds of the penis and what was left of the scrotum while nipping off scattered remnants of dead flesh. I had given Lance a strong 'hypo' before I began.

During the next two days, Lance showed no signs of infection. His scrotum and penis were irrigated every two hours, and he was given sulfa drugs. Pat again pressured me. "I'm sure I can do these things at home. I know Lance will do better at home. How about letting me try?"

I had found some exceptional nursing skills among mothers and grandmothers, probably because of their love and concern. But this was a problem that required limitless devotion. Pat would have to dedicate all her time to tending to her son. Around-the-clock care, every day of the week, could exhaust her. "We'll give it a try," I said with more enthusiasm than I felt, "but you will have to do the irrigation every two hours night and day and give him sulfa pills every four hours."

"I'm sure I can do that," Pat said with conviction.

"Another thing, Pat, you must make Lance drink at least 12 glasses of liquid a day, and half of them must be clear water. You must also keep a record of this as well the amount he urinates. This is very important."

"I'll do it. You can count on it." Again Pat spoke with assurance.

Days became weeks. Weeks ran into months. Pat sat with Lance, coaxed him, inveigled him, teased him, and generally nurtured him.

All this in addition to her irrigating, forcing liquids, measuring intake and output, and keeping records. She did it with a patience and competence that defies description. Eventually, Lance got well.

After graduating from high school, Lance studied to become an electrical engineer, obtained a good position with a national plastics firm, and then got married. Several years after adopting a child, he and his wife had two of their own.

Mothers surely make good nurses.

CHAPTER 59

"BUT WHAT ELSE CAN WE DO?"

The stubborn resistance of the average person to seek medical care troubled me. Even though the cost was low, some people couldn't afford medical care at any price and were too prideful to accept it for free. More than ever, I appreciated the extra time and help that the attending physicians at Minneapolis General Hospital had given me during my internship, for I was able to perform some procedures and operations that, otherwise, I could not have done. There were, however, many procedures I was incapable of doing, and this presented a problem. What does one say to an individual who refuses to travel to a specialist, even when his life or that of his child might hang in the balance?

Severe accidents were common due to the traumatic hazards of the mills, as well as those of the lumber and dairy industries. The combination of poor roads, severe winter conditions and low incomes created many difficult situations.

With the collaboration of all the local physicians, a program of visiting specialists was gradually established. Each physician would line up cases that needed consultation or surgery. When enough cases in a particular specialty had accumulated, a specialist in that field was called and a date set. The visiting doctor would spend the better part of the day consulting, operating and making suggestions as to treatment. Working with these specialists and assisting them at surgery also increased our own diagnostic and surgical skills.

In addition, all of our local physicians regularly attended refresher courses, choosing those that best filled their own needs. In spite of these highly beneficial aids, there were times when we were faced with situations for which we were unprepared but had to act.

"Please, Dr. Bill, come at once. My daughter is out of her head. She is seeing things that are not there and talking to herself. She is so hot and then shakes like she is freezing." I recognized the voice of Jennie Newell. Her daughter, Melissa, had been in my office the week before with an infected ear. I had prescribed sulfanilamide.

There was already a foot of snow on the ground and the weather forecaster predicted another foot. A high wind had caused the snow to block many roads. Even in town, the going was difficult. When I entered the Newell home, both parents accosted me excitedly. "What can we do? What can we do? Melissa is burning up."

Melissa was a very sick girl. She had a severe infection of the mastoid bone behind her ear. Today such infections are rare because of antibiotics. But, in those days, I saw many of them and referred them to Dr. Cooke in Eau Claire, 60 miles away. Dr. Cooke was a very charitable man who always accepted the cases I sent, knowing that many of them could not pay.

"That you, Bill?" he said in answer to my call. "What do you have for me this time?"

"Another mastoid, a hot one," I answered. "A 10-year-old girl with a fever of 105 degrees. The skin over the mastoid is not only tender but also edematous."

"Sounds like she's in trouble. Send her down."

"Can't do it. The roads are blocked. We have no ambulance, and she's in no condition to move in this blizzard. Can't you come here?" I appealed, knowing full well what his answer would be.

"How am I going to get up there if the roads are blocked?" Dr. Cooke chortled as though he were enjoying a private joke.

"That was kind of stupid of me, but I just don't know what to do. The snowplows worked long after dark but made no headway with the drifting snow, so they quit until morning."

"Looks like you are going to have to do it yourself, Bill. Have you ever done a mastoid operation?" he asked.

"No, but I've seen a few done."

"Well, from what you tell me, you had better get busy. Here's what you need." Dr. Cooke went over the operation and the instruments needed.

For a few moments, I sat by the phone, too numb to move, wondering what my next step would be. Melissa needed to have the pocket of pus in her mastoid released. I recalled my sister, Betty, and how she had nearly died from an acute mastoid infection. I reviewed what Dr. Cooke had told me. Yes, I had used a chisel and hammer before in repairing bones, but never on someone's head. Furthermore, how could I get Melissa to the hospital in this blinding snowstorm?

I called the hospital to talk to Sister Philip, our only anesthetist. She had not returned from Minneapolis because of the blizzard. To add to my frustration, three of the doctors were out of town and the fourth was sick in bed. I didn't need an assistant for the operation, but I did need someone to give open-drop ether. I called Dr. Sabin, a dentist.

"I need you, Floyd. I need you badly," I pleaded and explained the circumstances.

"Better get someone else. The only time I ever used ether was once in dental school; that was 20 years ago. I don't know anything about it."

"There is no one else. Please come. I'll start the anesthesia. I'll watch you and tell you how fast to drop the ether on the gauze mask, but I can't get along without you."

"I'll get there as soon as I can, but I'm not sure I'll be of any help."

"Thanks," I said, "and please stop at the hospital and pick up a sterile pack. I'll call and have it ready."

Up to this point, Melissa's parents had shown tremendous self-control, but overhearing my telephone conversations was just too much.

"Dr. Bill," they protested, "you have never done this operation and Dr. Sabin knows nothing about giving ether. Will Melissa be all right?"

"I think so, but what else can we do? Frankly, I don't like the situation any better than you do, but if we don't drain the mastoid, Melissa may develop not only a blood stream infection but also a possible brain abcess."

As I continued in my efforts to soothe the parents, Dr. Sabin arrived from the hospital with the surgical pack containing the instruments I needed. We placed sheets on the kitchen table, which was graced with a bright light directly overhead. Melissa's father placed her on the table. We strapped her to the table by hooking together several of her father's belts. I started the drop ether and, when Melissa was asleep, instructed Dr. Sabin at what rate to continue.

Actually, the operation was much easier than I had anticipated, once my reluctance to chisel and hammer on Melissa's head was overcome. But the sound and feel of hammer hitting chisel and the dull thump of the chisel cutting bone still tended to unnerve me. Soon, however, pus seeped out of the wound and then ran out. I placed a drain in the hole and covered the area with large, loose fluffs.

We placed Melissa back into her bed and watched her for an hour before I again took her temperature. Miraculously, it was down to 101 degrees. Circumstances had forced me into this situation, and I was greatly relieved by Melissa's improvement.

THE STING OF MY FIRST UNEXPECTED DEATH

It was 2:30 A.M. when the hospital call broke into my deep sleep. "Mrs. Haymes is gone," was the simple message. "When the nurse made her rounds, she noticed Mrs. Haymes seemed still. She wasn't breathing and had no pulse."

After dressing rapidly, putting pants and shirt over pajamas, I hurried to the hospital, wondering what might have caused Sonya Hayme's sudden death. There had been no evidence of cardiovascular-renal problems. Her heart, blood vessels, and kidneys were normal. Her former cancer of the large bowel had not recurred. Her surgery for a common duct stone six days before had gone well.

I had seen her only eight hours before, and had talked to her and promised that she could go home the next day. Why had she died?

Anxieties haunted me. A succession of images leaped through my mind. Every step of the operation reappeared in detail. Her bleeding during the operation had been minimal. Had a ligature slipped? Recollection of a minister who had died in a St. Paul hospital three days after an appendectomy came to me. I had witnessed the surgery while attending a continuing education's course. I had also witnessed the autopsy. A suture had slipped and he had hemorrhaged internally.

As I entered the hospital drive, my mind flashed back to the lifeless body of a sturdy 16-year-old boy I had seen in a Brooklyn, N.Y., hospital years before, while I was accompanying my father on his hospital rounds. Following a cast application for a simple fracture of his fibula, the lad had succumbed from a fat embolis, a small piece of fat that had clogged an artery. He was so handsome, so strong and so young. This left an indelible impression upon me, for I too was 16 at the time.

As I bounded up the hospital stairs, another past experience came to mind. Mr. Downs, whom I had known since I was old enough to remember, had hemorrhaged following a prostatectomy. At the time, I was a first-year medical student. His death had been so unexpected and I had known him so well.

My urgent steps, accelerated by my racing mind, brought me to Sonya's bedside. It was only ten minutes since I had been called, but I had traveled back in time many years, and now I was facing my first unexpected death. Sonya lay lifeless before me. A sense of helplessness swept over me. Why had she died? In almost two decades as a doctor, I had been witness to other deaths, but this was my first unexpected one.

Sitting on the edge of the bed, I forced my mind to an abrupt halt, allowing reason to take over. What about the family? How would I tell them? What could I tell them? If I felt so dejected, how would they feel? Since there was no evident cause of death, should I request an autopsy?

After some hesitation, I made the plunge and called Sonya's husband, Alan. He came at once. Though he seemed remarkably calm, he was understandably stricken by the suddenness of his wife's passing. He had planned to take her home on this very day. Before the operation, he had assured me that he was aware of the possible complications, yet recognized the urgent necessity for the operation.

After Alan had spent some time with Sonya alone, we talked, how long I can't recall. Baffled by Sonya's abrupt death, Alan and I delved into details of her medical past. We traced it back 17 years. At that time, following countless gallbladder attacks, she had gone into surgery expecting to have her gallbladder removed. While exploring her abdomen, however, I discovered a cancer of her large bowel. Although none of Sonya's complaints had been related to this cancerous growth, it was more important to remove the cancer than the gallbladder. I removed a section of her large bowel and brought the severed ends together. Sonya recovered nicely.

For 17 years, Sonya had been free of gallbladder attacks, perhaps because she had been careful to avoid all fats. During the last few weeks, she had suffered severe pains and became jaundiced.

Alan asked questions, partly from curiosity and partly to appease his suffering. "Why wasn't Sonya jaundiced previous to this episode?"

In Alan's emotional state, I felt it was essential that I answer his questions as clearly as possible.

"Sonya probably had a stone at the terminal end of her common bile duct for those many years. Its size and shape permitted the stone to move in what is called a ball-valve action, opening and closing the exit for the passage of bile into the intestines. Recently, it became impacted and totally closed this opening. Bile could not pass through, so Sonya became yellow with jaundice."

I could answer Alan's question readily, but I failed to answer my own questions. Why had Sonya died suddenly? What had brought her sudden death?

There were several moments of silence. Then Alan spoke. "For 17 years Sonya lived free of pain. They were good years. We might never have had them had you not found the cancer in her large bowel." He hesitated, then continued. "You have been our doctor. You have delivered all our children. You took care of Josie when she fell off the horse and broke her arm. You operated on Terry when he had appendicitis. You are like family to us."

It was a moment of empathy, more felt than spoken. My involvement in these experiences made me feel a genuine part of his thoughts. As he spoke, I realized that I was not an objective medical man seeking an autopsy for scientific analysis or to salve my conscience, but a subjectively involved partner, hoping to find an answer to the question that was perplexing us. Why had Sonya died so suddenly?

Alan and I discussed God, the need for faith, the purpose of living. Then abruptly, this usually calm man broke into sobs. His frame shook with each one. Tears streamed down his face. But he said nothing. At a complete loss for words, I also said nothing.

Gathering himself, Alan looked at me and broke the momentary silence with, "God has been good to me. Sonya was a good wife and mother. I have six fine children. Thank you, Doctor, for listening to me."

At that point, I couldn't bring myself to ask for an autopsy. The request must wait until morning. But I couldn't go back to bed. My mind was too active, reminiscing and questioning.

I returned home and sat outdoors, facing east. Spruce, hemlock and balsam framed a sky hung with countless stars. The scent of lilacs, carried by a faint breeze, was a tonic for my questioning and fatigued soul. An owl hooted a distant defiance.

I sat motionless. At times, the scene before me, with its vast heaven of stars, captivated me. At other times, the face of Sonya Haymes, as well as the face of her loving husband, appeared before me.

The vastness of the heavenly canopy provided sharp contrast to the petty life of man. "Here today and gone tomorrow," echoed through my mind. "Who am I, or any man, to alter plans made by One who has the power to shape the heavens and earth?"

The stars were fading. The eastern sky brightened perceptibly. A mourning dove signaled the death of night and the birth of a new day. Still shaken, my mind continued to agitate with a sense of defeat. It was not a sense of humiliation but a sense of humbleness.

In the east, a great ball of fire rose, inch by inch, creeping above the horizon to warm this side of the earth anew. Again I felt small, unimportant, insignificant. "Who am I to question?" This thought again rushed through my mind.

Blue jays squawked their shrill notes. Swallows swooped. Robins busied themselves feeding their young. All about, there was a bustle of activity. "All are a part of the plan, His plan," I thought. "You, too, are a part of His Plan — not a great part, but an integral part. To fulfill that plan, you must not question His plan but do your part as well as you can, always striving to do better." Somewhat renewed in spirit, I stood up but was still disturbed. "How do I know I have done my best?" I questioned. "Did Mrs. Haymes die because of something I did or did not do?"

Now I knew that the baffling conditions of her death had led to a feeling of insecurity within me. I had to admit that an autopsy was important to me. Yet, I knew I could not bring myself to force it upon this devoted husband.

Implemented by the truth of my own need to know, I met with Alan. I listed various advantages of an autopsy but did not conceal my own curiosity, nor its value to me.

Without hesitation, Alan consented. After the autopsy, I was relieved. Sonya Haymes had succumbed to a blood embolis. A blood embolis is created by a blood clot, a thrombus. Should a blood clot be released from its hold on the blood vessel where it was formed, it becomes an embolis, an ever-present hazard in surgery. An embolis may be shunted to the brain, to a lung, or to the heart, causing a stroke or death. Emboli can occur without warning.

This experience has remained with me as an important guidepost. It taught me not to be puffed up by easy success, as in Sonya's first operation for cancer, nor to be overwhelmed by unpredictable failure, as in Sonya's sudden death.

CHAPTER 6

"FERTILE VALLEY" and PROBLEM ARRIVALS

"Fertile Valley" was a nickname given to a town east of Ladysmith. It was a well-deserved name for multiple births were frequent there, as well as large families.

But one family in particular deserves full credit for the nickname. Anna Boyton and her husband had 17 children, nine daughters and eight sons. Each daughter had at least eight children, and one matched her mother's total of 17. The eight sons also had large families, but the statistics of their progeny are not known to me.

The name "Fertile Valley" originated in my office when one of the Boyton daughters tied her mother's record of 17. A chance remark about the town's unusual fertility blossomed into "Fertile Valley."

Yes, "Fertile Valley" boosted my obstetrical practice and at the same time, created for me a pediatric following as the babies became patients. One of Anna's daughters established another record, delivering nine children in six years with three single births and three sets of twins.

It became a source of amusement as increasing attention was drawn to the name "Fertile Valley" by my patients. Good-natured remarks were often passed between patients and office personnel: "Oh, yes, you are from 'Fertile Valley — are you planning twins or triplets?"

But on one occasion, embarrassment overcame me. I had just returned from my parents' 50th wedding anniversary. Mrs. Boyton was in my office and knew I had been away. As she questioned me about the trip, I responded with shameless pride, letting her know that all six of my siblings, their husbands and wives and 26 grandchildren had been present.

Pursing her lips and giving me a dubious look of amazement, she said, "Let's see, that would be 35 blood relatives in all."

Unfortunately for me, I pursued the subject. "We had quite a crowd in one house."

She glanced at me with a well-is-that-so expression and replied, "The mister and I had our 40th while you were gone. We had 75 of our kids and their kids in our house."

I was deservedly overwhelmed. I should have known better. No one in their right mind would have fallen into a duel with a woman from "Fertile Valley," not even unintentionally. Pride does come before a fall.

When I began my practice in Ladysmith, most babies were delivered at home. Although more than 70 percent were normal deliveries, the fear of an abnormal delivery always hung over me, for without available emergency equipment there was an element of risk to both mother and baby. And that fear was very real. Under the best hospital conditions, when the baby's bottom, shoulder or face come first, such presentations are most serious.

Whenever appropriate, I hinted at the comforts and safety features provided in the hospital at relatively low cost. In time, the ratio of hospital to home deliveries was reversed, but the process was slow and never completely attained during my medical career. Fortunately, the Lord of human origin devised the anatomy and physiology of women to be not only capable of perpetuating the species, but also of enduring the most difficult confinements, so, along with the women, I weathered many difficult deliveries.

There was one confinement, however, that I was most thankful occurred in the hospital and not in the home. Throughout her pregnancy, Betsy had been most cooperative, coming in to the office regularly and following my suggestions fully. All signs pointed to an uncomplicated delivery until three weeks before the expected date of confinement. On that day, the abdominal exam suggested a breech (bottom first) position, and a vaginal exam confirmed it. Betsy and her husband, Gordon, had agreed to a hospital delivery. Betsy was healthy, had an ample pelvis and an excellent emotional attitude.

When Betsy went into labor, she had typical uterine contractions. The baby's heart tones were regular and strong. Betsy's cardinal signs were normal. Examination revealed her cervix was more than six centimeters dilated. It was time for me to scrub, to be ready to turn the baby, if necessary. Betsy was taken to the delivery room. Her legs were put in stirrups, and the anesthetist was called.

Entering the delivery room under stressful conditions often gave me the impression of entering an arena of challenge. But this time, I was ill-prepared for the doubt and the chagrin that would assail me. With my gloved hand, I checked the dilated cervical orifice to discern the actual position of the breech. Something didn't feel right. With a scope, I retracted the vaginal walls. The presenting part still didn't feel like a breech. Had I been mistaken? Mentally reviewing my office examination, I recalled the position of the heart sounds and the feel of the anterior shoulder through Betsy's firm but well-stretched abdominal wall. Perhaps I had been mistaken, or perhaps the baby's position had changed. Anxious moments passed. Self-confidence slipped. Again, my rubber-gloved hand probed the now-eight centimeter dilated cervix. This time the answer was clear. Betsy had a face presentation, not a breech. Never having witnessed a face presentation, I froze momentarily. Memories of good old Professor Beck, my obstetrical professor, rose to the occasion. His admonition, "When you don't know what to do, do nothing" came to mind. So I sat down on the stool and gazed abstractly at the obstetrical tunnel, through which the infant must pass. My mind was retracing the pages of Dr. Beck's book on obstetrics, his multiple drawings, and his sound advice.

Suddenly the words and drawings of face presentations came bouncing back to me, giving me some reassurance. But then a new perplexing problem faced me. Anterior face presentations, I recalled, would deliver spontaneously, without help. Posterior face presentations would not. Or was it the other way around? What to do?

Betsy kept pushing with her pains. I sat watching, doing nothing except struggling to recall which presentation required interference — the anterior or the posterior?

I asked the anesthetist to check Betsy's heart rate and the infant's heart rate. She assured me they were excellent.

I continued to watch and wait. Betsy continued to push. As the cervix dilated completely, I injected novocain into the perineum and the vaginal walls. When the perineum ironed out, I performed an episiotomy to enlarge the opening. A puffy little face, seemingly without eyes or nose popped into view. (A few days later the eyes and nose appeared as the swelling receded.)

Suddenly, I knew. I had done the right thing by doing nothing. But I also knew that the result of my watchful waiting had been a stroke of luck, not a stroke of wisdom. And, if wisdom it was, it was not mine, but the wisdom of Dr. Beck.

CHAPTER 62

THE SHOT THAT WENT UNHEARD

"Come to get my deer hunting physical. I know it's a waste of time and money, but Helga won't let me go 'less I have one." These were Thor Peterson's words as he strode into my consultation room with the same slow drawl and slow steps as he had for more years than I care to remember.

Thor was 84. His six-foot frame was still well-muscled but bent and twisted with age and by an active life. The old gent hadn't missed a hunting season in all his years and had no intention of missing this one.

Helga, his wife, had stopped at my office two days earlier. "That old coot ain't in no condition to hunt and he knows it and you know it, Doc, so give him a quick check and tell him so." And with that she stomped out of the office.

It was difficult to disagree with her. Thor's joints were "out-of-whack" as he himself had often told me. His heart frequently skipped beats and his breath was short, even coming up a few steps. But it would have been impossible to dissuade him from hunting, and besides, Thor, for all his years, was remarkably young at heart, and his enthusiasm was remarkably contagious.

"This will be my 72nd hunting season. My Dad started me when I was 12 and I ain't missed one yet and I ain'ta goin' to." As he said these words, I recalled how often he had said them before.

"I got a place picked out. I'm plannin' to hide in an old white pine stump with peepholes that have rotted out. There's even a hole big enough for my gun to rest on. Don't hafta walk far, Doc, it's an old loggin' road south of Ingram. T'ain't far to this spring where the deer come to drink. The stump will protect me from the wind."

"Are you sure this is what you want to do?" I asked, knowing full well what he would say and had said for many years.

"Course I do, you oughta know that. What in hell you think I'm here for, to go to a turkey shoot?"

As I examined him, I marveled at his leg and arm strength, his flat stomach, but most of all, his exuberance. Each time he spoke, which was often, he turned his head towards me, his grey eyes would light up, his false teeth would clack and his face would become serious with a single purpose: "Thor was going to hunt on the morrow."

I wondered then and have often wondered since, how I or any man, physician or not, could have stood in the way of Thor's hunting. Which I didn't.

"Thor," I said, "you know as well as I do that you shouldn't, but I know as well as you do that you will. So at least go slow and be careful." And that's all I said.

"Sure will, Doc. I'll take my lunch and a thermos of soup and a jug of coffee. See you in a day or so. I'll bring you a roast. Would you like that?"

"You bet I would."

Three days slipped by. I thought often of the dire possibilities that might have befallen Thor. His craggy features, silver hair, drawling speech and mulish passion to hunt broke into my thoughts with regularity. Another three days went by and my concern for Thor continued. Though often tempted to call his home to quell my anxiety, I resisted. Only three more days of hunting season, I reasoned, and then Thor will call me.

But those last three days, Friday, Saturday and Sunday, dragged; they were made especially anxious ones for I had to take care of two gunshot wounds and one hunter who collapsed with a heart attack.

Sunday night, while debating whether or not to call Thor, the phone rang. It was Thor. In his typical slow speech, he said, "Got ya a roast, Doc. I'll have it ready for ya by Wednesday if you wanta stop in." Then he hung up.

My relief was instantaneous. Thor and his family had been patients for many years, some filled with grave problems and some joyful results. Though relieved, my curiosity was now greatly aroused. How did that old bugger get a deer, drag him out of the woods and get him home? I found it difficult to wait till Wednesday.

Wednesday came at last and at seven P.M. I drove three miles to Thor's home, set in a large stand of Norway pines. As I entered the yard, the sweet fragrance of a wood fire enveloped me. Thor's dog, a full-grown Newfoundland, nearly bowled me over as I stepped from the car. His greeting was friendly but overly generous. Almost at the same instant, the kitchen door opened and Thor's deep voice drawled, "Come in; got your roast and a story to tell ya."

Helga looked up as I came in, gave me a gracious smile and then murmured, "He got by with it again, but he shouldn't have and he knows it and so do you, Doctor Bill. Anyhow, come sit down by the fire and I'll get you some plum pudding I made and a cup of coffee."

Impatience was nipping at me. I wanted to hear Thor's story, but there was no way to hurry him. When he was ready, I knew he would tell me, but in his own laconic style. As we ate the pudding and drank the coffee, the Newfoundland assisted me in spilling my coffee. Helga apologized for the dog's behavior while I muttered my apologies for being so clumsy. Thor's deepset grey eyes seemed amused with it all but he said nothing. Then, after the mess was cleaned up, he began.

"Well, now, Doctor Bill, I got somethin' to tell ya. In all my born days, I never heard of such things as happened to me. I can't believe it yet."

Helga interrupted. "This is not like you, Thor; get on with it."

"You know, I never saw a deer till Sunday, the last day of the season. Early each morning I climbed up into that tree stump and sat there on a stool I had put in there before the deer season began. There was a nice peephole to the northwest where the spring lay. Just below the peephole was an opening about a foot around where I rested my gun. There was another opening to the south and one to the east so I got a pretty good look around.

"I didn't really get cold but maybe a little stiff. Then I'd get up and move around a bit, have a cup of coffee and some donuts."

"How could you move in that stump?" I asked.

"It was a pretty good-sized stump, one from the old days. Maybe five feet around inside. Enough room to move around with my knapsack and stool."

"Sorry to interrupt, just curious to find out how you managed," I apologized.

Thor went on. "Every day, all eight days and till late afternoon on Sunday, the last day, I watched and saw nothing except an old 'porky' eating the bark off some trees. It didn't bother me none the first days 'cause I had studied the area and I knew from the deer signs that deer came to drink here. But, on the last few days, I was getting itchy, wondering if I should give it up.

"But I didn't, much as I was provoked to. I kept tellin' myself to be patient. 'Thor,' I said 'you got the time, lots of it, so just hold your horses.' And I'm glad I did.

"You know, Doc, since you took out my prostrate, I don't hafta go much. I can hold it, but about twice a day I had to crawl out and pee. I hated to go out, but I just couldn't pee inside that stump."

Thor hesitated and looked up at the ceiling. "You know," he went on, "except for those peepholes through which I could see the spring and a tamarack swamp and the old loggin' road, all I had to see was the sky. 'Course I was glad that except for the sky spittin' a few snowflakes, the weather was good.

"We—ell, Sunday afternoon was passing slow-like. I still had hopes but not much. I was thinkin' about Helga's cookin' and hankerin' to be by a warm fire. My eyes closed for an instant or so but they was aimin' like my gun towards the spring. Somehow, they opened again and there stood a great buck. I rubbed my eyes, but it was no dream. That buck held his head high and looked around, stepped forward a few paces and looked again in all directions. It was so clear I could've counted his prongs, but I was too excited. 'Hold on, Thor,' I said, 'you've waited too long to spoil it now!' So I watched and as he stepped to the spring and stooped to drink, I pressed the trigger."

Thor stopped, looked straight at me, drew his face into a wry knot and then exclaimed, "But I heard two shots, not one. I jumped out of that stump as fast as I could and went over to claim my deer. Two fellows beat me to it. A great argument took place. I knew I had shot the deer and, sure enough, where I had aimed, a bullet had penetrated the chest. The other fellows both claimed the deer and both had fired into the abdomen and, sure enough, there was a bullet hole there too. I was a little puzzled 'cause I only heard two shots but figured two of the three shots must have gone off at the same time.

"We discussed the situation for some time. They were really nice fellows, both came from Sheboygan and had hunted here before. Finally one said, 'We got a deer Thursday. We can split it and let this old man take this one.' Now I don't like being called an 'old man,' but 'long as they was goin' to let me have the deer, I said nothin'.

"They sure were nice fellows. They cleaned my deer, dragged it down the loggin' road and put it on my pickup truck. Never had it so good. I chawed with them a bit, thanked them and drove home. Helga had dinner ready and we ate."

Thor hesitated, picked up his pipe from a small table and then stood up. "Helga, where have ya put my tobaccy pouch? You women are all alike. Always movin' things."

Helga turned her head abruptly. "You men are all alike. Always lookin' for some'un to blame. Your pouch is right in your pocket. I can see it bulgin' from here."

Thor placed his large hand over his right side, gingerly felt his tobacco pouch and hesitantly produced it. He swallowed hard and lit his pipe as his face flushed red; but, to cover his embarrassment, he closed his eyes and concentrated on sending forth great billows of smoke.

Helga, accustomed to her husband's antics and always ready to say her piece, spoke up: "Doctor Bill wants to hear the rest of your story, not watch you hide behind your smoke screen."

"All right, woman! All right!" Enveloped in a great cloud of smoke, he sat down and continued his story. "When we finished dinner, I told Helga I'd shot a big buck, eight prongs on the right side and seven on the left. It was a big bugger, at least 200 pounds. I explained to her how I never knew those two fellas was hidin' nearby."

Thor hesitated again, quite obviously reluctant to finish his tale. Helga eyed him up and down. "Come on, you great white hunter, Doc ain't goin' to tell no one. In his business, he's used to keepin' secrets."

Thor glanced at his wife, ran his tongue over his lips, took a deep breath and started again. "We–ell, I went out and hung that buck up in the shed and brought in my gun to clean it. First, I looked in the chamber and I couldn't believe it. There it sat, an unfired shell. I pressed the lever and ejected six unfired shells from the magazine of my Winchester. I counted them again and again.

"I couldn't believe it, Doc, but it was true. Apparently, my shell had not gone off. Something musta gone wrong with the firing pin. And now I know why I only heard two shots, not three; mine didn't go off. Some hunter I am, Doc; I got my deer and never even fired a shot."

This story was printed in the Wisconsin Outdoor Journal, Oct/Nov, 1990.

CHAPTER 63

THE PAINS FOR SURVIVAL

As I entered the hospital vestibule on Warren's third post-operative day, I was met with the shrill wailing of a woman. The alarming cries came from the waiting room and belonged to Warren's wife, Nancy. She ran up to meet me and literally showered me with tears and moans of utter dejection. "Warren has given up! Warren has given up! He says he knows he is going to die. He is sure he is going to die."

The visitors in the waiting room were visibly disturbed by Nancy's shrieks. One woman, however, had real compassion written on her face. Apparently she understood Nancy's distress. I approached her and asked if she could go for a brief walk with Nancy. She could and she did, which added a degree of composure to the hospital, patients, visitors, and Nancy, too.

I walked up the hall to Warren's room. He was half sitting up in bed, his face tight and almost expressionless. His half-closed eyes avoided mine. Nancy's wails still echoed in my ears: "Warren has given up! Warren has given up!"

For 35 years, I had tended Warren. He suffered from recurrent bouts of rheumatoid arthritis. Many of his joints would swell, redden, get hot and tender, and throb agonizingly. Warren was an excellent carpenter, and his arthritis became a real problem in his work. He built houses and barns and did repair work. His hobby was putting together small pieces of different kinds of wood into mosaics, creating vases, bowls, lamps, and even tables. He and Nancy maintained the brightest flower garden in the county, and their vegetable garden was the equal of the best around.

Only a month before, Warren suffered through an excruciating episode involving multiple joints. He had been looking forward to gardening and wanted to finish a mosaic game table for me. In addition, he had contracted to build two barns. His days became long and his nights longer, but as I increased his dosage of cortisone, the swelling and pains in his joints subsided. Then all hell broke loose. Warren's gallbladder ruptured, requiring immediate surgical drainage. At the same time, he had a marked flare-up of his arthritis. His temperature spiked to 104 degrees, his abdominal pains were intense and his joints swelled.

It was now Warren's third post-operative day. Between glances at Warren's face and his swollen limbs, I studied his chart. His temperature had lowered to 102 degrees. His pulse was 90 and his respirations 18. There was cause for renewed hope. Urine elimination was adequate and had almost returned to its normal color. In addition, he had had an excellent bowel evacuation, light brown in color. Drainage from his abdomen had lessened and was less purulent.

I sat on the edge of Warren's bed and tried to communicate with this man I had known so long. He seemed far away. Earnestly, I tried to convey the positive signs of improvement I had found. Warren's eyes were now closed. He seemed not to listen and said nothing.

Again I noticed his swollen left hand with its enormously swollen fingers. Warren had abnormally large hands, but as I stared, his left hand seemed to grow even larger and more inflamed. His left arm, wrist and hand looked like one huge bee sting. I thought of the pain he must be suffering, of the sense of hopelessness he must be feeling, and I thought of the two barns he had contracted to build. Again I tried to communicate.

"Warren, I'm really pleased. Your condition has improved remarkably. In another day or two, I'll have you walking up the hall."

There was no sign that Warren had heard or cared. His eyes remained closed. I thought of his indomitable will, of how he persisted in everything he did even when conditions became difficult. "You have always been a fighter, Warren. What's happened to your pluck?" I said.

Again there was no response. Nancy was right; Warren had despaired, given up. I rose from the bed and went to the window, desperately seeking a solution. A prayer, silent but sincere, followed. As I glanced aimlessly out the window, a hawk, sitting on a high-wire pole, suddenly swooped toward the ground. What the hawk sought or what it caught, I did not see. But the hawk's swift act of violence conveyed to me an instant picture of nature's struggle for survival.

There was no reason why Warren should not survive, except that he had surrendered. All signs pointed to a successful outcome, but Warren had lost his desire to live. Warren was defeating himself. How could Warren be brought out of his despair and encouraged to fight? What had happened to his indomitable will? Why had he quit his struggle to live?

Perhaps it was coincidence, perhaps it was an answer to my silent prayer, but the hawk's abrupt swooping with outspread talons, as violent as it might appear, was an act of survival. Suddenly I knew Warren needed something to stir him out of his utter despair in order to survive.

Slowly I advanced toward the bed and drew up a chair. Carefully I entered the fingers of my right hand through his swollen, partially flexed left hand. Warren's eyes remained closed, his face reflected his "I don't care" attitude. I grasped his hand with gradually increasing pressure. As I increased the intensity of my grasp, I felt his hand and then his forearm muscles tighten slightly. His eyes remained closed. Again I increased the force of my grip. The muscles of his entire frame quivered. Then he sat bolt upright. He glared at me, first with disbelief that I would perform such a ghastly deed on a good friend and then with complete defiance. His face, flamed with anger, matched the red of his inflamed joints. Still silent, his eyes flashed with amazing vitality. His right hand and arm struck out at me with more determination than effectiveness.

I shriveled up inside, aghast at my own role, but continued to squeeze relentlessly. Warren spoke up, "What kind of a doctor are you? You call yourself my friend and then come in and hurt me? G.. d... you! What are you doing to me?" He spoke with vehemence, condemning me to the eternal fires of damnation. His invectives were more heated than his joints.

Warren was now in marked pain from my grasp. I spoke loudly and firmly. "So, Warren, you have not given up. You have lots of fight left in you."

Withdrawing my hand, I stared him full in the face. His glowering abated. His flush of anger receded. His muscles relaxed. He pulled his left hand, which I had so relentlessly squeezed, closer to him. He sputtered out a few words, "Why did you hafta do that to me?"

Cautiously, I responded, "Don't you know why?"

He looked at me again. His eyes had lost their defiance and anger. With a small, somewhat forced smile, he said, "Yeah, I guess I do."

Leaving the hospital ten days later, he thanked me in his own quiet way. But many times after that, he expressed his gratitude with carrots, beets, lettuce, beans, and squash left at my door. Often beautiful flowers were left for my wife. There was never a note; somehow, I just knew who was responsible. His final memento was the completed game table, in the center of which was a checkerboard made of different varieties of wood.

CHAPTER 64

A COSTLY LESSON

"Your old friend, Mrs. Jefferson, is here," Peggy announced as she escorted her into the consultation room

Miriam Jefferson's silver hair framed a face marked with the deep lines of a full life. Her thin face reflected both sides of her personality, for her eyes twinkled as readily with humor as her mouth turned down with sorrow. For 25 years she had shared with me her ups and downs, her family worries and tribulations. Talking with her had always been a pleasure. She came across as a woman who had established a sound hold on life, one who had invested a great deal in it and extracted a great deal from it.

But it was obvious she had changed since I last saw her. She was pale, thinner than usual, and had lost her lively spirit and her spry step.

"Come, sit down, and let's get reacquainted," I said, offering her a chair.

"Myra brought me, you know, my daughter. Can't say why. I'm just no good anymore. Ever since my husband died, I've been living with her and her family," Miriam said in a tired, raspy voice.

"What seems to be the trouble?" I asked, leaning over her and taking her hand so I could feel her pulse.

"I'm just tuckered out. I'm off my feed. I can't sleep, and besides, I'm no use to anyone."

Miriam's pulse was a bit fast, but regular. I sat down, disturbed by the change in her appearance but even more so by her broken spirit. At this point, her daughter came in.

"What have you noticed about your Mom?" I asked, hoping Myra's daily observations might be a key to the problem.

"Mom can't read. Her eyes have gotten worse. We tried a change of glasses. It didn't help. We got some large-print editions of *Reader's Digest*, but that didn't help either. I know she's lost weight, but she refuses to eat, " Myra said with desperation. "Gosh, Dr. Bill, we've tried everything we know, but Mom doesn't seem to care one way or the other."

I checked Miriam's blood. Her hemoglobin was 5.8 grams, less than half the normal amount and as low as I had ever encountered in a person still up and about. My scales showed she had lost ten pounds, considerable for a person whose normal weight was less than a hundred.

"Myra, did this change in your mother happen suddenly or gradually?"

"It started soon after Mom came to live with us a year ago and gradually got worse."

I was concerned that Miriam might have developed a cancer or a chronic disease, but after a complete exam and further history, I could find no physical cause for her loss of weight, anemia or listlessness.

"Miriam, how often do you see old friends?" I asked.

"You know I don't drive, Dr. Bill. Besides, Myra is too busy with farmwork to take me. I just stay at home."

"What do you do?"

"Nothing, Dr. Bill, nothing. I can't knit or crochet like I used to. My fingers are too stiff and full of bumps. My eyes won't let me read."

Perhaps I had missed something, but I was increasingly convinced that Miriam Jefferson was lonely, that she felt useless and without purpose. Always a go-getter, a spirited individual, she had no place to go and no one with whom to share her loneliness. She had changed from the woman I had known, the woman who had possessed a sound hold on life. She needed something to make her rest and sleep. But, most of all, she needed something to soothe her troubled spirit. She needed to be wanted.

Wine in proper dosage can be an adequate tranquilizer and an excellent appetixer in the elderly. It doesn't take more than one or two tablespoons before meals. With an increased appetite, the blood is often rejuvenated. Having used it successfully in several cases, I decided to give it a try here. So I arranged for Miriam to have a tablespoon of wine three times daily, ten minutes before meals.

One month later, mother and daughter returned. Improvement was obvious. Encouraged by her reawakened spirit, appetite, and mounting hemoglobin, I again prescribed the same wine dosage.

Things went well. Every month for two years, Mrs. Jefferson returned. She seemed like her old self. But one summer afternoon, a very hot and sticky one, her daughter called, anxiously requesting that I come to her home, some 30 miles out of town. Mrs. Jefferson had fallen down a flight of stairs.

On arrival, it was immediately evident that Mrs. Jefferson had broken the bone in her right thigh, her femur. She had numerous bruises, a large lump on her right temple and smelled of alcohol. I easily lifted this less-than-100-pound lady and placed her on the back seat of my car. I had splinted her leg with a Thomas ring splint, part of the regular equipment I kept in my car.

At the hospital X-rays revealed a long spiral fracture of the upper two-thirds of her right femur. I set the bone and put her leg in a cast.

In the ensuing days, I often felt a sense of guilt. Miriam had fallen down stairs, but she had smelled of alcohol. Had she taken too much wine? Was this why she fell? Had her daughter been too busy to oversee her mother's intake of wine?

As Miriam gradually grew stronger and started to use a walker to get about, I pressured her gently. "How much wine did you take at home?" At first she declined to answer. But I pursued the question, and a few days later she admitted that she had "upped the ante," as she put it, to four tablespoons. "And sometimes five or six, it made me feel so good," she said with a sly smile.

Before Mrs. Jefferson went home, Myra and I had a serious conference. It became obvious that Myra felt as guilty as I did. We acknowledged to each other that we had both been remiss. Myra should have spent more time with her mother and should have overseen her mother 's wine intake. I should never have prescribed the wine without the assurance that Myra would supervise its use.

Four-and-a-half months after her fracture, Mrs. Jefferson was up and about at home. Myra carefully allotted the wine before meals. She also took the time to take her mother to visit her friends and read to her twice daily. Miriam flourished under this loving attention and lived till she was 89.

For many years, Myra was an infrequent visitor to my office, but when she came, she would reminisce about her mother, repeating how she had neglected her. She assured me that her mother's accident had taught her to be more concerned and loving with all her family members.

I never completely lost my sense of guilt either. Miriam's broken leg, her thin face framed with silver and her intake of wine — "I upped the ante" — often flashed through my mind. This memory was a constant reminder, a stamp of caution when prescribing for the elderly, to use minimal dosage and maximum supervision.

SHE'S TOO FAT FOR ME

Rhonda Rankin was huge when I first met her. In the following ten years, she continued to gain. Though short of stature, barely five feet, her weight on my office scales was well over 200 pounds. Rhonda's huge rolls of fat made even a routine office examination difficult. Rhonda was a fun person and we had a good relationship, but her structural makeup — the enormity of her flesh — was a handicap that I did not choose to face on the surgical table.

Mother Nature contrived otherwise. On a bitterly cold January night, Rhonda was brought into the hospital with unremitting abdominal pain and vomiting. She had intestinal obstruction. Several attempts made to pass a Miller-Abbott tube were unsuccessful. This special tube, when passed to the point of the obstruction, sometimes releases it. Rhonda could not tolerate the tube. Surgery became necessary.

What an experience that proved to be! Rhonda had fat deposits everywhere. Opening her abdomen, in itself, was a major operation. Once inside, I found fat hanging from her organs like stalactites. Exploring her abdomen to find the source of the obstruction was like searching for it in a huge bowl of jello. Everything literally bounced with each touch of my gloved hands. Finally, I noted a dark area of the intestines, caused by a kink in the bowel where it had twisted on itself. After I released the kink, the intestines' dark color gradually returned to pink. I took a few supportive stitches to prevent its recurrence and prepared to close her up.

Now the real problem began. The inner abdominal lining, the peritoneum, was lacy. When I attempted to pull its edges together, the stitches tore through. To enclose the bulging abdominal contents within this thin, lacy peritoneum was like wrapping a quart of jello into a pint-sized envelope made of tissue paper. It was a tedious task, one that sorely tested me and one I vowed to avoid in the future.

Ten years later, Rhonda was still gaining. My office scales were limited to 300 pounds, and Rhonda surpassed this limit. Though she was beyond the menopause, she had begun to "spot." A dilation and curettage of the uterus revealed cancer. The accepted treatment was radiation, then the removal of the uterus, followed by more radiation. With clear-cut memories of Rhonda's former operation, I was certain her operation required the services of a team of skilled surgeons. Certainly, I wanted no part of it.

Rhonda, her husband, Merle, and I conferred. "You will need radiation," I began. "Then your entire womb must be removed to be sure as possible to remove the mother cancer cells in your womb. Then you should have more radiation."

"Why the radiation?" Rhonda asked.

"The radiation before surgery is designed to limit the spread of the cancer, and the radiation afterwards is to eradicate any remaining daughter cancer cells."

"Can't that be done here?" Merle asked.

"We do not have therapeutic X-ray machines here," I responded.

"But you can do the surgery, can't you?" Rhonda asked.

"Thanks for your vote of confidence, Rhonda, but you will need a team of specialists to ensure that the best job is done."

With the consent of Rhonda and her husband, I made an appointment at a surgical center in Minneapolis. A few days later I received a phone call. "Bill, this is Dr. Kline, Ethan Kline. Mrs. Rankin has had her preoperative dosage of radiation. We are sending your patient back for surgery. After you remove the uterus, send her back for more radiation."

How well I remember that moment. How well I recall my instant reply. "Oh, no, you don't, Ethan! You have the personnel. It's your problem now."

Then I realized Ethan was being ethical, and I was recalling only too well my operative experience with Rhonda. With this, my words moderated and my tones became subdued. "Ethan, I've been inside this woman's abdomen. It's huge. It was a nightmare. Please indulge me. Believe me, this is a job for a team of specialists. Besides, I will consider it a great personal favor."

Rhonda remained at the surgical center, where her hysterectomy was done and was followed with the necessary radiation. How well I remember the phone call informing me that she would soon be returning home to my care. "You old S.O.B." Ethan said. "Never have we encountered a more difficult case. It took two teams — four of us — to do the job. Be good enough not to favor us with another case like that — at least, not right away."

215

CHAPTER 66

"WHO MADE MARY SUCH A MONSTER?"

It was to be one of those very special days. Easter had come early and Christi, our eldest, was home on vacation. The entire family, all seven of us, had plans to ski at Telemark, and I had been looking forward to this day for some time. Leaving my bed early, I double-checked our equipment and started breakfast in order to get an early start.

With a cup of coffee in my hand, I gazed out the window and was once again thankful that Gussie and I had agreed to live here in the north country. Long shadows stretched to the nortwest. Rays of the rising sun pierced the leafless canopy of birch, basswood, and maple, nibbling at the lacy fingers of snow. Stalactites of ice hung like sabers, bending light into a dazzling array of colors. Evergreens, in marked contrast to the white quilt that covered their feet, were nudged by the soft whisper of a breeze. Absorbed as I was, the usual savoring of my morning coffee was lost on me, and I barely heard the phone ring.

"This is Tim, you know — Tim Powell. I've gotta talk to you."

"Tim, this is Sunday. Can't it wait until tomorrow? I've planned to take my family skiing."

"Gosh, Dr. Bill, I need to talk to someone. I'm ready to give up. You won't believe it, but Mary has turned into a monster." Tim's voice became louder, "She's impossible. She's a monster."

"What do you mean, Tim?" I asked.

"I'm ready to end it all, Dr. Bill." Tim's voice broke, but he continued. "Mary tells me what to do. She threatens to leave and take the children with her."

I remembered bringing Tim into the world, and Mary, too. Mary had been a most difficult face presentation. Twenty years or so later, I attended their wedding. Tim and Mary had four children, whom I delivered. The long night I spent when their daughter, Donna, had a ruptured appendix came to mind, as well as the spring day when their son, Pete, was run over by the farm tractor. Miraculously, he was spared from severe injury by the remnants of snow and the soft, partially thawed ground.

"O.K., Tim," I said, trying not to sound as reluctant as I felt. "Come as soon as you can. I'll be waiting."

In half an hour, Tim arrived. As we entered a room where we could talk in private, Tim started at once. "That Mary, she won't listen to my ideas. She acts like a big boss. She refuses to help with the farm chores, won't even go to the barn. She's a monster. What can I do, Dr. Bill?"

I wanted to reason with him, but I knew from past experience that he could be extremely bullheaded. Being reasonable was not Tim's strong suit, and, in his present mood, I knew reasoning would fall on deaf ears. Besides, I still wanted to spend the day with my family. With certain desperation, I suddenly turned on him and firmly asked. "Who made Mary such a monster?"

I studied Tim's ruggedly handsome face. He looked so dejected but seemed entirely indifferent to my question. So I continued, "Did you ever consider that you may have made her into this monster you speak of? What have you done to her in these years you have lived together?"

Tim stared at the floor. The muscles of his face tightened. He drew his hands into tight fists. His frame seemed to bristle with resentment at my remark. I pressed on. "I recall your wedding. Two happier people I have never seen Your children's births were surrounded with affection. I can't forget the deep love you two had for each other. What happened to that love? Was Mary totally responsible? Were you always so right, so perfect, so blameless? Or, did you make her into the monster you say she is?"

Tim glanced at me with disbelief. A quizzical smile played on his lips. His mouth opened but no sound came out. A light of possible comprehension came into his eyes and drove me to continue. "Tim," I said, mustering all the courage I could, ". . . marriage is like that. Each partner contributes something to the marriage and each other. In the same way, each may detract from the marriage and from each other. Consider your responsibility. This is a real test of maturity. Perhaps your wife has turned into a monster. But, perhaps you helped to make her that way."

Tim looked at me sheepishly, but did not speak. I continued. "Tim, I know I'm a better man today because of the woman I married. In some ways, I'm sure my wife is a better woman because of the man she married. Go home, Tim. Go and resolve to share with Mary those many fine qualities you possess. Stop making a monster of her."

Tim stood up, stretched to his full height, and thrust out his hand. As he gripped mine, tears filled his eyes. "What a fool I've been" he stammered, "an utter fool. Thanks, Doc. I'll try. No, I'll do better than that. I'll do it."

I hate to be called "Doc," but this time I didn't mind at all. Nor do I mind even now, for Mary and Tim are proud grandparents of four boys and two girls. And he still calls me "Doc."

CHAPTER 67

NATURAL PHYSIOTHERAPY

More than 60 years ago, I observed grizzly bears, crippled with arthritis, settle into hot springs in a remote corner of Yellowstone Park. Sparked by some inner drive, these lame behemoths had learned the benefits of this daily hydrotherapy. Apparently, they had selected the most suitable water temperature, 1,200 feet downstream from where the springs gushed from the ground. My companion and I tried it, when bear-unoccupied, of course, and found it remarkably relaxing to the muscles that had carried us over miles of rough terrain.

Years later, recalling the daily pilgrimage of those crippled grizzlies, I recommended simple hot baths and hot packs as a fundamental approach to the multiple aches of my patients.

Whirlpool baths and other forms of hydrotherapy were not available in our location, nor would my patients have been able to afford them if they were. In fact, some did not possess bathtubs and others not even running water. And so, with a little persuasion from me, cattle watering troughs became their tubs and the warm water was supplied from large pails heated over open fires or on wood burning stoves in their kitchens. One family adopted this as a weekly bath routine, drawing lots to decide turns. Hot baths and hot packs were no panacea for hard-worked muscles, but, along with aspirin, they definitely relieved many an ache and made possible a return to work and the resumption of family income.

There is nothing new about physiotherapy (physical therapy). It is as ancient as man, who has long valued exercise and massage for the relief of aches and pains. Today, however, it seems that physiotherapy is more dependent on fancy equipment than on simple, natural activities. Most of my patients had to depend on self-help physiotherapy, which made use of simple daily activities.

Much was accomplished by motivating the patient's independent spirit to dress and feed himself, to wash clothes and to walk, hobble or crawl. I suggested hand-washing dishes to men and women recovering from hand injuries, and, at my suggestion, women taught their husbands and sons to knit, which speeded the recovery of their finger flexibility.

Joseph Palowcyk was sitting up in bed when I arrived. He was tossing about in obvious pain. His right arm, with bones protruding through the skin, was swinging from side to side, much like a pendulum. It was immediately evident that he needed hospitalization, but neither he nor his wife spoke English, and I understood very little Polish.

It was not until Martha returned with a neighbor, who spoke both Polish and English, that I learned what had happened. Joseph had fallen from the hayloft two days before. Martha had washed his shoulder and arm with a laundry soap and put his arm in a sling.

Martha's stubborn insistence that he remain at home was soon overcome with the help of the neighbor as translator. As we drove to the hospital, I wondered how he had withstood two days of what must have been severe pain, for he had a comminuted and compound fracture of his humerus at the shoulder and of his radius and ulna at the elbow. My admiration for his fortitude was mixed with apprehension, not only for the mending of the bones but also for the grave danger to his life. For two day his bones had been exposed to conditions that did not protect his wounds from infection.

At the hospital, I inserted a metal plate to bring together the broken ends of the humerus along with a metal band to hold the multiple fragments together. I removed the head of the radius and, after realigning the ulna, fixed it with screws. Sulfa powder was placed in the wound; antibiotics were not yet available. Then I closed the wound.

Why no infection occurred remains a mystery. Twelve days later, Joseph left the hospital with his semi-flexed arm in plaster splints from shoulder to the base of his fingers. His arm was further supported by a sling. Twice a week for six weeks, he came to the office, where I gingerly removed the plaster splints, inspected the arm, and replaced both splints and wrappings. During this early post-operative period, he was encouraged to do frequent finger motions. Communication between us had improved as Joseph and Martha taught me some Polish and I taught them some English.

After six weeks, as bone healing appeared adequate for increased mobility, I cautiously moved Joseph's shoulder and elbow joints and encouraged him to attempt some slight motions. Still reluctant to turn over this delicate maneuver to Joseph and his wife, I replaced the wrappings. A week later, however, fearful that his elbow and shoulder would remain too fixed to be of any use, I showed him and his wife how to pursue gradual activity. It was then that I learned that Joseph had been helping Martha to hand strip their 32 cows for a month, using only his left hand.

The following week revealed no progress in mobility of shoulder or arm. By now, I feared that Joseph's arm would never regain mobility, but I refused to settle for a completely useless arm. As he was dressing, I noted that Martha assisted him; in fact, she practically dressed him. Somehow I managed to get it across to her that this she must not do. Then I asked if she fed him. She did. Again I insisted he should feed himself. To be certain that Martha and Joseph understood the importance of this, I called in a Polish patient from the waiting room. He spoke to them and assured me that they understood.

Weeks followed. Joseph dressed and fed himself. Using his left arm, he placed small logs on a sawhorse. With a Swede saw, he made firewood.

Six months after the accident, Joseph had between 30 and 35 degrees range of motion of his elbow. All shoulder motions were limited to 15 degrees. Bone healing was complete. Again I obtained the help of a Polish patient to be sure the Palowcyks would understand.

"Tell them," I said, "that the arm and shoulder will always remain stiff unless he does two things: use hot soaks and active motion. He must do the moving, not Martha."

That evening I went to their home and showed them how to soak the elbow and shoulder with hot bath towels, jars filled with hot water, and a large piece of plastic. "Most important," I emphasized, "Joseph must use his arm, not baby it." I asked them to return in a month, but they never showed up.

More than a year passed. One warm summer day, as I was returning from a country call, my car windows were open to absorb the beauty and fragrance of the outdoors. Suddenly, I heard the repeated sounds of an ax. When I looked toward the sound, the wood-chopper's swinging figure and the brick-sided house seized my attention. "Can that be Joseph or has his son returned from service?" I wondered.

Impatiently, I turned the car around, drove into the driveway and rushed to the ax wielder. It was Joseph. He grinned at me, somewhat amused at my enthusiastic greeting. Still impatient, I hurried him into the house. He stripped to the waist. I had been astonished to see him chopping wood, but what I found was even more astounding.

For all intents and purposes, Joseph could use his right arm as well as before the fall. His range of motion was limited by less than eight degrees. I could hardly contain my excitement, which he failed to fully understand.

Obviously, the best physiotherapy is that which is motivated by necessity. Joseph did what he had to do.

PUFFED UP WITH MYSELF

No question about it. I was puffed up with myself. I had made an accurate diagnosis on Carmen Hilger. She had an unmistakable ulceration of the lower esophagus due to a reflux, or flowing back, of hydrochloric acid from her stomach. Yes, when I learned she had previously been to several specialists who had not diagnosed her problem, I was puffed up.

Then I recalled that only three months before I had sent Edith McIntyre to one of these specialists, feeling that his special know-how would be most helpful in making a diagnosis that stumped me. Apparently this was a wise decision, for the patient returned quite happy to learn that she had pernicious anemia, which responds well to treatment. But I was not happy when she turned to me and said, in a rather contemptuous tone, "You know, Dr. Bill, the specialist said you should have known that I had pernicious anemia."

Yes, since I had been diligent in assessing Edith's condition, this statement was a hard pill to swallow. When I had last seen Edith, her anemia was only slight and her blood smear was not typical of pernicious anemia. There was no formication of her legs, (a feeling like pins and needles), no achlorhydria (absence of acid in the stomach) and no change of reflexes or vibration; but the specialist saw her three months after I had seen her.

"Yes, Edith," I responded, "Dr. Schulte is a good man. That is why I sent you to him. I'm happy that we can now make you better with pills and shots." I said this because it was the proper thing to say, but I had felt as though Dr. Schulte had knifed me in the back. Yes, underneath I resented his remark.

All primary physicians are placed in an awkward position. Only after some diseases have developed are they easy to diagnose. To make a simile, some common plants look much alike as they break the earth's surface and their first two leaves unfurl, so much alike that the average gardener cannot truly distinguish one from the other. At this stage in the plant's development, even an agronomist would find it difficult or impossible to distinguish. Not till the plant begins to differentiate does it reveal its unique characteristics.

Many medical condition are just as difficult to distinguish in their early stages, and the primary physician (general practitioner, family doctor, internist, pediatrician) is wise to seek the opinion of the specialist. Such consultations with men and women experienced in special fields of medicine provide a genuine source of information that may serve to assure an earlier diagnosis and thus ensure proper treatment.

Even the specialist, however, (the dermatologist, gynecologist, oncologist, surgeon, and so on) may not be able to make and early diagnosis, for the characteristic changes of the disease may be slow to progress or the tumor slow to grow. In fact, some conditions remain ambiguous even at the later stages of their development. Thus, consultations with specialists, while they afford an important source of diagnostic information, are not flawless.

Usually, time elapses between the primary physician's request for consultation and the actual consultation. While this lapse of time is usually minimal—a day or a week—in some cases it is considerable. In Edith's case, it was three months. During this lapse of time, the disease may have had sufficient time to grow, to differentiate like the plant emerging from the earth. This can place the primary physician in an awkward position, for the diagnosis now may have become very obvious, as in Edith's case. The primary physician then appears to have been rather stupid or unobserving. The consultant, if experienced and modest, does not flaunt his effortless diagnosis. Unfortunately, the arrogant consultant will. As in Edith's case, he may say, "Your doctor should have known this."

But now, the opposite was true. Carmen Hilger had been seen by several specialists, none of whom had diagnosed her esophageal ulceration. However, they had not seen her for at least seven weeks, and her condition was now in full bloom. It was now perfectly obvious that Carmen had a reflux of acid which had ulcerated her esophagus. The situation was an ego booster until I recalled my resentment at the specialist who had said, "Your doctor should have known this."

My puffed-up feelings subsided as I realized my diagnosis was anything but spectacular and there was no cause to indulge in self-inflation.

RAPPORT

One day, while in a dentist's office, I overheard a brief conversation between a dentist and his patient.

"I don't like the way you do things around here," the woman began. "My fillings come loose. I'm always having toothaches, and it hurts the way you stick needles into my gums."

"I'm sorry, madam," the dentist replied.

"Sorry, indeed. What good does being sorry do?"

Without another word, the dentist called in his receptionist.

"Mary," he said in a soft voice, "Mrs. Linton needs to have a reference. Please suggest several dentists for her to call." Then he addressed Mrs. Linton. "Mary will help you find a dentist you can be happy with. There will be no charge for today."

I knew the dentist well enough to ask, "Why did you do that, Bert?" His answer was simple, "No use fighting dissatisfied patients. It only gets worse. They're not happy, and I'm not happy."

It didn't take me long to learn the truth of Bert's remarks. Susan Breager was clearly such a patient for me. Attempts to communicate with her proved futile. Every suggestion made by me was contradicted.

"Your blood pressure is normal," I began after a complete examination.

"Then why do I have these terrible headaches?" Before I could complete my answer, she interrupted, "And why does my heart beat so fast? And why am I so dizzy?" She went on repeating all the symptoms she had already listed for me.

"Mrs. Breager, you are having menopausal symptoms. You are experiencing the unpleasant symptoms many women have at your age."

"Couldn't be. Nellie, my good friend, never had headaches like I have. She never got dizzy, like I do. She never had her heart beat fast like mine."

"All women don't react the same. Some women are lucky. Their menses just taper off and then cease without any real discomforts."

"But I've had this dizziness and these headaches for a year now, and my heart beats at night, keeping me awake. But I haven't had any menses for ten months," Mrs. Breager continued as she scowled with obvious unacceptance of my explanations.

"Women vary a great deal both in their start and their shut down of menses. They also vary their cycle changes. While most start at 13, some start as early as ten years. Most women stop menstruating at around 45 years of age, but some stop earlier and some go even beyond 50." I explained.

"My mother never had symptoms like mine, and my sister, Carol, she didn't either."

Mrs. Breager had a point, a point difficult for me to get across to her. How could I tell this unyielding woman that her symptoms were tied up with her disposition? I had often observed that some women's menopausal symptoms were exaggerated by a high-strung emotional makeup, and Mrs. Breager definitely fit this pattern.

I proceeded cautiously. "Susan — I hope you don't mind my calling you Susan — it must be very uncomfortable when you get these nervous spells and headaches and your heart beats fast and you feel flushed."

"That's not it at all. My husband calls me nervous just like you do. I'm not. Something's really wrong, and you just don't understand. You're like all men— you think we women haven't got a brain in our heads." With that, Mrs. Breager stood up with an attitude of defiance.

Clearly this woman and I had no rapport, and equally obvious was her need to find such a relationship.

"Susan, I know a woman gynecologist to whom you might entrust your problem. Would you consider traveling 60 miles to see her?". Mrs. Breager agreed; I made the appointment with a sense of relief.

My dentist friend, Bert, had taught me a valuable lesson—the importance of rapport. More and more I realized there are sufficient medical and surgical hazards to surmount in treating patients without taking on personality conflicts, but it was on Mrs. Purcell's fourth prenatal visit that I became thoroughly convinced that she and I lacked rapport.

"I don't eat much. Besides, I can't starve my baby. Mom tells me I should eat enough for two." Mrs. Purcell spoke emphatically.

I tried to persuade her otherwise. "Angela, the little one needs nourishment, good nourishment, but it's not how much you eat but what you eat that counts. I gave you a diet slip. For the baby's health, as well as his satisfactory growth, please follow it. Actually, it will be better for your health as well."

Mrs. Purcell also frowned on my mention of an exercise program. "Angela, you have gained 12 pounds already. Not only should you eat less but you should also exercise as I indicated on the prenatal care sheet I gave you."

She bristled, "Your scales must be wrong. At home, my scales say I've gained only two pounds and I don't need any more exercise. I get enough just milking cows. Besides, I don't have the time."

"Angela, my scales are balanced scales and are quite accurate. I know milking is important, but a half-mile walk twice a day would be good for you, not only to keep you limber and help keep your weight down, but exercise would also help you to handle your labor better."

Angela bristled again. "I'm in good shape. All that modern diet and exercise stuff is for the birds. I don't know why you insist on my coming in each month anyhow."

"The Wisconsin Medical Society, through its obstetrical committee, has discovered that the biggest cause of infant deaths is lack of prenatal care for the mother" I said.

"Oh, I can't believe that. I think the whole thing is silly. My mother never saw the doctor till she was in labor. She had five of us kids and never had any trouble."

It seemed unwise to fight her. I recommended another doctor.

A month later, I had a most enjoyable experience which emphasized the positive value of rapport between patient and doctor.

Mrs. Dubinski was a Polish woman of 65, but her physical condition was that of a much younger woman. She was broad of face and her hair was streaked with gray. She spoke in short, excited bursts, each brief response emphasized by flashing eyes and gesturing hands. Her affability was contagious and our rapport spontaneous.

"I have a great heaviness down here," she said pointing to her lower abdomen. She grinned. "I feel like pregnant, but I can't be. I have no period 16 years, not till now."

"How often have you passed blood and how much?" I asked.

"Last three months, much times. Sometimes dirty my underclothes. Once I got it on the rug." She grinned again, but not with shyness or embarrassment. She felt comfortable with me while conveying her personal problems, and her trust made me feel comfortable, as well.

An abdominal and pelvic examination showed that Mrs. Dubinski had a large fibroid tumor of her uterus, almost 3/4 the size of a basketball. Bumps protruding through the muscular layer of the uterus were easily felt. Showing her pictures from a textbook, I explained to her the possible sources of her bleeding.

"You could be bleeding because of fibroids in your uterus if they have penetrated the mucosal layer of the uterus, or the mucosa might be bleeding because of a cancerous growth, or you could have a growth on the cervix, the neck of the womb. In order to be certain, it will be necessary to do a D & C — that means dilating your cervix and scraping the inner lining of your uterus so that it can be studied under a microscope."

"Sure, sure, you do it, Dr. Bill. I understand. Pictures help me understand."

"Think about it. Talk to your husband. If the scrapings are not cancerous, then your uterus should be removed. This will not only lighten the heaviness you feel, but will also stop the bleeding."

The following day, Mrs. Dubinski returned with her husband. Once again, I explained the situation in detail and then suggested to Mrs. Dubinski that she get a second opinion.

"Oh, no," she said. "You take care of me. Nobody else."

"If that's what you want, then I'll do the scraping on Monday. If there are no signs of malignancy, we'll go ahead. I'll remove your womb on Wednesday."

Although up to this point, her husband, Earl, had remained silent, he now stood up and, waving his arms violently, shouted, "No, no, no! My wife go to city. Have operation there!"

Mrs. Dubinski answered just as loudly. "No, no, Dr. Bill operate me. He only doctor touch me."

But Earl retorted, "No, you go to city. Da bigga da garage, da more da tools!"

A heated argument followed. Mrs. Dubinski repeated her faith in me, and Earl continued to protest vehemently.

Finally, at my suggestion, they went home to decide, but the following day they were back. On entering the consultation room, Mrs. Dubinski spoke at once. "You operate, Dr. Bill. I want you operate. Tell me when."

Although her English was broken, Mrs. Dubinski and I communicated readily. But it went further than that. Perhaps my explanation of her condition and my detailed description of possible sources of her bleeding made her aware that I cared. Our personalities were never in conflict—they merged. From the confident look on her face, it was obvious that she had no fear of the operation, and when she said, "I want you operate. Tell me when," I also felt confident, for I knew she had faith in me. A definite rapport existed between us.

Arrangements were made for the D & C, which was done. The resulting pathological study showed no malignancy, and the removal of the fibroid uterus was scheduled. Mrs. Dubinski turned to me, and, with her pale blue eyes looking directly at me, she said, "Tomorrow my big day, my good day. Tomorrow I lose my big tumor? Yes, Dr. Bill?" Again, I could see she was trying to share her feelings and emotions and that she was fully prepared to go through with the operation.

The following morning, the day of the operation, Mr. Dubinski met me as I entered the hospital corridor, and, with a worried look on his face, he blurted out, "My wife die, no pay, Dr. Bill!"

A short time later, as Mrs. Dubinski was being wheeled into the operating room, I looked down at her. As I touched her hand, she opened her eyes and then winked at me. I winked back.

Mrs. Dubinski's operation went well and she recuperated rapidly, returning home in five days. Ten days after the operation, she came to my office to have her stitches removed. Her first remark when she saw me was, "I tell you everything go good, so everything go good. Yes, Dr. Bill?"

Three months after the operation, I received full payment of my bill, $150, with a short note: "Thanks, my wife good, signed Earl."

CHAPTER 70

HE COULDN'T FORGET

At one time, Norbert Brockway was a devoted husband, a loving father, and a much respected member of the community. After his wife, Alice, died, he became an alcoholic and, by many, was considered a dirty bum.

Norbert had been a handsome man who always managed a smile and never seemed in a hurry. Alice, with her delicate features and blonde hair that fell softly over her shoulders, had a figure that was the envy of women and the delight of men, but it was her blue, dancing eyes that first drew attention. The Brockways made a pleasing couple.

When Norbert and Alice were in their late 40's, Belinda, their only child, married and moved to Minneapolis. A few days later, Alice had convulsions, one after the other. The abrupt onset of the convulsions suggested an aneurysm, a "bubble" in the wall of a blood vessel of her head, rather than a tumor or tissue growth. Because the convulsions were unremitting, I feared that the "bubble" had already ruptured.

Fearing the worst and with little hope, I called a vascular surgeon in Minneapolis who had successfully operated on two of my patients with cerebral aneurysms. Within eight hours he opened Alice's skull and attempted to stem the blood flow and repair the artery. His efforts were in vain. Alice died on the operating table.

Belinda and her husband, Jim, stayed with Norbert for a week after the funeral. Norbert began to drink heavily soon after they returned to Minneapolis. In a few months, his unshaven, disheveled and generally unclean appearance became a daily affair. Few who had known him could believe it was the same man. As his pleasing personality and sense of responsibility vanished, most citizens left him alone. His only companion was his bottle.

Norbert was frequently jailed overnight and, on several occasions, was hospitalized for delirium tremens because of his excessive drinking. On one of his hospital admissions, after his frightening hallucinations had subsided, we talked,

Norbert and I. I urged him to join Alcoholics Anonymous, but to no avail. Norbert made it clear that he didn't care. The memory of Alice with her blond hair and blue eyes, constantly haunted him. He insisted that only when he was intoxicated did he find relief. Suicide by violent means was out of character for this man, but I felt sure that Norbert hoped alcohol would finish him off.

Life, however, had different plans for this once-gracious and responsible man. Ten years of almost daily intoxication did not finish him, but did manage to render him increasingly more crude and disgustingly dirty. No one sought him out, not even his daughter, and he sought out no one.

One Saturday, Norbert struggled up the stairs to my second-story office. Although reeking of alcohol, his voice was strong and articulate, and his hands did not shake. He had pains in his chest and back. His ribs, at least a half-dozen on each side, were tender, and he had lost 20 pounds. Norbert was the picture of pathos. His face was gaunt and skull-like; his emaciation and pallor accentuated his deep-set eyes. His bones protruded not only in his limbs but also in his chest, where the spaces between his ribs looked like a series of parallel canals. X-rays of his ribs, vertebrae, and skull revealed all were "moth-eaten" in appearance. Cancer of the prostate gland had spread, eroding bony tissue in almost circular patterns.

During the time I was examining him, Norbert rambled on, probably talking more in that half hour than he had in several years. He told me about his life from his childhood to the present. But whenever his thoughts wandered, they always returned to Alice, with her blue eyes and her blonde hair. Her abrupt departure from his life had never ceased to hurt. He had not accepted her death. The clear image of his beloved never faded.

As I listened, I recalled the previously wholesome, gracious, and talented man who was now wracked with cancer and still haunted by regret and sorrow for one he had so loved. Even now, as sick as he was, his need to express himself and to alleviate his inner hurt was more important than relief from his physical pain. And so, I listened. The misery, so long held within him, had finally burst its self-imposed bonds. When at last he sat quiet, he was as exhausted as if he had just completed a marathon, but his face was relaxed and his eyes looked into mine with a restful gratitude.

Then it was my turn to talk — to discuss his condition with frankness and to urge him to go to the hospital. At first he refused, but finally agreed.

Within a week, his weight decreased rapidly and his frame became like a skeleton. Because of his pain, sedatives and morphine were increasingly essential. Norbert was quiet, patient, and even pleasant. He had finally accepted his lot — Alice's death.

But I was angry and distraught. No one visited Norbert except nurses, hospital Sisters and myself. His daughter and son-in-law, though notified of his condition, had not come to visit him. I located their telephone number and called them. After some intense moments of controlled indignation, I exacted a promise form Belinda that she would come the following day.

Belinda bustled into my consultation room, very upset. "What has my father ever done for me?" she said without sitting down. "All he has done is humiliate me. I don't owe him a thing."" Her husband, Jim, nodded his head in silent agreement.

I was tempted to tell Belinda of her father's ten years of agony, of his inability to cope with her mother's death, but thought better of it. Harnessing my emotions, I gazed at her and spoke softly, "Belinda, this is your father. No matter how his actions have seemed to you, he is still your father and he needs you now. He needs the warmth that only you, his daughter, can give. Are you and your husband going to continue to avoid him when he needs your understanding and love?"

Belinda fell into a chair. As if to support her, Jim stood behind her. Belinda's face softened, and tears fell from her eyes.

Then I continued, "It's not too late. Go see him now."

Belinda raised her head, then raised her moist eyes that had been staring at the floor. She choked out two words: "We'll go." After a few seconds of silence she asked, "But what can I say?"

"Don't plan what to say. Say whatever seems right. Just be his daughter."

Belinda and Jim spent six days with Norbert, who relinquished his meager hold on life at the end of the sixth day. After settling Norbert's affairs, they returned to Minneapolis.

A month later, a foul winter day was brightened by Belinda and Jim's appearance in my office. They presented me with a tie clasp and matching cuff links, which bore the medical insignia — a caduceus. I treasure this gift, a reminder of their look of gratitude that required no words.

.

CHAPTER 71

STRANGE HELPERS

It had been a long night. I could not sleep. The scorched bodies of Mrs. Jeffrey Holloday and her three children repeatedly came to mind. Two of the children had died in the fire. Mrs. Holloday and her daughter, Nadine, were in the hospital with severe burns that covered more than 60 percent of their bodies. For two days it had been touch and go. Mother and daughter barely clung to life. Daily changes of Vaseline dressings almost seemed an imposition, they caused so much pain.

It was now five days since the fire. It looked as if Nadine and her mother might make it, but their discomfort was constant. Each time I changed the dressings, there was the problem of exfoliation—huge chunks of skin were peeling off and there was a strong odor of decaying flesh. As I tossed in bed, I thought there must be an easier way to get rid of the decaying flesh than to pick it off with forceps and scissors with each change of the dressings.

It was four o'clock. The morning light of May was peeking through my window. I decided to get up and roam through my growing young forest. I had now planted over 200 evergreens, most of them 12 to 15 feet in height and a dozen or so over 25 feet. I had started my trout stream. Water from a well dug in the cellar trickled over a small waterfall into a large pool faced with rocks. The water then passed into a series of shallow pools and on into the Flambeau River. Wild iris, marsh marigold, and arrowhead, snapdragons, and watercress edged the pools, making habitat for various forms of insect life, which in turn provided natural food for the trout I had brought home alive from local streams.

The rat-a-tat-tat of a downy woodpecker broke the morning silence as he hammered his beak into the trunk of a hemlock. A pair of mourning doves cooed blissfully on the limb of a spruce. A flying squirrel whirred through the air, navigating a 30-foot leap with remarkable ease. Images of the burn victims were receding from my mind as I became absorbed in my little forest and stream and its inhabitants. The golden tips of the evergreens were emerging from their winter's nap into new growth. The bright yellow of the marsh marigolds was reflected in the water. A trout dimpled the surface. My professional anxieties had completely faded in the vibrant awakening of life all about me.

I wandered from spot to spot, engrossed in the ever-changing ways of nature and at the same time occupied in thoughts of changes I hoped to make, such as enlarging a pool or adding more plants and trees. My concentration was so complete that for several moments I was unaware of a foot-long trout that had jumped out of the pool and lay at my feet. It was a brown trout that evidently had lain there for at least a day, it's belly alive with maggots.

Images of Mrs. Holloday and Nadine came rushing back and how they suffered through each change of dressing and the removal of their decaying flesh. An article I had read, describing how maggots were used years ago with great success, flashed through my mind. I stared down at the dead trout, its belly bulging with maggots. The temptation was strong, but I could not make up my mind. I returned to the house to eat breakfast alone. It was still not yet 5:00 a.m.

I tried to eat, but the agony of mother and daughter with each dressing change and the possible benefit of the maggots obsessed me. I jumped up and went outside, convinced it was worth a try. I reasoned that if I was going to use the maggots, it would be best to do it at this early hour, when there was less chance of being observed in the act. Using an old knife, I opened the trout's belly and gathered an abundance of maggots into a damp cloth.

Mrs. Holloday and her daughter were at the end of the hospital hall, where the morning light was still dim. Both were asleep. Ever so gently, I lifted some of the Vaseline dressings. With a pair of forceps, I placed maggot after maggot where the decaying flesh was most ample and smelled the worst.

A sense of enormous guilt came over me and remained till I returned to their bedsides at seven o'clock that evening. As I lifted a few dressings, it was evident that the maggots had been busy. Neither patient complained, and the nurses probably had not noticed, for they said nothing.

The following day, I looked again and was amazed at the change in the appearance of the skin, which looked so much cleaner. Most of the decaying flesh was gone. Two days later, I decided it was time for a complete look. As I removed the dressings, the nurse assisting me almost jumped out of her skin. "Look," she screamed. "Look at all those things crawling about. What are they?"

I never explained what they were or how they got there, but by removing the decaying flesh, the maggots made Nadine and her mother more comfortable and appeared to hasten the healing process.

CHAPTER 72

DON'T ROCK THE BOAT

There is a little gem of a lake, still clear and clean after many years of bathing and fishing in its waters and picnicking on its shores. Countless families have come to share this tiny lake's special attractions. Its spring-fed waters are encircled with huge hemlocks, towering pines, and a smattering of birch. Although only ten acres in size, the lake has surrendered many a bass and walleye and occasionally one of trophy size. This is Harvest Lake, the scene of an incident that helped resolve a sticky problem.

Paula and Boyd Jenkins were regular visitors to my office. She had diabetes and he, epilepsy. They had first met in my office when only youngsters and often recalled romping in the waiting room and chasing each other up and down the stairs to my second-floor office. As adults, they continued to return for professional counsel. Fearing their children might inherit diabetes or epilepsy, they planned someday to adopt rather than have children of their own, but kept putting it off.

Paula's father, who had gone west seeking higher wages, was killed when he was crushed between two freight cars and, without invitation, Paula's mother, Edith, moved into her daughter's home.

Edith was a self-assured, well-disciplined woman. Unfortunately, her self-confidence became overbearing. She took over her daughter's household, giving daily instuctions to Paula and Boyd. "Today, I want you to paint the kitchen, Boyd. Go to town and buy some off-white paint. Paula, pick some carrots, beans and lettuce. Then help me clean the refrigerator. Go now, we haven't all day."

Paula bore up under the duress, even though her mother left few decisions to Paula herself. But each time Edith hovered over Boyd like an army sergeant giving orders, Paula winced.

From the time of their childhoof meeting in my office, on through grammar school and high school, Paula and Boyd had developed one of those unusualy smooth relationships. Their union was blessed with tranquility, which now was being threatened. In their anxiety, they consulted me.

I brought up the subject of adoption in hopes that an infant might soften the home situation, but their ardor for adoption had been chilled by the tensions that persisted in their home.

"We are beside ouselves. We just don't know what to do," Paula said. "I know she's my mother, but she rules the roost. It's been a long winter with her in the house."

"Paula is putting it mildly," Boyd added. "Because it's her mother, I just don't say anything at home, but I'd sure like to. She sticks to us like glue. We don't have a minute alone. Now that the ice is out of Harvest Lake, we want to spend our Sundays there, but Mom insists on joining us."

"For several years, Boyd and I have gone to Harvest Lake on Sundays," Paula said. "It's a special day for us. What can we do, Dr. Bill?"

What could I suggest? How could Paula deny her own mother? Various ideas came to mind, but when I thought what I might do if this were my mother, I hesitated to mention them.

Boyd looked at Paula. His eyes narrowed and his lips became taut. "Paula," he said. "We've got to tell Dr. Bill the whole story. It's your mother, so you should tell him how she threatens us."

Paula nodded her head. "OK, I'll tell him. When we've tried to get Mom to let Boyd and me have time alone, she pouts, 'You don't love me anymore. No one cares about me. You want me to die!'"

"I'm glad you told me," I said. "This is a real problem. I'd like to think on it. Can you come back tomorrow?"

When they returned the following day, I suggested a long-range plan. On the surface it appeared inhuman, and we were about to abandon it, when Paula spoke up with finality. "We've got to give it a try. We can't go on like this."

The following Sunday, all three went to Harvest Lake. Mother Edith received much attention and the best seat in the boat and at the campsite. Her gloomy attitude and autocratic manner faded. "She never threatened, 'I might as well be dead.' She sat like a queen surrounded by her vassals," Paula reported.

For two Sundays, Queen Edith absorbed the attention showered upon her. On the third Sunday, Paula feigned a headache and sore throat. Boyd appeared sympathetic: "I'll stay home and take care of you," he offered.

"No," Paula insisted. "You go and take Mother with you."

After proper offers to remain home and take care of Paula, Mother Edith agreed to go with Boyd. When they arrived at Harvest Lake, Boyd put the small dory in the water. It was still early in the morning, a good time to try for bass before the lake was disturbed by the Sunday crowd. When close to the middle of the lake, Boyd stood up and started casting while Mother Edith sat in the stern, fishing with a minnow supported by a bobber.

"Sit down, you boob. You want to turn us over?" Edith shouted.

Resolutely, Boyd kept his fully erect position and continued casting.

"What's the matter with you? You know I can't swim. You want me to drown?"

Boyd lurched slightly to the left with each cast and to the right with each back-cast. The boat rocked gently from side to side.

Edith set her pole down and grabbed the sides of the boat. "You damn fool. You're rocking the boat. Sit down, damn it. I can't swim."

Gradually, still not uttering a sound, Boyd increased the sway of the boat by extending his side-to-side lurching. With some of his more extreme movements, he managed to get a little water into the boat.

Edith screamed, "Sit down, you no-good son-in-law. What are you trying to do, drown me? For God's sake and mine too, sit down damn it. I can't swim."

Boyd spoke for the first time, "What difference does it make if you drown here or die someplace else? You are always threatening to kill yourself." With that, he tilted the boat even more with his side-to-side motions. Several inches of water lapped into the boat.

Edith gripped the boat more tightly. With her eyes and voice full of tears, she whimpered, "Please, Boyd, sit down, I'm scared. Take me home. I'll do anything you ask."

Boyd sat down facing her. "You are a good woman. You were a good wife and mother. But you are a helluva mother-in-law." With that, he stood up and rocked the boat violently.

"Please, Boyd, please," Edith begged. "I'll do anything you say, just stop rocking the boat."

Boyd moved closer to the back seat on which Edith sat petrified. He continued to rock the boat. "Here's your chance," he said. "You want to die; go ahead."

Then, noting the genuine fright in her eyes, he quietly sat down once more. The boat continued to teeter sideways in gradually diminishing arcs. Edith sat still, her eyes closed and her mouth trembling.

"Look at me," he demanded. "You are the damn fool, not me. Your daughter and I have tolerated you because you are her mother. But no more. We can't have someone live with us who wants to rule the roost—our roost, not yours. We can't have someone always threatening to kill herself if we don't do what she says. We want to live, to be happy, to have time to ourselves. Sunday should be our day alone, Paula's and mine."

Several minutes passed. A car pulled up on the gravel road to the picnic grounds, then another and another. Couples sat on the wooden benches. Others entered the water to swim. A boat was dropped from a cartop into the water. Boyd and Edith sat gazing at each other.

Edith spoke first. "Boyd, you are right. I have been a fool, and I've been unfair. Since my husband died, I've relied on you two for everything, even to support my self-centered ego."

Boyd stood up once again. His face was still drawn with anxiety. "Mother, you can stay with us, but let Paula and me live and breathe freely. Find some friends and interests of your own. Live your life and don't smother ours."

The two of them went home, not arm in arm, but each with the hope of a new and lasting friendship. Strangely, it worked. Edith's eyes had been opened. Home for all three became peaceful. There was no need for resentment, as Edith no longer demanded assistance, but requested it. In time, she developed outside friendships that gave her a life of her own. On Sundays, Paula and Boyd went to Harvest Lake and Edith went to church with friends.

Edith no longer "rocked the boat" at home and Boyd no longer needed to "rock the boat" at Harvest Lake. Edith had finally surrendered her self-centered dominance.

CHAPTER 73

A MOMENT SPANS THIRTY YEARS

The very moment she opened her eyes, I knew I had seen those eyes before. My reaction was instantaneous — those were the same saucy, laughing eyes I had once known years ago. But where and when?

She had been brought to the hospital unconscious, and according to the chart, her name was Mazie Canfield. She and her husband, Gordon, were touring from Vermont to California and had just been in a car accident. Gordon was only bruised, but Mazie had a severe concussion. I remained by her bedside to observe her, fearing her condition might get worse.

It was three hours after she was brought into the hospital that Mazie muttered a few indistinct sounds, but soon thereafter she spoke clearly, asking for her husband, and then opened her eyes. Yes, even under these conditions, her eyes were full of merriment. I was both relieved and amazed, but at once became possessed with the conviction that I had seen those saucy, laughing eyes before.

Mazie's pulse, blood pressure, and temperature were monitored by nurses, but I frequently returned to her room, obsessed by the notion that her laughing eyes were a part of my past, and I became plagued with curiosity to find out.

On Mazie's second hospital day, as she shot me a glance, the past 30 years suddenly unrolled. I could see those same saucy, laughing eyes in the face of a teenage girl I had once known. She had been somewhat of a problem for Tom, Carl, Mousey, and me. We fellows had felt very secretive about some of our teenage pursuits but somehow Mazie managed to tag along, and there was little we could do to evade her.

Mazie didn't like to play with girls. She preferred boys. Her hair was cut short in a boyish bob. She wore trousers and a shirt, which would raise no eyebrows today but was unknown then. In time, we accepted her as just another one of the boys, and she held up her end even in the pranks we played and the unusual outings we took, some of which were rather devilish and even dangerous. One Halloween, seeking mischief, we placed all the available neighborhood porch and patio furniture up on telephone poles. A particularly unpleasant neighbor who had often yelled bloody murder at us was repaid with a bundle of 'ripe' fish left on his front porch.

As I said, we just accepted her as one of the guys. She fished with us, carried worms and dead minnows in her pockets, waded through swamps, rode a canoe on the crest of ocean waves, and bicycled 20 miles for a new adventure. We got to the point where we no longer tried to shake her off but even relied on her to bring along a little extra lunch and cookies.

But the last adventure with Mazie of the laughing eyes proved the most memorable. We four males had sworn a special oath not to tell her what we had planned. We were going skinny-dipping at a local beach at midnight. Even though we had accepted her as a guy, underneath we reckoned she was a girl and we just didn't want her along. None of us ever found out how she got there, but shortly after we were in the water, she dove in, as bare as we. We swam farther and farther out, but she came after us. We dove under water and swam till we were out of breath. She followed. We finally gave up and hurried back to shore. Mazie lingered in the water as we rushed to dress.

Our male curiosity aroused, we examined Mazie's small pile of clothes and found them to be no different from our own — shirt, trousers, boxer shorts, and undershirt. In those days, we usually went barefoot.

Yes, Mazie was just another guy to us. We never saw her any other way. She dressed like one of us, ate like one of us, and shared our rowdy and smelly ways. And here she was, my patient in a hospital 1,200 miles away from where I had known her before, 30 or more years later, and still with the same saucy, laughing eyes.

Several days had passed. Mazie was ready to be released from the hospital and was eager to go. I sat by her bed and abruptly startled her by a plunge back into our childhood.

"Mary Brandon" I said, using her maiden name. "Do you remember Carl Hutton, Tom Andrews and Mousey Gebhart?"

"Why sure," she answered, and then her eyes turned quizzical. "Are you Bill Bauer?"

We spent a full hour recalling many of our teenage experiences before her husband came to get her. As she started down the hospital corridor, I observed that she was a very feminine, stylishly dressed woman. At the moment, I could little imagine the tomboy I once had known, but as she turned to wave good-bye, her saucy, laughing eyes caught mine, and I saw the teenage tomboy once again.

CHAPTER 74

A TRIAL OF FRIENDSHIP

"This is Mick, Dr. Bill. My niece fell down our steps, and her leg is all twisted. I'm sure her leg is busted. We've got her in the car. Can you meet us at the hospital?"

I met them there. His niece had a compound fracture of both bones of her right leg. The bones had ruptured the skin. After cleansing the area with soap and water, I swabbed it with merthiolate antiseptic and then set the fractured bones into satisfactory apposition and encased her leg in plaster, leaving a small opening for drainage should infection develop.

"Mick, your niece should do well, but there's a good chance of infection setting in because the bone has punctured the skin." I explained. "That's why I left this hole in the cast. She will have to be watched carefully."

"You should know, Dr. Bill, that she's only going to be here another week. She's visiting us from California."

"Better have her stay in the hospital a couple of days to see how she gets along, Mick. We will give her some sulfa medicine and hope her leg doesn't get infected."

A week later, Mick's niece, Ellen, returned to California. There had been no signs of infection. She took with her a summary of her care and X-rays of her right leg. Soon thereafter, I received a letter from a California lawyer, informing me that I was being sued for malpractice. Deeply concerned, I consulted my attorney, Jacob Howard. We were old friends; our families had often picnicked together. He and I played golf in the same foursome, and our wives belonged to the same bridge club. We also attended the same church and were as close is spirit as it seemed possible.

Jacob was a man of considerable self-possession and quiet dignity with a lean, Lincolnesque figure. In characteristic fashion, he assured me there was nothing to worry about. I had never been sued before, and of course I was worried—worried I would have to go to California to face trial, worried about the time I would be away from my practice, worried about expensive legal fees, and worried about the outcome of the trial.

But my self-possessed attorney repeatedly assured me all would be well. At first, the California court demanded that I appear, but Jacob arranged for a deposition to be made, sworn to, signed, and sent to the California court. This was carried out with aplomb by my tall, dignified attorney, Jacob Howard. Since Jacob and his family were going on a two-week's vacation to California, he assured me that, if necessary, he would render his professional services to the California court.

When Jacob returned from California, he reported all had gone well. "After all," he said, "you followed all established medical procedures in treating your patient."

Attorney Howard was right. I lost neither money nor time, but a week later I received a bill—a legal fee from my good friend, Jacob, for $10,000. Upset by the size of the bill, I determined to sit on it for a week.

The week passed. It was a Saturday night. The bridge-potluck supper club, to which we and our wives belonged, met. The usual eight couples were present. During dinner, I looked at my friend often but detected no sign of a change in attitude nor a difference in Jacob's self-assured posture. But, later, during the evening of bridge, when Jacob and I were at the same table, I spoke out, quietly but with unmistakable firmness, heard by all.

"Jacob," I said, "wasn't $10,000 an extraordinary fee?"

"Bill," Jacob responded with a touch of smugness as he shuffled the deck, "no, I don't think so. I will send you an itemized bill."

I said no more. Within two days, I received the itemized bill. Items listed included travel expenses to and from California, research into similar suits, the cost of making and sending the deposition, and a long series of other items, including stationery, postage, secretarial work, and so on.

The following day, I sent attorney Jacob a check for $10,000, money which I had borrowed from a local bank. No more was said, but I often thought I had been artfully imposed upon and reckoned that time might right the situation.

Fourteen months later, early one sub-zero morning, I was awakened by an urgent telephone call. "Come at once, come at once," pleaded my good friend and attorney, Jacob Howard. "My wife is doubled up with pain, is pale as a ghost, and is retching something awful."

Friend Jacob had not exaggerated Mrs. Howard's condition. She was suffering from acute empyema of the gallbladder. I sent her to the hospital at once, and after ten days of a medical regimen, the gallbladder was surgically drained. Four days later, she went home. After a few office visits, Mrs. Howard was discharged from further care but admonished that later surgery might be required.

I sent attorney Howard a bill for my services. It was for $10,000. Ironically, he received my bill the same day as our usual monthly bridge-potluck supper date.

All eight couples were present. Supper was completed. No words were spoken between Jacob and me, except for our initial greeting. Bridge tables were set out, cards and scorecards laid upon them. With the draw of the partners, Jacob and I were relegated to the same table. I glanced at my attorney with diffidence, hesitant to assert myself. The usually self-possessed Jacob avoided my eyes, then lustily exclaimed, "That was a g— d—— awful bill you sent. What kind of doctor are you anyway? No way am I going to pay you $10,000. Some friend you are, robbing your own pal."

I looked straight into Jacob's eyes. It was obvious that he felt and reacted to my searching look, for his eyes dropped, his lips trembled perceptibly, and he stiffened. In clear tones, soft but heard by all, I said, "Jacob, I will send you an itemized bill."

Nothing further was said; the subject appeared sealed, shut off from further discussion. However, attorney Jacob's menacing words hung over the group for most of the evening. The usual light banter, exchanged among old friends, was absent. Even on parting, it was apparent that the air was still charged. Yet no one voiced an opinion, for one and all prudently avoided taking sides, though each, no doubt, wondered about and was concerned with the eventual outcome.

The following day, I sent my itemized bill as promised. I considered it a deserved response to attorney Jacob's impersonal legal fee of $10,000. The bill read:

Night call to Howard residence	$15.00
Fourteen hospital visits @ $5.00	70.00
Surgical drainage of gallbladder	100.00
Eight office calls @ $5.00	40.00
STAYING UP AT NIGHT WORRYING ABOUT YOUR WIFE	$9,775.00
TOTAL	$10,000.00

It was paid without another word.

CHAPTER 75

TRUTH CAN BE A HARSH BEDFELLOW

Her hair hung straight over her forehead and ears. Her eyes were downcast. The listless expression of her face remained unchanged, even as she said, "Hello, Doctor." Her posture was one of complete dejection. It was obvious she was short of spirit and heavy with fear.

Reaching deep inside for words of assurance, I faced Cynthia Kasten with the warmest smile I could muster. This scene in her hospital room was being enacted for the third day. Again, I was attempting to replace despair with hope, depression with cheer, and fear with confidence.

My words went unheard, my smile unseen. Why, I wondered, was Cynthia so desperately afraid? After all, she had not yet been told that she had cancer of her right breast. Her husband knew. Her grown children knew. But they had requested that the diagnosis be withheld from her until she had settled into the hospital routine; for of a certainty, she had a highly apprehensive nature.

After more that two decades of treating her, I could attest to her extremely sensitive disposition, so readily agitated. When a baseball that had strayed from its mark broke her bathroom window, she was in a tizzy for more than a week. When a visiting daughter, helping her in the kitchen, cut her finger, Mrs. Kasten expanded her solicitude by fainting and then remaining in bed for the rest of the day. When her husband was two hours late from a golf game, in her anxiety, she made numerous phone calls in a voice nearing hysteria. Not having delivered any of her children, I often wondered how she had endured childbirth three times.

Sitting by her bed, with one large hand enveloping hers, I asked her what was bothering her. She trembled but did not answer. I did not want to even mention the word, "fear," so I sidestepped it by asking her why she was trembling. Was it that she was cold?

Her eyes remained downcast. Her lids fluttered but did not open. She did not speak, but her face drew so taut I could distinguish her facial muscles.

Convinced that Mrs. Kasten was consumed with fear, and that once again, I could not allay that fear by kindly counsel, I chatted about her family, her bridge club, and her hopes for a flower garden come May. She nodded silently with her head, but spoke no words.

Dismayed at my own inability to exact any positive influence on Cynthia, I finally retreated and at once telephoned her husband, Martin, requesting that the family meet with me. Two hours later, the four of them were in my consultation room.

We again spoke candidly of our concern. We re-established the need for nurses around the clock and the necessity for tranquilizers. There was registered a unanimous feeling that Cynthia should not be told the truth about her diagnosis at that time. The three special nurses had all been apprised of the family's request that Cynthia not be told.

Curiosity, both personal and professional, consumed me. Why was Cynthia so distraught, so utterly frozen in fear?

This led me to review every conversation, every medication, and every person involved in Cynthia's care. It was a slow process, for all the people related to her care were not present at the same time. This meant questioning the personnel of all three eight-hour shifts.

Tiptoeing into Cynthia's room at 3:30 a.m., I noted the special nurse, Hannah, sitting in a chair by the window, reading under a dim light. Cynthia was motionless and appeared to be asleep. I quietly signaled the nurse to step outside into the hall.

We went over the chart—Cynthia's pulse, respirations, temperature—what medical personnel refer to as the cardinal signs. All were normal. This was a preliminary to numerous questions regarding Cynthia's attitude and what, if any, conversation Hannah had had with Cynthia.

Hannah was a nurse of solid proportions and solid convictions. Past experience should have forewarned me. Hannah was one who spoke her piece. The truth of what she believed, thought, or lived came out of her undistilled. Attending Cynthia proved to be no exception.

Yes, Hannah had told Cynthia the truth. "After all, Cynthia had a right to know."

Shortly, we returned to Cynthia's room. She lay in the same position as when we had left. She appeared so motionless. I bent over her. There were no sounds. I felt for her pulse. There was none. Grasping my stethoscope, I listened over her heart. There were no heart sounds. Cynthia was gone. She had died in her sleep.

Truth can be a harsh bedfellow. Hannah had no right to take it upon herself to inform Cynthia of the truth. Perhaps we all need to know, have the right to know, and thus should be told the truth. However, like the treatment for any disease, there is a time to treat and a time to hold back. The choice should be made by the one who is in charge, the responsible party—in this case, the doctor. Fear in itself is a disease that can kill. It killed Cynthia.

The expression "scared to death" had more real meaning than meets the eye, as an autopsy on Cynthia revealed. The stress of fear had led to an acute coronary occlusion.

CHAPTER 76

A BORN CONNIVER

It was at precisely 3:00 p.m. on a Tuesday that a telephone call compelled me to respond at once. The wind was rattling the fluorescent sign that faced the building, and rain was pounding the roof. Between claps of thunder, the office waiting room was strangely quiet. The usual babble of voices was reduced to an occasional whisper. The office lights, turned on because of the ghastly darkness, had quit because of a power failure. Peggy was busy searching for candles when the phone rang. I picked it up and heard a plaintive voice say, "Please, please, Dr. Bill, come at once. We've made a terrible mistake. Mother is out in this storm and hasn't returned."

It was Linda, Janet Carter's daughter. I pictured her distress, for the family and I were involved in a bold plan to cure Janet of her malingering. "I'll come at once," I said and set out on what became a long 30-minute drive to the Carter farmhouse. At the first fork in the road, blinded by a burst of hail, I swerved into the ditch. It seemed best to sit and wait.

As the lightning flashed and hail pelted the hood and roof of my car, the years rolled back. I saw Janet as I had first encountered her, a happy-go-lucky youngster of 14, vivacious and pretty, yet willful and sly by turns. I soon learned she could pout, draw tears, act hurt or smile with uncanny facility. Always ready for mischief but never ready to accept blame, she managed to glide through her growing-up years and marry.

Her husband, Tom, was an average, hardworking individual. He was quite the opposite of Janet. Where she was attractive, he was plain. Where she was fickle, he was dependable.

Following the birth of their first daughter, Janet remained an invalid much longer than was warranted, even by the most liberal medical yardstick. She complained of swelling where none could be seen. Pains, aches, and stiffness, being subjective, were difficult to deny, as seemingly absurd as they appeared to me. Her many symptoms carried over for several weeks, during which time her dependable husband took over the household chores in addition to his own job at the mill. Though suspicious that Janet was malingering, what could I do?

A year later, Janet delivered a second daughter. A similar episode of unaccountable symptoms developed. It was three months before Janet again took on her own chores.

Measles, mumps, chicken pox, a broken arm, and a severely slashed hand kept me in touch with the Carters as the young girls entered their teens. Cassie and Linda had acquired their mother's radiant good looks and their father's stability. They had gradually accepted increasing domestic responsibility as it was pushed upon them by their mother. Conflicts, however, were arising. The daughters, now of high school age, were getting involved in outside activities, and less time and effort were available for domestic responsibilities. They complained to their father. "Why should we have to do our mother's work?"

Janet started to complain of low back pain, then pain in the frontal pelvic area. Not long after this, she said her legs felt numb and then her feet. Two weeks later, she insisted she was helpless, that her legs refused to move. She took to a wheelchair. But there were no neurological signs. Her reflexes remained normal. I was convinced Janet was trying to acquire a secondary value at the expense of a primary one—no domestic work—by appearing paralyzed.

The girls became of little help with the household chores, and Tom's stability began to crumble as he was swamped with the increasing burdens of domesticity. The house became a nightmare of unwashed sheets, blankets, clothing, pots, pans, and dishes. One Sunday afternoon, the girls had begged me to come. "Pa is angry. We just don't know what to do. Ma has become a real problem, and Pa threatens to leave. Please come, Dr. Bill."

Tom and the girls were in the kitchen when I arrived. Their words were loud and heated.

"Where's Janet?" I asked.

"She is out in her wheelchair. She's been real good at using it and sometimes stays out for several hours," Cassie said. "When we want her to come in, we ring this cowbell. I'll ring it now, and she will come in a few minutes."

"No, don't ring it. I'll go find her," I said. Cautiously wandering in the direction Janet had taken, I found her standing erect, her back leaning against a large maple tree. She was facing the sun receding in the west. I watched her for a few minutes. Suddenly, she was startled by a squirrel leaping from branch to branch. Looking about anxiously, she rushed to her wheelchair.

Quietly, trying not to be seen, I returned to the house.

"Did you find Ma?" Linda asked.

"Yes, I did, but I didn't bring her back with me."

"Why not?" Cassie asked.

I didn't know how to answer. What could I say? How could I tell them what I had suspected all along—that their mother had been deceiving them, that she was a fraud? I decided it would be better for them to find out for themselves. "Your mother needs your help, your understanding. She has a serious problem that is difficult to explain. Perhaps if you see it for yourselves, you will understand it better."

244

"How can we do that?" Tom asked.

"Well, it won't be easy, but if you really want to understand her problem and perhaps help to cure it, then I'll suggest a method," I said, now confident that Janet was malingering and needed to be caught red-handed. "We must all agree to the plan or it won't work."

After all three agreed to stick to the plan, I went on, "Your mother wanders through the woods in her wheelchair and returns when the cowbell is rung, but if a storm is brewing, one of you runs to get her. Is that right? I suggest when the next storm starts, your mother be allowed to return home on her own, that no one go after her."

Reluctantly, all three had agreed.

It was still as black as midnight. The hail no longer pounded on the hood and roof of my car. I had only been in the ditch ten minutes, but my mind had traced back through the high points of Janet Carter's life. Cassie's plaintive voice still rang in my ears: "Please, please, Dr. Bill, come at once. We've made a terrible mistake. Mother is out in this storm and hasn't returned." A sense of enormous guilt swept over me. I had been so sure that Janet was a malingerer. What had happened? It was still raining. What if Janet was still out in this rain? I hated to think about it.

I went out into the rain, jacked up the right rear wheel, stuck a wire pad under the wheel, and the car came out of the ditch with the first trial.

On my arrival at the farmhouse, both girls met me at the kitchen door. Their father, whom they also called, was waiting impatiently. "What are we gonna do now?" he shouted. "That's some plan you had. Janet's probably drowned by now in all that rain, or frozen to death. We must have been crazy to have listened to you."

"I'll go find her. I'm already soaked." I spoke without confidence, for I also pictured Janet sitting, wet and cold in her wheelchair.

"I'll go with you," Tom muttered, his face set with determination. We were about to leave by the kitchen door, which was close to the ramp Janet used for her wheelchair exit, when I heard a sound between claps of thunder. "Was that a moan?" I asked.

"I didn't hear anything," Tom said.

Then Linda shouted, "I heard it!"

We hurried down to the basement. The door to the outside, just beneath the ramp, was partially open and moving in the wind. As the lightning flashed, there stood Janet, wet and shivering, huddled in a corner.

Gasping wildly, the girls rushed to her. Few words were spoken. Janet was carried upstairs, bathed, and put to bed. Obviously, she had walked home. The wheelchair, unable to navigate the slippery, wet ground, had betrayed her.

It was an eye-opener for Tom and the girls to realize that Janet was not paralyzed, that she could walk. They no longer felt compelled to cater to her whims and were free of her conniving manipulations. Now that her secret was out, Janet had to adjust to a new way of life. No longer could she escape from her domestic duties through the wheelchair.

CHAPTER 77

GUILTY CONSCIENCE?

Mrs. Jackson was a remarkable woman. Though 73, she carried herself with dignified assurance, reflecting to others that she approved of herself. And she did, in spite of many recent setbacks. She also had a sense of humor, which helped her as well as others to momentarily escape from harsh reality.

Mrs. Jackson was small framed and spindle-legged, but agile. Like most Norwegians I knew, she was warmhearted and enjoyed the company of other people. Often, her pleasant conversation prolonged her office visit, making if difficult to bring the visit to a close.

This remarkable woman lived alone in a farmhouse after her husband died. One sister lived two miles east and another sister three miles west, but Mrs. Jackson staunchly refused to abandon the farm and give up her independence.

In spite of her self-reliant spirit, she remained dependent on her sisters for transportation. She had no car and never had learned to drive. Somehow, her sisters were always available when needed.

Mary was her first name, but I always referred to her as Mrs. Jackson for, in spite of her informality, she seemed to cherish her married name.

Year after year, Mrs. Jackson visited me at monthly intervals. She had an irregular heartbeat known as auricular fibrillation with occasional bouts of cardiac decompensation. When her spindly legs swelled and she developed a cough, she came in more often. She had learned these signs signified a need for medical regulation.

In December of each year, Mrs. Jackson failed to appear. During the Christmas holidays, three daughters and a son descended upon her, insisting that she see a specialist in the Twin Cities.

When she reappeared in January, she always handed me a long list of instructions she was to follow, including an all-rice, no-salt diet. In addition, there were eight extra pills to be taken daily. It was a complicated schedule to follow.

Each January without fail, Mary Jackson handed me the instructions, but her first words were, "Dr. Bill, you are not going to keep me on that all-rice diet, are you?"

And as regularly, I'd promise her that I wouldn't keep her on such a diet. I had learned that as people get older, they did not require stringent diets, except under dire circumstances. Living alone was enough of a dampening experience on one's spirit without being confined to an unvarying diet of rice. In fact, there was more hope for cooperation with a semi-restricted, low-salt diet than with the monotony of an all-rice diet.

I had also learned that elderly people, limited in their activity, did not require a host of medications. Actually, they did better with a well-chosen few, for their body responses appeared better and a complicated schedule of multiple medications proved too confusing.

Yes, cooperation is an essential ingredient between physician and patient, and this is what Mrs. Jackson and I had developed. Our mutual confidence in each other inspired this cooperation.

Blessed with this cooperative spirit, many years passed without serious complications. Except for her annual pilgrimage to the Twin Cities, Mrs. Jackson remained a regular monthly visitor to my office.

One January, soon after returning from the Twin Cities, Mrs. Jackson delivered her often repeated request, "Dr. Bill, you are not going to keep me on that all-rice diet, are you?" But then she went on, "Why do I put up with this unnecessary expensive trip to the Twin Cities?"

I watched her silently as she grimaced, as if in pain. I soon realized she needed to speak her piece and release some inner disturbance that troubled her.

"I love my children, but why do they always insist on taking me to see a specialist? I'll never follow all those awful rules he imposes on me, anyhow. Besides, it's an expensive trip. My children don't pay for it—I have to. Gosh almighty, I just don't understand why they insist on taking me. Why can't they just visit me and let it go at that?"

Her question was not rhetorical. She wanted and needed an answer. She had gone to the Twin Cities seven Decembers and felt an accumulated dissatisfaction. But how to answer?

In my own mind, I had an answer—a logical one. These children, mature grownups, all four of them, never visited their mother except to take her yearly to see a specialist. Were they relieving their guilt at not visiting their mother during the year by demonstrating this desire to have her health checked by a specialist.

And if so, why did they not pay for the medical bill?

It was a strange enigma, but if baffling to me, it must have been even more so to this dear lady. To suggest that her offspring were relieving their guilt by this annual pilgrimage would only add to her discomfort.

Furthermore, I did not want Mrs. Jackson or her family to feel that I resented her annual visits to a specialist.

Yes, it was a dilemma which I finally met head on. Mrs. Jackson needed a straightforward answer and I gave it to her.

"Next December," I began, "when your children are about to take you to the Twin Cities, you insist that they will be responsible to pay the bill." I avoided saying why.

"But then they won't take me," Mrs. Jackson said with vehemence.

"So what" I responded, "You have made it clear to me that you don't want to go."

"That's true," she replied and said no more.

Perhaps she had interpreted the situation as I had. If so, she didn't let on.

Another year passed. Mrs. Jackson appeared every month, including December.

When she came in December, my curiosity was high, but I said nothing. Just before leaving the office, she looked me full in the face and said, "Children, even when grown, can really get under your skin. It's hard to understand them at times. They show their love in strange ways. Anyhow, I told them I wasn't going to the Twin Cities unless they paid. They wouldn't pay, so here I am. Actually, I'm glad, Dr. Bill, for then we'd be wasting their money instead of mine."

CHAPTER 78

A TWELVE-YEAR-OLD ENIGMA

"Before you see your next patient, the social worker wants to talk to you. It's Colleen Jacobson, the one you like, the one with the red hair," Peggy teased. I did like Colleen. She was so thorough and yet so brief. She gave more information in fewer words than most women and indeed most men.

Colleen got right to the heart of the problem. "Maureen is a 12-and-a-half-year-old girl who, I'm afraid, is pregnant. She has had no menses for three months and was reported frequenting bars with men. She lives with her father, who is never at home. She is absent from school as much as she is present. She is not interested in school nor in any of its activities. This is no life for a 12-year old girl."

"I agree, but skipping three periods in a 12-year-old girl means nothing," I said.

"But she's had regular periods since she was nine," Colleen replied. "Doesn't that mean something?"

"It can, especially if she is of Mediterranean stock. Sometimes girls of Mediterranean stock menstruate early. Why don't you bring her in?"

Maureen Stevens entered the room submissively, eyes to the ground, head lowered and back bent. After she seated herself, she gave a furtive glance about the room, crossed her shapely legs and again looked at the floor. In spite of her cowed appearance, she was an unusually attractive female. Her dark hair fell in wavy tresses about her shoulders. As she reluctantly raised her head to answer questions, I noted her dark brown eyes, her white teeth and her clear, olive-colored skin. Maureen was indeed shapely. No one would have guessed that she was only 12-and-a-half years of age.

"What does your father do?" I asked.

"I don' t know. I hardly ever see him," she replied, then looked at the social worker as if for help.

There was little doubt that Maureen felt very uncomfortable. How could I make a 12-year-old girl, wrapped in an 18-year-old body, open up and talk to me? I needed to gain her confidence, to question her in private. For this reason I requested that Colleen step into the waiting room.

Again I studied Maureen as she sat across from me. Her low-cut dress revealed her well-formed breasts. She sat with her shapely legs crossed. This was not the portrait of a 12-year-old girl. What could I do to make her talk? To gain her confidence? I had to know the truth. Was she actually pregnant? Had she had sexual intercourse?

"Where is your mother?" I asked.

"She ran away. I haven't see her since I was eight."

"Don't you like school? What about your girlfriends?" I asked, hoping I could find some means of starting a conversation.

"I don't like school. I have no girlfriends." Maureen spoke in a monotone that I could barely hear.

I was getting nowhere and had to make a decision. I would be frank—pleasantly so, but frank. "Maureen" I said, "you and I have a problem. The social worker is interested in you and your future. She fears you are pregnant. You deny having had intercourse, so you probably aren't. But you and I must prove that you are not pregnant, so I need your help to find out."

Maureen looked up. Her dark brown eyes sought mine. It was the appealing look of a 12-year-old, pleading to be understood. "What do you want me to do?" she whispered.

"We must do a pregnancy test. If it is negative, we will do it again to be sure. All you need do is bring in the first urine you pass tomorrow. Please help by doing everything right. I'm going to depend on you so I can do my job properly. Will you do that for me?"

Again Maureen looked up. Our eyes met and she smiled. "I can do that," she said and rose from her chair.

I watched her as she walked out. No longer did she present the cowed appearance as when she entered. Nor did she have the animated stride of a 12-year-old youngster. With head held high, she left the room with the measured steps of a young woman.

A week passed before I saw her again. The pregnancy test was positive. An examination was obviously necessary. I explained this to Maureen but assured her that there would be no need to hurt her.

After the nurse had Maureen on the examining table, I reentered the room. Standing beside this 12-year-old 'woman,' I explained that I would first examine her breasts, then her abdomen and then her pelvis. I reassured her, "I will not hurt you. If anything hurts even a little bit, you let me know."

With that, I examined her full, well-rounded breasts. The superficial veins appeared engorged and the primary areola of pigmentation was darker than normal. These were positive signs of pregnancy. Was this girl telling the truth? Perhaps she did have intercourse.

I proceeded to examine her abdomen. In spite of her cooperation, I could find nothing. Now came the hardest part. Even the thought of doing a vaginal examination on a 12-year-old girl is a hurdle to cross. I put Maureen's legs in stirrups. She did not seem to object. Then came a shocker. As I started to examine her vagina, I found her hymen was intact. She was a virgin. Yet, the vagina was highly congested. It had a purplish hue, another sign of pregnancy.

It seemed I had entered a blind alley. Three positive signs of a pregnancy and yet an intact hymen. The situation was ambiguous, to say the least.

I walked to the head of the examining table and told Maureen that I would not examine her through the vagina but instead would do so through the rectum. "This will hurt a little," I explained, "but I'll be as gentle as possible."

With one finger in the rectum and one hand on the lower abdomen, I felt a slightly enlarged ovoid uterus. This also suggested pregnancy. Then, on the right side of the uterus, I felt a small mass, also ovoid in shape. Perhaps Maureen had an ectopic pregnancy in the right tube. Why then an intact hymen?

While Maureen dressed, the social worker bombarded me with questions, questions I was not yet prepared to answer. In the medical literature, I had read of pregnancies with questionable causes. I recalled one where a 15-year-old girl followed an older brother into a bathtub. Another questionable cause of pregnancy was external intercourse without penile entry. I mused for some time.

There were tumors of the ovary to consider. Was the mass I felt on the right side of the uterus a tumor? A growth of the ovary? If it was an ovarian tumor, was it malignant?

The more I thought of an ovarian tumor, the more I was convinced that this was the answer to Maureen's problem. The positive signs of pregnancy could be explained by an ovarian tumor which had caused an elaboration of the same hormones that occur in pregnancy.

Armed with these thoughts, I conferred with the social worker. The diagnosis could not be confirmed without surgery, yet, I was reluctant to open up Maureen's abdomen. What should we do?

Though Maureen had the appearance of a 18-year-old, she was still only 12 years old. Though bright, she was still a child. I stalled for time. I wanted to talk to her father. I wanted to be sure it was not a pregnancy, yet I realized that if the tumor was malignant, waiting might risk Maureen's life.

Her father was corralled. As suspected, he was of little help. A father who permitted a 12-year-old girl free rein was not about to change into a responsible parent. He didn't seem to care, one way or another, what we did.

After another positive pregnancy test, I made up my mind that we owed Maureen a surgical "look in." Her father signed the consent and the operation was authorized by the county judge.

Maureen had a malignant tumor* of the right ovary. It was slightly larger than a baseball. There were no signs of spread into adjoining tissues or lymph glands. Within five days, Maureen was back at school.

The social worker kept me posted for a year. Maureen had developed a better social life and a better attitude at school. When I last saw her, 14 months after

*Dyssemenoma

251

the operation, she was still an eye catcher, a very attractive young woman.

Three years later, a California physician wrote me, requesting records of Maureen's operation. Two years after that, a Michigan physician also requested this information. I never again saw Maureen, however; the 12-year-old girl in an 18-year-old body.

PART FOUR

"What have I got, Dr. Bill?" What's my diagnosis?" I quite frequently answered these questions with "I don't know." In truth, I didn't know. If I could begin my medical career over again with the knowledge I have gained over 50 years, I could say "I don't know" less often, but I would still have to say it.

There is so much we physicians don't know. There are so many unanswered questions. Medical science is not an exact science. Unfortunately, the public has unrealistic expectations of our ability to diagnose and heal. May these chapters reveal how often physicians must say "I don't know," and must ask themselves, "What is best to do?"

Table of Contents

Part Four

CHAPTER 79

IT PAYS TO PICK GOOD ANCESTORS

It was a Sunday morning, bright and clear, with promise of an early spring. Birds, back from their southern pilgrimage, were announcing their return with lusty enthusiasm. While I was musing about the forces that control the migration of birds, suddenly the phone rang.

"Dr. Bill," a woman's voice said, "this is Mrs. Navis. You know, Mona. Could you come out to the farm this morning? I know it's Sunday, but our son, Frankie, had a nasty cut on his leg that's swollen and red. I think his heart is beating awful fast, and he feels awfully hot."

"I'll be there," I said, and, as I hung up the phone, a little blonde, curly-headed three-year-old peeked out at me from the doorway. It was Christine, our first-born. In seconds, she was sitting on my lap.

"Daddy, it's Sunday. You don't have to go to work today, do you?"

"Yes, I guess I do. I'm going up to the Blue Hills to see a man who has a sick leg. Want to come?"

Christine glanced at me with one of those looks that all fathers cherish. "You will really let me come?"

In 15 minutes we were on our way, my companion chatting unrestrainedly the entire 20-odd miles to the farm. "What do you hafta do? Why is his leg sick? What do farmers do? What do cows eat? How does the cow make milk? Do cows make cream?"

When we arrived, Christine came into the farmhouse with me. While I looked at Frankie's leg, she besieged Mrs. Navis with a volley of questions.

Frankie had developed a nasty infection in his wound that required a thorough cleansing. I asked for some boiled water. Then, using a large syringe, I irrigated the wound but did not dress it. "Keep it open, except at night, when you can bandage it loosely with some gauze I will leave with you."

Mr. and Mrs. Navis wanted assurance that the ugly-looking wound would heal, but, of course, I couldn't give such assurance. "He's young and his healing powers are good. I'll give him a shot to prevent lockjaw and another to prevent gas gangrene. Keep his leg elevated and irrigate it three times a day, but be sure to use boiled water. And Mona, give Frankie two of these pills every four hours. They should help fight the infection. Call me tomorrow and let me know how he is doing."

"Thanks, Dr. Bill," both parents said in unison. "Will you stay for breakfast?"

"I'd like that," I said, for I had been tantalized by the savory smells coming from the top of the wood-burning stove. I also wanted to know my patients better. To share a meal was an invitation to do just that.

Pancakes, sausages, fried eggs and bacon, doughnuts, and buttered toast were piled on the table. Before the coffee was poured, we bowed our heads as Mona said 'Grace.' "We thank You for this day, Father, and for this food and ask you to give wisdom to this young doctor and strength to our son, Frankie. Amen."

Then Mona passed the food. Both she and her husband, Albert, helped themselves to generous portions of everything, and I did the same. Christine ate a single egg and two pieces of bacon. Then she had a doughnut and a glass of milk. Frankie, who remained in bed, was given only liquids.

When I finished eating, I lit a cigarette. "Land sakes, you, a doctor, smoking cigarettes? You want to die at an early age?" Mona said, with feeling.

I was stunned and didn't know what to say, but I managed a feeble, "You are right. I'll put the cigarette out, if it bothers you."

Albert spoke up, "Oh, no, go ahead. We are just surprised that you smoke. You seem a rather sensible young man."

Then Albert changed the subject. He spoke of surplus foods. "So many people in the world go to bed hungry. It seems a shame that the government urges fruit growers to plow under grapefruit. I suppose you heard how some farmers are urged to burn excess potatoes. I heard it on the radio last night." Then he turned to me, "What do you think of the price support program, Dr. Bill?"

I knew Albert was being tactful, but already embarrassed by the cigarette incident and insufficiently informed about farm programs, I said, "From the little I know, I'd hate to venture an opinion, but it doesn't seem right to destroy food while so many need it."

Albert went on discussing the value of county agricultural agents, how he and Mona were third-generation farmers in this same Blue Hills area, and that two of their married sons were now farming in the Red River Valley of Minnesota. "You should see the size of their farms—oceans of grain, hundreds of acres. They don't share a farm combine with neighbors like we do at harvest time. They each own two."

And so, on the conversation went. When there was a lull, my curiosity about the size of the breakfast tempted me to ask, "Do you always eat such a big breakfast?"

"Always have," Mona answered.

This was in the early '40s. Town and city people still took cream and whole milk from the milkman. The milk industry was still battling the value of butter over oleomargarine. But evidence was mounting to indicate that coronary heart disease was associated with a high fat intake.

"Tell me, Albert, how old are you?"

"I'm 70 and Mona is 69."

"I'm curious and hope you don't mind my asking, but how old were your parents when they died?"

"Oh, they are still alive. They live down yonder." Albert pointed down the valley toward the east. "Father is 89 and Mother is 87."

I turned to Mona, "How old were your parents when they died, or are they also still alive?"

Mona looked at me and laughed, "Oh, they are alive enough. In fact, they come around at haying time. Dad helps in the field and Mom helps me here in the kitchen. They are both 87."

I didn't want to offend these considerate people with my probing, but I was anxious to get more information. Mona and Albert were obviously healthy, even though they ate high-cholesterol foods. Their parents were long-lived. Did they also eat high-cholesterol foods, I wondered.

"Do you mind if I ask you some more questions? You are surprised that I smoke, and I am surprised at the kind of breakfasts you eat. What about your parents: Do they eat breakfasts like this?"

Again Mona answered, "Oh, sure, they always have. Of course, Dad is down to eating only two eggs each morning and Mom's appetite isn't what it used to be."

"My father and mother have cut down a trifle too," Albert broke in, "but I guess you gotta expect that when you get older."

I was astonished. Here were farmers and their parents who daily ate eggs, bacon, doughnuts, pancakes, buttered toast — all high-cholesterol foods, and yet they were long-lived and free of heart disease. I was astonished and must have revealed my amazement, for both Mona and Albert went on to tell that their brothers and sisters were all still alive and in good health.

It was time to go home. Christine and I said our good-byes and thanked our hosts for breakfast. On the trip home, while Christine napped, I mulled over what I had learned about this family and their diet. What kept Albert and Mona free from heart disease in spite of excessive cholesterol intake?

Though somewhat overweight, the Navises got plenty of exercise and didn't smoke, but surely the key was having good ancestors. And that is a matter of luck.

It is now more than 50 years since I made that Sunday trip to the Blue Hills. Frankie's leg eventually healed, but astonishment at the breakfasts the Navises ate never left me. To this day, I am certain that research and statistical evidence have not yet solved the riddle of coronary heart disease, for over these 50 years I have seen too many contradictions: thin people who died of coronary heart disease and fat people who lived long lives, non-smokers who died of coronary heart disease and smokers who lived to ripe old ages. Some people who exercised died early and some who didn't exercise lived long lives.

One thing I am sure — it pays to pick good ancestors.

IN THIS AGE OF COMPUTERS, WHY BOTHER TO TAKE A MEDICAL HISTORY?

Claude and Yvonne Bateau had been in my consultation room for half an hour. As they fired question after question at me, escape seemed impossible. I didn't mind answering their questions, but I was disturbed because they didn't seem to listen to my answers. It had been the same many times before. When I removed their daughter, Celeste's, tonsils, it had taken hours of explaining and repeating the same explanations.

"Why must the tonsils come out?" Claude had asked.

"Tonsils are the first line of defense against throat infections, but when the tonsils act as a reservoir to incubate germs, they should be removed," I had responded.

"But if they were put there to safeguard against infection, why remove them?"

"When the tonsils no longer act to defend but act as a focus of infection, they should be removed."

"But why? Didn't the Lord know what He was doing?"

"Of course He did; but it is something like removing a toe or a foot or a leg when that part becomes diseased and no longer functions properly. It is removed to spare the rest of the body."

"I don't understand how the tonsils can hurt the rest of the body."

"Let's put it this way," I said with a wry smile. "A septic tank collects materials that would contaminate our homes, but the septic tank, when overly full, becomes a hazard and needs to be emptied. The same is true of tonsils. It is believed that one of the potential sources of germs that cause rheumatic fever is the tonsils that have been overworked."

This question-and-answer session had continued for almost an hour, but Claude and Yvonne remained unconvinced. Two days later, we spent another 40 minutes and a week later another half hour with the same abortive result. All of this took place before the antibiotics which have practically eliminated the necessity for removing tonsils.

Explaining didn't really bother me. I was accustomed to that role. It was the fact that they would ask questions and then seemed more bent on asking another question rather than listening to my answers.

One morning at 5:00 a.m., Claude called, "We've made up our minds; can you take out Celeste's tonsils today?"

It seemed a rather strange way to make an appointment for a tonsillectomy, but if I could arrange it, I thought maybe it would be better to put myself out and end this long, drawn-out, indecisive farce. "I'll call you back," I said as cheerfully as I could, considering the hour.

I called the hospital and made arrangements to do the surgery at 7:00 a.m. and explained why. Then I called Claude back and told him that Celeste should have nothing by mouth, not even water, and to be at the hospital at 6:00 a.m. He agreed, and I was surprised that he asked no questions.

Fifteen minutes later, my doorbell rang. It was Claude and Yvonne. "We must talk to you. Are we doing the right thing? Must the tonsils come out?"

"I thought you had made up your minds."

"Well, we wanted to be sure."

I coaxed myself to be patient, once again answered their questions, and an hour later removed Celeste's tonsils.

Now, it was a year later. Yvonne had suffered from severe backaches and had felt progressively weaker for three months, but had not sought medical attention. In her soft, nasal twang, she pleaded, "What could cause such a thing to happen? I've never been sick."

Claude burst in, "No, we've always been healthy. We eat well, don't smoke, don't drink, and work hard."

"Have you fallen? Have you done any unusual lifting?" I was looking for a history of possible trauma, but could find none.

"Yvonne, the nurse will help you to get ready to be examined."

Reluctantly, she undressed and lay on the examining table. As I approached her, Claude stood up and, in a defiant tone, said, "Why can't you just give her some medicine?"

I hesitated to answer. It had been a tough day. The office was still loaded with patients and I was tired. The memories of the long struggle to remove Celeste's tonsils came rushing back to me. I couldn't bear the thought that the next hour would probably be consumed by these two asking questions. For a long moment, I stared at them while summing up what I knew about them. They were French Canadians who had lived in Rusk County for only six years. With hard work, they had turned a marginal dairy farm into a profitable one, but had remained isolated from other people. Though intelligent, they were acquainted with little save the requirements and mechanics of their own farm.

Both were deeply tanned, had firm bodies that bore witness to their hard labor, and stood with exaggerated erectness. Claude's leathery face was prematurely creased, adding emphasis to his scowls as well as his grins. Yvonne, on the other hand, retained the soft look of a young woman both in her eyes and in her skin. He was almost bald, and she had long hair rolled up into a tight knot. Whenever they spoke, which was often, their pale blue eyes would seek mine with almost child-like appeal. There was both an intensity and a simplicity about them which was undeniably entreating.

I finally answered, "I can't treat something without knowing what it is."

"Well, go ahead and get it over with, but I can't understand all this monkeying around." Claude said, with one of his deep scowls.

While Claude hovered over Yvonne, she glanced up at me. Her eyes held a singular appeal which I interpreted as a call for help. Something within me softened as I prepared for a long, drawn-out ordeal.

"You know, Claude," I muttered half to myself, "there was a French doctor by the name of Charcot — Jean Martin Charcot, a well-known French neurologist. He said something very wise, 'The diagnosis is the best trump in the scheme of treatment.'"

Claude was all attention now. "A Frenchman said that?" He eyed me carefully. "A Frenchman said that? Sounds great, but what does it mean?"

"It means a doctor must recognize a disease to properly treat it. You see, Claude, a physician does not just spin a wheel or use a computer to diagnose a patient's disease. Even with the best of medical personnel and the best laboratory techniques, some diagnoses remain obscure."

"Then why all that examining and all those questions about our family and our habits? What has my wife's grandfather or uncle got to do with it?"

For the first time, I realized that Claude and Yvonne had little knowledge of the reasons why a doctor did the things he did. Like everything else about them, there was a simplicity in their health philosophy. In spite of my anxiety to complete my office schedule, I relaxed and tried to explain. And, so for the first time, both of them listened, and intently so.

"Heritage is important," I said. "For example, cancer of the large bowel is most common among Americans and least common among the Japanese. However, if Japanese follow an American diet, they often develop cancer of the large bowel. Breast cancer is five times more common in women with a family history of breast cancer. Women who had multiple sex partners in their teenage years are more likely to get cervical cancer. This sort of information can only be obtained by taking the time to question the patient. A good physical is of enormous value, but a good knowledge of the patient's habits and heritage are often the key to a diagnosis."

Both remained silent, looking at me like children first introduced to a new and wondrous toy. I went on, "Yvonne, your back is tender, your skin is pale, you feel weak. Even though you claim you eat well, you are probably anemic." I turned to look at Claude. He was still silent and obviously taking it all in.

Taking Yvonne's hand, I said, "Since you deny hurting your back, you may have what is called a pathological fracture, due to a diseased bone. We should take an X-ray of your lumbar vertebrae. The nurse will also check your blood and urine."

"OK, Dr. Bill," she said, "Go ahead."

When the nurse had completed checking the blood and urine and had taken the X-rays, I returned to the room. Claude and Yvonne both looked up at me expectantly but said nothing.

Considering their simple health philosophy, I decided it was time to be direct. "Yvonne, you may have a most serious condition. You do have a pathological fracture of two lumbar vertebrae. You are anemic. Your urine contains a protein, called Bence Jones' protein, which suggests multiple myeloma. To be sure of a proper diagnosis, let's draw some of your blood. If the blood protein is high, we can be certain of the diagnosis, and as Dr. Charcot, the French neurologist, said, "be certain we are treating you properly."

Yvonne did have multiple myeloma, a malignant disease. She was treated with both chemotherapy and radiation, to which she responded reasonably well and lived comfortably for several years.

Never again during our relationship as patients and doctor did Claude or Yvonne Bateau swamp me with interminable questions. Was it because I had been patient with them? Was it because they finally understood that a doctor needed to know all he could about a patient's background? Or, was it because they felt a prideful kinship with the French physician, Dr. Charcot, who said, "The diagnosis is the best trump in the scheme of treatment."

CHAPTER 81

WHAT IS THE MYSTIQUE OF HEALING?

After 50 years, I am still fascinated by the mystique of healing, for healing so often occurs following treatments that scientists and doctors are unwilling to acknowledge. On the surface, countless forms of treatment appear unwarranted, yet some of them, at times, have proven efficacious. Summarily denying the value of a treatment because it seems scientifically illogical suggests a dearth of observation and experience. Witness the testimonials of many who claim benefits from wearing a copper bracelet to relieve arthritic pains. Consider the seemingly magical merits of a placebo. Even though double-blind tests have proven some treatments useless, the treatments continue to be utilized by a host of supporters. Acupuncture also has many advocates, although apparently without scientific basis. It appears to me that any form of treatment, unless explicitly proven hazardous, should not be abandoned as entirely invalid.

Over the years, some discernment of the mystique of healing has gradually evolved. Elaborate mechanisms within us are constantly defending us against disease. Other mechanisms are geared for repair. Many times healing is accomplished, not because of prescribed treatment but in spite of it. Acceptance of this truth helps physicians to abet, not hinder, the natural healing and reparative powers of the patient's body. At times, therefore, this requires doing absolutely nothing in order to avoid doing anything that might interfere with the body's own healing mechanism.

Many of the protective mechanisms within us have long been understood. One of these is the veritable army of white blood cells that are ready to do battle against infection. Some of these cells mobilize slowly, like the infantry, and some mobilize quickly, like the cavalry. Another mechanism is the antigen-antibody system that can build up a specific immunity against each disease or foreign substance that invades our bodies.

We have also recognized the power of mind over body[1], the influence of sug-

---

[1] *See Chapter 82.*

gestion (with or without hypnosis), and the enormous value of positive thinking. Until recently, however, these benefits have remained theoretical, a matter of observation and conjecture rather than scientifically proven facts.

It was during the span of my medical career that some of the benefits of positive thinking were confirmed scientifically. By studying the blood of patients with positive attitudes, conjecture became accepted fact. It was found that patients with positive attitudes healed more rapidly and that this more rapid healing was associated with the release of corticosteroids into their blood. Patients with positive attitudes also had a lowered sensitivity to pain, which was found to be associated with the presence of endorphins in their blood. Thus, even laetrile, though proven ineffective, may offer value by replacing despair with hope and giving the patient a more positive attitude. However, it must be recognized that laetrile has often been found to be dangerous because it was prepared in contaminated vessels and sometimes contained cyanide.

There is now sufficient proof that a person's inner chemistry is altered for good or bad by response to love or hate[2], to calm or panic, to confidence or despair. Thus, medical personnel try to fulfill the emotional as well as physical needs of their patients by replacing fear with confidence, despair with hope, and depression with cheer.

It is interesting to note that 2,000 years ago, Hippocrates, the father of medicine, understood that medical care is a dual process. One part of the process is provided by the physician with his skills. The other is the innate healing powers of the patient, whose powers can be evoked and augmented by an empathetic physician.

There are times when the physician inadvertently robs the patient of a positive attitude. Caught between his legal and moral obligations[3], the physician is called upon to decide how and how much to tell his patient before surgery. Will the physician's fear of suit influence his decision to detail all dangers? Will the dangers of anesthesia and surgery, elaborately detailed to safeguard the physician from potential suit, bring harm to his patient by increasing the patient's fears? Is the art of medicine and the patient's welfare being compromised by the fear of litigation?

In order to more fully comprehend the mystique of healing and treatment, it is necessary to maintain an open mind. Discounting a treatment as useless, without established proof that it is dangerous, is not only unfair but also unreasonable. During the 18th century, a witch doctor living on the outskirts of London was the only one successful in reducing anasarca (fluid in body tissue). William Withering, a young physician, free from prejudice but frustrated by his inability to aid patients with anasarca, unobtrusively followed the witch doctor as she gathered the multiple herbs that composed her healing brew. Eventually, he gathered all of them and concocted a separate broth from each. These broths were then tried individually on patients with anasarca. To his amazement and

---

[2] *See Chapter 81.*

[3] *See Chapter 86.*

delight, the brew concocted from the foxglove markedly reduced fluid swelling. In 1785, William Withering introduced digitalis, extracted from the foxglove, as a useful aid to heart patients. It is still used today and represents substantial evidence that all of us should remain unprejudiced.

Sometimes, however, it is difficult to remain open-minded, free to accept or refute the potential value of unorthodox treatments and still retain a skilled responsibility to our patients. Believe me, it can be an enigma. The persuasive influence of the patient's loved ones and even neighbors must be contended with. Emotionalism with all of its irrational overtones, must be faced. Each case is different, deserving of individual consideration.

However, I have found some basic principles worthy of attention: unorthodox treatments should never be substituted for treatments proven sound, and, of course, any treatments that have been proved hazardous should be avoided. It became evident that under no circumstances should I deny a patient the comfort of hope, even if all medically known treatments had failed. But I continued to caution my patients against wasting precious hours in the grasp of a quack. At times, it took much tactful persuasion to convince a patient to accept sound treatment rather that outright quackery. Too many charlatans are very adept at disguising their lack of medical knowledge with a certain charisma and glibness, convincing the desperate patient that they have something to offer. One of my patients with terminal cancer paid a quack $10 a day for the suggestion that he sit in his room and face in the direction of the sun for one hour morning and evening.

A further challenge for the physician comes when convincing evidence urgently presses for medical or surgical care and the patient's family has chosen chiropractic treatments. One day a boy of eight years came to my office with his mother. For the previous two years, he had suffered from a torticollis, an involuntary contraction of his neck muscles which pulled his head to his right side, his chin almost touching his right shoulder. His mother, obviously in a hurry, demanded a prescription for vitamins as suggested by her chiropractor.

After a cursory examination of the boy, I suspected a brain lesion and insisted on taking an elaborate history. Annoyed at the time consumed, the mother impatiently repeated her request for vitamins. I assured her that she could get vitamins without a prescription but tried to persuade her to let me give her son a complete neurological examination. She rose defiantly. "It's a waste of time. I've been to other doctors and clinics. Nothing helped until we went to the chiropractor."

She went on to tell me that her son's chin had been firmly fixed almost over his right shoulder, and that after some eight dozen manipulations, it was now improved by more than 18 degrees.

Something beyond my understanding determined the course of my action, for it surprised even me. I went over to the door locked it and then put the key in my pocket. "Now, open the door," I said.

Looking a bit startled, she said, "You know I can't. It's locked."

"Here, you take the key. Put it in your purse," I said. Then, as she watched, I put my shoulder to the door and forced it open, taking the door jamb with it.

"Why did you do that?" the mother questioned, astonished by my action.

"To convince you that your lad's muscles are locked in position by something in his head. The chiropractor is forcing the locked muscles as I forced open the door."

With a deep sigh, she sat down and seemed to resign herself to the long, drawn-out examination. Thirty minutes later, I informed her that her son had a brain tumor, from which the pressure had created a torticollis. Realizing the need for expediency, I called the University Hospital in Madison, Wisconsin to arrange for almost immediate brain surgery. Half an hour later, mother and son were on their way to Madison via ambulance.

The patients in my outer office were upset by my violent action, but soothing words assured them that I sill possessed my wits. My anxiety for the boy had produced a drastic attempt to save him, but it proved futile—possibly not too little, but definitely too late.

The date of the operation remains fixed in my mind—August 8. The surgeon found an inoperable tumor, a glioma. The boy died September 8. At the family's request, I removed the tumor at autopsy. I hoped that this experience would spread by word-of-mouth and convince others to seek proper and early medical assistance.

This episode caused me considerable loss of sleep. This handsome eight-year-old lad kept popping into my thoughts. What could we, as physicians, do to prevent such casualties, such premature and perhaps unnecessary deaths?

About three months later, at 8:00 p.m., Mrs. Gibbons called me from Davenport, Iowa. Her 27-year-old daughter was returning to Ladysmith by ambulance. She would arrive in five or six hours. Would I see her?

Night seemed a strange time to travel and 2:00 a.m. a strange time to expect an examination, but Mrs. Gibbons was so distressed that I agreed.

The Gibbons family, parents and four children, had been my patients for many years. All four children had married and established their own homes, but Bernice, the 27-year-old daughter, had returned home soon after her divorce.

As soon as the ambulance arrived, Mrs. Gibbons called me, and I went to her home. When I arrived, I was told Bernice's story. Six months before, Bernice had started chiropractic adjustments because of sore muscles in the left side of her neck. When the local chiropractor felt he could no longer help her, he sent her to Rice Lake, Wisconsin for further treatments. When treatments there were unsuccessful, Bernice was sent to Davenport, Iowa, considered the center for chiropractic manipulation at that time. She was told that the center was equipped with a 'special machine' that would help her. Twice daily over a period of two months, Bernice had 'machine' therapy. Mrs. Gibbons had remained in Davenport with her daughter.

My examination, even there at her home and at that early morning hour, definitely pointed to a 'brain tumor.' Surgery two days later was performed in Minneapolis but was too late. The tumor was, by then, inoperable.

My nightmares continued. The need to find a comfortable answer haunted me. What can anyone do to solve what appears insolvable? Who am I, with my limited skills, to speak against chiropractors, acupuncture, copper bracelets, or laetrile?

Then I read a book, *"At Your Own Risk,"* a treatise revealing the training and the philosophy of chiropractic. After reading it, I was astonished at how clearly it denounced chiropractors. With concerned interest, I reread the book and arrived at the conclusion that if revelations in the book were not true, the author and publisher would have been sued for millions.

A week or so after completing the book for the second time, a chiropractor called me at 9:00 p.m. and requested that I come to his office. Ten minutes later, I was in the chiropractor's office. A man lay sprawled, unconscious, on the floor. It was soon obvious to me that the man had fainted. He responded well to spirits of ammonia. While chatting with the chiropractor, I perused his records on the patient. The recorded diagnosis was 'dislocated lumbar vertebrae.' The 65-year-old man had undergone weekly adjustments for two years without remission of his back pain.

The chiropractor introduced me to the patient when he regained consciousness. Later, before I left, the man asked if I would see him in my office the next day. The chiropractor agreed to this request. A rectal exam and an X-ray the following day made the diagnosis of prostatic cancer with metastases (spread) to the pelvic bones and vertebrae.

My concerns continued. How do chiropractors obtain their testimonials? The answer finally walked right into my office. A 40-year-old man came in, listing toward his port side. He announced that he had rheumatic fever and had been treated by a chiropractor 16 times without improvement. His only symptoms were pain in the lower lumber area, in the left shoulder, and in the right arm. When I examined him, all I found was a slight tenderness in the same areas. Blood tests, including sedimentation rate, were negative.

I recalled that, over a period of years, I had observed this man helping support the Security State Bank building by sitting on the front ledge. He frequented this spot with such a regularity that he was considered a fixture. Now I learned that several days before consulting the chiropractor, he had shoveled coal for a local dray outfit. After the second day of shoveling, his soreness was intense. He decided, on his own, that his intense pain was causd by rheumatic fever and sought the help of the chiropractor, who agreed with his self-made diagnosis.

Actually, the man had developed sore muscles of his back, left shoulder, and right arm from shoveling coal. Unaccustomed to usage, his muscles had recoiled from this sudden burst of activity. He did not have rheumatic fever. He had sore muscles. This suggested to me how testimonials are obtained. The patient, self-convinced he has cancer or rheumatic fever or heart trouble is treated for cancer or rheumatic fever or heart trouble. His recovery then becomes a miracle.

Had my 44-year-old man with self-diagnosed rheumatic fever been treated with sugar pills, bedrest, aspirin, or a few more chiropractic manipulations, he would have recovered completely. As it was, he recovered with my treatment—aspirin and continuing to shovel coal. His muscles grew accustomed to activity and aspirin relieved his pain.

Though still distressed by my inability to prevent what appears to be improper treatments, I am forced to recall how many people remain totally convinced that their chiropractor has cured them of all manner of aches, pains and diseases. Though a patient's positive attitude, whether being treated by a physician, a chiropractor, or an outright quack, is beneficial, I am amazed at the bald confidence of some bold healers. Even the medicine man in the jungle can sometimes allay pain and alleviate suffering by putting fear to rest.

This is the mystique of healing, some of which we may never comprehend.

CHAPTER 82

WHAT IS THE MEANING OF FAITH
TO THE PATIENT?

Perhaps it seems out of order to consider the religious aspects of patients' lives, but I found that no aspect of their comfort or getting well should be neglected. Many people have come to grips with religion and have gained a comfortable outlook on life and death because of their specific beliefs. Experience taught me that, in the elderly and those about to face death, this inner comfort from their faith should not be interfered with.

There are many routes from Chicago to New York, some long, some rough, and some with many detours. There are many highways to Heaven. Since no one has returned to prove there is but one way, I wonder who has the right to insist that their way is the only way?

Beulah Collins said it well in the Los Angeles Times:

> *"Several cotton farmers were whiling away a winter afternoon around the pot-bellied stove. They soon became entangled in a heated discussion on the merits of their respective religions. The eldest of the farmers had been sitting quietly, just listening, when the group turned to him and demanded, 'Who's right, old Jim? Which one of these religions is the right one?'*
>
> *"'Well,' said Jim thoughtfully, 'you know that there are three ways to get from here to the cotton gin. You can go right over the big hill. That's shorter, but it's a powerful climb. You can go around the east side of the hill. That's not so far, but the road is rougher'n tarnation. Or, you can go around the west side of the hill, which is the longest way but the easiest.'*
>
> *'But, you know,' he said, looking them squarely in the eye. 'When you get there, the gin man won't ask you how you came. He just asks, 'Man, how good is your cotton?'"*

Gwen Muller was in her early 80's. She had the face of an angel and a disposition to match. Her four children obviously adored her, as did her baker's dozen of grandchildren. Her husband, Hiram, had passed on four years before.

Gwen was in the hospital because of cancer of the pancreas. She had moments of great misery which made frequent 'hypos' necessary. Most of the time she was clear-headed and sharp, but while under the influence of a 'hypo', her usually detailed memory was blurred.

Gwen's faith was obviously strong. Over the years, I had often witnessed clear evidence of its durability. She had not only survived the loss of two sons in the Vietnam War but also had been the stalwart support for the rest of the family. Gwen was not just a churchgoer, she was a firm believer who addressed her problems to God, seeking answers from Him. Gwen's attitude was far from complacent. She was a strong-minded individual but truly believed her strength came from God.

One evening, a phone call from Harriet, one of Gwen's daughters, shook me. Her mother had been visited in the hospital several times by a neighbor who was of a different religious sect. This neighbor had tried to persuade her mother to change her faith.

Harriet was very upset. "Mother's faith in God has supported her throughout her life. Her life has exemplified her faith and has been a real inspiration to all of us. Mother has been calm during this painful trial of facing cancer, unafraid to die. She has responded to this neighbor with remarkable tact, but we can see Mother is wearying of this neighbor's fervent efforts to change her faith.

"Tonight was just too much. The neighbor brought her clergyman. The two of them spent an hour urging Mother to change before it was too late. At the time of their visit, Mother was under the influence of her 'hypo'. When they left, my sister and I went back into the room. We have never seen Mother so distressed. She was not herself at all. She was bitter, insecure, and angry. Isn't there something we can do, Doctor?"

"Of course, Harriet. I'll take care of it right away. I'm sure your mother will not be disturbed again, but if she is, let me know at once."

I went to the hospital and posted a sign on the door. In large plain letters, the sign read: "FAMILY ONLY!"

Gwen was soon her old self once more as she embraced her family. Once again, she revealed confidence in the trip we must all make some day.

WAS IT THEIR LOVE?

Mavis Morris was very upset with her son-in-law. "I just can't understand him," she said. "He's so unfeeling and so rude. Yesterday at breakfast, my husband was drooling at the mouth. He often does that. He can't help it since his stroke two years ago. Dave, my son-in-law, rose from his chair and said, 'He's disgusting. Why don't you put him away?'

"When Dave made remarks like that before, I said nothing, but this time I couldn't help myself. I turned to Dave and said, 'If you don't like it, don't bother to come here. That's my husband you are talking about. He's a good man. He has been a good father and husband, and he can't help it that he drools.'"

. Mavis hesitated as tears ran down her cheeks and dropped from her chin. "The worst part of it was that my daughter, Karen, was still in bed. She doesn't understand how really rude Dave can be and how it hurts me to see my husband treated so callously, as though he were some horrible beast."

I looked at Mavis, her face drawn and wet with tears. She and her husband, Chuck, had worked side by side in the fields and in the barn. For more than 30 years, they had struggled together to make ends meet and had managed to send both Karen and their son, Peter, to college, though at great sacrifice to themselves. I also recalled their great pride when Karen won a scholarship and Peter was elected captain of the swimming team.

Only two years before, at the age of 58, Chuck Morris had suffered a severe stroke, which made his right side almost completely paralyzed. With amazing persistence and tender care, Mavis had brought Chuck back from the land of hopelessness and helplessness. Chuck still dragged his right leg, but he had learned to use his left hand, even to write, and with a little help, dressed and fed himself. Being voiceless from the stroke, he carried a small pad and pencil in his left pocket for communication.

"Mavis, I agree, you have a problem," I began, "a real problem. You don't want to lose your daughter or her love, but you feel a responsibility to your husband.

Certainly, you are entitled to protect him from flagrant abuse. Your daughter should and will show loyalty to her husband when you tell her how you feel, but underneath she will work it out. After all, she is your daughter and was brought up to show respect and love."

I wasn't sure when Mavis left that I had really helped her, but she seemed slightly more at peace with herself.

Some half-dozen months later, I was called to the farm by Mavis. "Chuck asked me to call. He wants to talk to you," she said over the phone. "You know, with his pencil and pad."

When I arrived, the three of us sat at the kitchen table sharing a freshly baked apple pie and coffee. When we had finished, Chuck held up his left hand and pointed to the bedroom. Mavis interpreted this for me. "He wants you to go into the bedroom."

All three of us started for the bedroom. Just as we were about to enter, Chuck held up his left hand to his wife and, shaking his head side-ways, indicating he did not want her to come in. He then made it clear that he wanted us to sit down on the bed together. Then he drew out his pad and pencil.

"I'm a mess," he wrote, "and a nuisance. My Mavis has to baby me like an infant. It's not fair. She has many good years left, and I don't want to cheat her from enjoying them. I really don't know what to do. I hope you can suggest something."

This came like a bombshell to me. I was completely unprepared for such a statement. I sat there observing Chuck, attempting to find some sort of an answer or just something to say, but couldn't.

Chuck took a new sheet and wrote, "Please help me. I love Mavis, but can't show that love. I'm so restricted that there is no way I can reciprocate her many considerations."

Again I remained silent. What could I say or do?

Chuck took another fresh sheet from his pad, "Dr. Bill, you have known us for more than 30 years. We have tried to do our best for each other and our children, Mavis and I." He wrote this very deliberately as though it was a painful thing to do and then wrote, "I can't go on like this. It hurts me each hour of each day to see her enslaved by my incapacitation."

The situation was awkward at best. Chuck was right, I had been through many personal experiences with his family and could not help but feel a strong kinship. At the same time, I was astonished that this truly incapacitated man so clearly revealed his thoughts. His love for his wife obviously transcended all else.

Chuck stared at me, his left eye wide open and his right half closed because of his stroke. He was waiting for me to say something wise, something that would answer his deep concern—or at least something. But I could come up with nothing.

After a long silence, he wrote, "I'm not afraid to die. If I could find a simple way to do it, one that would bring no shame to Mavis, I would."

Again I was amazed. Chuck was not complaining of his disabilities, that his speech therapy had failed, that he could not use the right side of his body and limbs. He was concerned for his Mavis, that she had so much to live for and yet was burdened with his incapacity.

No, I had no wise advice for this man, physically disabled but emotionally whole, not concerned for himself but for the one he loved. Finally, feeling the necessity to say something, to let Chuck know that I was responding to his appeal, I said, "I'd like to think about it, Chuck. Please let me have a day or so and I'll come back and let you know."

Chuck wrote once more. "Thanks, I'll be waiting to hear."

I went out to my car, distressed by my inability to add even a fraction of comfort to this thoughtful man. Mavis stuck her head in the window of the car as I was about leave. "What's the problem?" she asked.

Perhaps unwisely, but perplexed to the core, I answered, "Please come to see me tomorrow. We'll talk about it. Come about 11:00 a. m."

Mavis was there when I came from an out-in-the-country house call. Although I had given the problem considerable thought, I still was uncertain of what to say.

"Well, Dr. Bill, what was the urgent problem Chuck talked over with you?"

"Mavis, I almost wish we were total strangers. It would be easier to discuss it with you. I just don't know where to begin."

"Being friends should mean something, Dr. Bill."

"Yes, it does. Although I'm infringing on Chuck's rights of privacy to tell you, I believe you should know. Chuck feels he's devouring your life, exhausting you each day with his many needs."

"Oh, it's not that bad. He does require a lot of personal attention, but I'm strong and I can handle it."

"Mavis, I know you can and I admire the way you do it. But we must think it out from Chuck's point-of-view. He loves you, and it hurts him to see you exhausting yourself just to satisfy his needs."

"I see what you mean, Dr. Bill. But what can I do? I won't put him in a nursing home. He's been a good husband to me and a good father to our children. You know I love him. What can I do?"

"I wish I had an easy answer, but I don't. Chuck has had physical therapy with limited success and speech therapy with no success. Perhaps you can give it a try. Just working with him might encourage him to try harder."

"I don't understand, Dr. Bill. What can I do? If the speech therapist couldn't improve his condition, how can I?"

"Mavis, it's your love that might inspire him to do the seemingly impossible. Working with him day after day may stimulate processes in his nerves and muscles that we don't fully understand."

"But how do I go about it?"

"Remember, Mavis, my method is unconventional and it may not work, but I'm convinced that it is worth trying. Language is an interesting accumulation of sounds made up of simple ones. When each syllable is clearly sounded, the English language becomes almost musical."

"I'm not sure what you're getting at," Mavis said with the wistful look of a child anxious to grasp what is meant.

"Mavis, say the following one-syllable words after me, but say them clearly and slowly: at, cat, hat, bat, sat, fat, mat, pat, rat." She did.

"Good, but say them even slower; exaggerate the enunciation. Make the c long, and the h long, and the b long, and the s long, and the f long, and the m long, and the p long and the r long. Do it again. Make the s hiss, make your lips really press out the b." Again, she did.

"Now, you are getting the idea. Make it a friendly game between you and Chuck."

"I understand, but is that all?"

"No, now try it with 'it': bit, flit, nit, hit, kit, lit, mitt, pit, sit, and so on. The real value of this method, as I see it, is that Chuck tries to imitate what you say, but the difficulty is lessened because it is only one syllable. I will give you a number of one-syllable words that will do the same thing. This is a method or pronouncing simple consonants and simple vowels. Later we can build on this with two-syllable words, and on up."

Mavis started to show some enthusiasm for trying this out on Chuck. I didn't reveal Chuck's dire thoughts about possible suicide. There did not seem any point in doing so, but I felt that this threat was sufficient reason to talk to Mavis.

The following day, I went back to the farm to see Chuck. Before he could write words on his pad, I confronted him, "I've got an idea which I hope you will give a try. It's worked for other people, and with your determination, I'm sure it will work for you. I'll spell it out to Mavis and she will work with you several times a day with one-syllable words for you to repeat. When no one is around, hold a mirror in front of you with your left hand, and watch your tongue and lips as you practice saying the words. You are too good a man to give up on. Will you oblige me and give my unconventional method a try?"

I looked at Chuck. His questioning eyes looked intently at me. Then his mouth, crooked from his stroke, slowly framed a half-smile and he shook his head, nodding assent.

"Good," I said, "I'll explain it to Mavis and come to see you again in a week."

The week slipped by, and as I approached the farm, I felt a strong reluctance to enter. What if there had been no improvement? Would Chuck lose interest? Would his disappointment shut off the possibility of further effort?

Summoning up my courage to confront Chuck, I entered the house and approached him. "How is it going?" I asked.

Chuck went for his pad, but before he could write an answer, Mavis said, "Good, Dr. Bill, he purses his lips, sticks out his tongue and hisses at me. I'm sure in another week he will say words."

Two weeks went by before I had an opportunity to get back to Chuck. Mavis had called and said she had a surprise she wanted me to see. Chuck was at the table when I entered. "We see, me, he, be, tea," he said with characteristic determination and then gave me his distorted but friendly smile.

I stayed for a full hour while Mavis had Chuck repeat numerous lists of one syllable words he had memorized. It was apparent that the two of them had developed their former closeness and camaraderie which had been interrupted by the stroke.

"We think we are ready for two syllable words," Mavis said. "What do you think, Dr. Bill?"

Weeks and months passed. Chuck's speech improved fantastically under Mavis' patient tutelage. Although it never returned to prestroke clarity and was slow, his speech was adequate for Chuck to engage in conversation. And with his renewed ability to communicate, Chuck seemed to blossom. He no longer spent most of each day sitting alone in a chair. He followed his wife around the house, conversing with her and then one day, as if by magic, he felt some sensation in his right hand and arm. In his excitement, he tripped and fell. Mavis called me, concerned that Chuck had broken some bones.

Though bruised, Chuck had not broken bones. He told me of his twinges of feeling in his arm and hand and asked if something might be done to restore movement.

Realizing it was more than two years since his initial stroke, it seemed cruel to give him hope. On the other hand, realizing what had been accomplished for his speech by persistence and love, it seemed cruel not to offer encouragement. After all, I was fully aware that there is much that does not follow a given pattern in medicine, so much that science can't explain.

"No harm in giving it a try. You and Mavis are such a good team, why not?"

To this day, I can't account for the seemingly miraculous changes that came about in Chuck's limbs. Better than seventy percent of sensation and motion came back to his right arm. His right leg did not fare as well, but thirty percent of sensation and motion was restored. Equally miraculous was Chuck's attitude. Once again he entered the world of other people, leaving his solitary world far behind.

Yes, I suggested gentle massage, hot baths and both passive and active exercises. Perhaps these did help; but I am certain that the teamwork of Mavis and Chuck and their persistence were truly responsible — their love that would not let go.

CHAPTER 84

CAN LOVE AND FORGIVENESS HEAL?
ARE ENVY AND HATE DESTRUCTIVE?

Over the years, I have watched the power of envy and hate destroy individuals, marriages, and families, but I have also observed the healing power of love and forgiveness.

Oscar wept copiously. Between sobs, he would catch his breath and gasp a few words. Piecing together the relevant bits of his ramblings was difficult.

Oscar's only son, Joseph, was on drugs and had gambled away large sums of money. Oscar was beside himself. His son's behavior had completely upset him, for he had trusted his son to manage his two dry cleaning establishments. One of them had failed, and the other was on the verge of bankruptcy.

As Oscar gradually controlled himself, he detailed the circumstances. He had turned over the full responsibility of his business to his 43-year-old son. Joe had agreed to send Oscar 40 percent of the net profit monthly. This would be sufficient income for Oscar to retire.

My friend, Oscar, was a soft-spoken man of 75. I knew him well. I had never heard him speak unkindly of anyone nor heard anyone speak unkindly of him. For this kindly man to suffer from his own son's misbehavior was a tragedy.

Although Oscar now had a grip on himself, whenever he mentioned his son by name, tears would start anew, but Joe was never condemned. Oscar still loved his son and blamed himself. "I was eager to retire. Maybe Joe was not ready to take over the business. Maybe I made it too easy for him."

At this point, Oscar's wife, Verna, entered the consultation room. "That Joe," she cried, "He has upset our household. Oscar will have to go back to work. We can't live on Social Security alone."

Again I noted no harsh condemnation of Joe, no vindictive remarks. In fact, I wondered why they sought my advice, for aside from their hurt, they were handling the problem in a healthy way, relieving their loss with tears but not with hatred.

The realization of why they had come dawned slowly. They had come to share their problem with me, not as a physician but as a friend. Before their problem was fully resolved, I was doubly glad they had shared it with me. Their lack of hatred and recrimination was a revelation of Christian faith in action.

Yes, I was envious of their ability to weep without rancor, but, as time went on and Oscar returned to work, I was even more impressed that love is the strongest force known to man. In his own quiet way, Oscar's warm, friendly spirit salvaged one of his dry cleaning shops. Over a period of three years, Joe's gambling debts were paid and Joe was rehabilitated. Without condemnation, Joe was restored to his position as manager of the dry cleaning shop.

Oscar is again retired. Every so often, I meet him on a trout stream or I stop at his cabin and soak up the warmth of this couple, Oscar and Verna, who taught me so much about the constructive force of love.

* * *

Iris was sick, really sick. Pneumonia involved both lungs, and Iris gasped for breath. To some extent, oxygen eased her breathing and morphine eased her pain, but she lay listless on her hospital bed, her eyes turned to the ceiling.

Her husband, Tony, came every day and sat by her side. He tried to talk to her but with little success. At first it seemed that she was unaware of his presence, but after a few days, it was obvious that she was avoiding him. She responded to my questions clearly though briefly.

"Are you feeling better?" I asked.

"Uh-huh."

"Is the pain better?"

"Uh-huh."

"Want to see your children? I can bring them to the door."

"Sure."

Iris was a farmer's wife. For a dozen years, she had kept house, milked cows, and helped with numerous farm chores. In between these tasks, she had brought four children into the world but had had little time for herself. Before marriage, Iris had been a secretary to one of the business executives in Ladysmith, had enjoyed skiing and bowling, and was an avid reader. There had been no time for these pleasures in the last dozen years.

Tony was a large man who spoke frankly, sometimes in the manner of an Army sergeant giving orders. According to his wife, he commanded rather than requested, and this led to friction between them. The children, she said, resented him and were afraid of him.

As her pneumonia improved, I expected that Iris would talk to her husband, but when he came, she continued to turn away. Tony, however, patiently sat in a chair by her bedside.

One day, Tony approached me. "How is Iris?" he asked.

"Much better, physically, but apparently she needs something I can't give her."

276

"What's that, Dr. Bill?"

"She needs something to make her want to get well, to get out of the hospital and back on the farm."

"Well, she has me and the children."

"She knows that, Tony, but she needs the assurance of love. She needs to know she is wanted and needed, not as a machine to do chores, but as a person."

"Never thought of that, Dr. Bill. What can I do? I've been here every day, and she won't even talk to me," Tony pleaded.

"Tell her how much you have missed her and the many wonderful things she has done in the last dozen years. Let your love speak out. Let her know how much you care."

What Tony said or how he said it I never learned, but Iris improved miraculously. Two days later, she was sitting in a chair with Tony beside her. On the third day, they walked up and down the hall hand-in-hand, and the next day Iris went home.

Love is a powerful medicine.

* * *

Sally sat down across the desk from me, her eyes apprehensive and imploring by turns. She leaned forward in her chair, her whole being seemingly intent on reaching me. With anxiety in her voice, she said, "I've skipped two periods, Dr. Bill. If my folks found out, they'd skin me alive. What am I going to do?"

I had brought Sally into the world and had treated her for a host of childhood diseases as well as a broken neck caused by a farm accident. Now she was 17, a senior in high school, and she had an excellent reputation.

I studied her face carefully before responding. Sally was an attractive girl with deep brown eyes, a facile smile, and dark brown hair that hung to her shoulders. But her usual easy smile was gone. Her face was drawn tight with apprehension.

"Sally," I began, "have you had intercourse?"

"Only once, Dr. Bill, three months ago. I know it was wrong, but it just happened."

"We'll have to do a pregnancy test and examine you, Sally, to find out if you are pregnant."

When the exam was completed, Sally blurted out, "Well, am I , Dr. Bill?"

"I found no signs of pregnancy, Sally, but I'll need to have a sample of your urine, the first one you pass tomorrow morning. You bring it to the office, and come see me in a few days."

It was a late Friday afternoon when Sally returned. She was so fidgety in the waiting room that Peggy, my office nurse, brought her into the consultation room before her turn. She was hardly in the room when she asked, "What did the test show, Dr. Bill? Am I pregnant?"

"Calm down, Sally. You are not pregnant. Skipping a period or two sometimes happens without a good reason."

"Are you sure nothing is really wrong?" she asked.

"No, I can't be sure. There are other things that can cause periods to stop, but since I found nothing wrong when I examined you, let's see what happens."

"OK, Dr. Bill. I'll let you know," and Sally started to leave the room.

"Hold on, Sally. I feel the need to talk to you. You know that there are many responsibilities as well as hazards to going all the way with boys. Boys will say, 'If you really loved me, you'd let me!' This is a common argument boys will use. Don't be taken in by such foolishness. Your have a good future and don't want it to be spoiled by a pregnancy you are not ready for emotionally. Venereal diseases can not only cause severe illnesses, but can also create conditions within you that will prevent you from having a baby when you are ready for it. Hold off, Sally. Have fun, the kind of fun girls your age should have, but save a close physical relationship for marriage."

"I will, Dr. Bill, and thanks. I've learned my lesson. You won't tell my folks, will you?"

"No, but I hope you realize that had you been pregnant, it would have been advisable to tell them. Believe it or not, your best friends are your Mother and Dad. They would be upset, even angry, but remember they are still your best friends."

"I'll remember, but I'm glad we didn't have to tell them. What do you think caused my periods to stop?"

"Have you had serious worries? Have you been frightened? I know you were afraid you were pregnant, but did you have any serious scares or worries other than that? Strange things happen within our bodies when we get uptight, as you young folks call it. We doctors call it stress."

"Gosh, no, but I'll think about it. Anyhow, thanks again."

As she started to leave, I called after her, "Let's see what happens. Come in again in about four weeks."

A month passed. Sally did not return. Then another month passed. Late one afternoon, as the office force was preparing to close-up, Sally rushed in, her face flushed with excitement. She asked if I would see her. "It's very important, Dr. Bill. Please, I've got to talk to you."

"All right, Sally, come in and I'll listen," I said as we walked into the consultation room.

"Remember when I came in a few months ago and I was worried sick?"

"Yes, I haven't forgotten, but what is the trouble today that seems so urgent?"

"Well, I skipped another period, but I haven't let any boy touch me. So I began thinking about what you told me about worrying and fright and stress, as you called it. Dr. Bill, I think I know why my periods stopped."

"Tell me about it."

"It has to do with Betty Miller. I know she comes to see you pretty often."

"What about Betty?" I asked, leaning forward and putting my elbows on the desk.

"I've done a terrible thing, and I've worried about it. I've been jealous of Betty ever since school started, and maybe that's what stopped my periods. You know what a nice girl Betty is. Well, we have become good friends in the last two months, but I used to hate her.

"About a year ago, her folks bought a farm just across from ours. They came from Chicago, and Betty seemed so—well, you know—sophisticated-like. She had much better clothes and stuff. She had all the boys looking at her, and the girls too. Sure, she was nice and everybody liked her, but I guess I was jealous. I was used to being looked up to, but after she came to school, I was no longer the center of attention. She was. I didn't like it for sure and got awful moody and envied her. She made me sick, and it was then I skipped my first period."

I had often seen Betty in the office and could easily picture how Sally felt. Betty's appearance was striking. She always drew stares. Her very blonde hair swept back from her smooth forehead and her widely-spaced blue eyes drew immediate attention, but her erect bearing and air of confidence turned their attention into stares. Betty obviously had stirred up envy, that green-eyed monster, in Sally.

Sally went on, "One day, about a month after I first came to see you, I noticed that Betty got a lot of mail. I was envious of that, too, for I seldom get mail. She gets lots of letters and packages. Well, her mailbox and ours are on the same side of the road, right next to each other. Our mail carrier usually comes late in the afternoon. I saw Betty's name clearly written on a letter from her Grandma, Reva Bixby. I grabbed it and ran into the house, steamed it open, and read it."

"I was so ashamed and felt just awful when I read that Betty had cancer. Her Grandma wrote an awful nice letter, telling Bety how proud she was to have such a wonderful granddaughter and that she knew the treatments would cure her."

Sally again looked up at me and then dropped her eyes as she continued, "Gosh, Dr. Bill, I never felt so dirty in my life. I sat and cried for a long time. Then I sealed the letter and put it back in the mailbox, hoping no one would notice. I haven't told a soul but kept it secret to myself.

"One day at school, I looked at Betty. I saw something I hadn't noticed before — how really nice she treated everyone. She was so nice to me, even though I was really nasty to her, and here I'd been envious of her. She deserved to be looked up to and I didn't. That night I went for a long walk, and I cried and cried. I decided I wanted Betty as a friend.

"Since then, I have stopped being envious of her. I think of how she never told anyone about her cancer, never complained about it, and never seemed to feel sorry for herself. You know, Dr. Bill, I know it was wrong to open that letter, but I'm glad I did it. Betty and I are good friends now, and my periods have come back. Don't you think my envy and hatred of Betty caused them to stop?'

"I really don't know, Sally. Could be. Let's see what happens in the next few months, but your envy and your worrying could have done it, I suppose."

Sally sat back in her chair with a big sigh. She had unloaded herself and was obviously relieved. She rose slowly, promising she would come back if she had another skipped period. But she never did.

* * *

Her eyes were almost swollen shut. Her upper lip was twice its normal size. Black and blue spots were on her forehead, cheeks, arms, and legs. Two ribs were broken on her right side.

Valerie was hurt. Her physical hurt was obvious. Her emotional hurt was equally obvious. She had been beaten by her husband. And this was not the first time.

While patching Valerie, I tried to draw her out. Reluctantly, she began, "I really loved him, but now I hate him. This is the last time I'm going to take it."

I reminded her that she had voiced the same thought three times before. "But this time I mean it." she said.

"You also told me that three times before. In fact, I recall advising you to seek help before someone was seriously hurt or killed, and each time you promised you would."

"But I just couldn't bring myself to do it," Valerie muttered.

Once again, I advised her that marital counseling was the least she should do, but actually she should separate from her husband until he had had psychiatric treatment.

She looked at me and sobbed, then broke out with a tirade of hatred for her husband, Andy. "He is a bully. I despise him. Everything I do is wrong. Everything I say is wrong. I can't please him. He is an SOB. I wish I had never married him."

When Valerie calmed down, we talked. She had gone into marriage in good faith and felt betrayed. Every attempt to start over had been defeated by a new beating, and the emotional wound had penetrated deeper.

This time, the result of our talk was fruitful. Valerie left her husband, a temporary separation. In time, however, she decided on divorce. Perhaps this was the best solution. Some people rub each other the wrong way and can't resolve their differences. They are incapable of communicating with each other. The divorce did not wipe out Valerie's bitter hatred.

A year went by. One day, Valerie came to my office with a long list of complaints. She had headaches every day. Some days, she felt so weak she could hardly get out of bed. Accomplishing her daily tasks exhausted her. She had used up all of her sick leave and now was likely to lose her job.

Valerie had aches that seemed to migrate from limb to body and limb to limb. There was no definite pattern and no evident swelling or tenderness. At times she was dizzy and at times short of breath.

Physical examination and a few laboratory tests done in the office produced no positive findings.

Inadvertently, I asked, "Have you seen Andy? How is he? I haven't seen him since your divorce."

I had opened Pandora's box. Valerie ranted for several minutes. "That no-good S.O.B. I hate him. He has stolen the best years of my life. He is now going with another woman and will ruin her life. He's no good, and I'm going to warn this other woman that he is rotten."

It was apparent that Valerie had never permitted her emotional wounds to heal. Her hatred was gnawing at her, destroying her from within, not unlike cancer.

"Valerie, " I began, "I know you pretty well. I gave you your first spanking when you were born and were too stubborn to breathe. I think you are now too stubborn to forgive."

"Why should I forgive that g.. d.... S.O.B. ?" she screamed. "How can I forgive him all those beatings he gave me? How can I forgive him all those fears I have? I still wake up at night frightened."

"You are not alone," I answered. "There are many who have been beaten, including children and old folks, as well. In fact, most of us have hurts, deep hurts from close ones who have betrayed us."

"I'll never forgive him. I hate him!" she exclaimed, heaving with sobs.

"Forgiving is not easy, not for anyone. But it is the only way to rid yourself of the hatred that is eating you. Your hatred no longer hurts him—it hurts you. You are destroying yourself and your future life."

Valerie looked up at me with disbelieving eyes. "I can't and won't," she said with firm finality. "Good-bye, Dr. Bill. I don't mean to be rude, but you don't make any sense at all." With that, she rose and left.

Three weeks later, Valerie returned. Her headaches were worse. Her appetite was gone, and her abdomen pained most of the time. Recalling her resistance to my designation of her physical disorders as psychosomatic, I spent considerable time asking details of all her symptoms and gave her a most thorough examination. I could not find a single physical link connected to her symptoms.

"Valerie, perhaps you should go to a clinic and let a group of doctors check you. I can't find anything physically wrong. Do you want me to make an appointment for you?"

I made the appointment. A week later, she returned. "The clinic doctors couldn't find anything wrong either," she said. "What now? I can't go on like this."

I started warily. "Valerie, there are some hurts we can ignore. But when we have been unfairly hurt, we can't easily dismiss them. The hurts remain and won't disappear until we, ourselves, remove them.

"Years ago, I had such a hurt. I yielded to it, made no effort to remove it. I let it grow within me. It gnawed at me every day and even some nights. As my hatred grew, my dreams and daily images became more vicious. My relationships with others, even my loved ones, became distressful.

"After a year of this hating, unable to be at peace with myself or others, I decided it was time to do something about it. My hate needed healing. It had become dangerous to me and to those I loved.

"I needed the power of forgiveness, total forgiveness. At first, I could not get myself to do this. After all, the person who had betrayed me deserved my hatred. I felt very righteous about hating him.

"However, when I realized that the hate was becoming malignant, that it was destroying me and affecting those I loved, I knew that no matter how difficult, I needed to give it my full attention.

"Each day I started the agonizing battle of forgiveness. Each day my sense of self-righteousness interfered. Each day I felt and saw and heard the wrongs that had been done me.

"Then one day a separation took place. I saw the person who had hurt me as a fallible human being who needed love, compassion, and understanding, as we all do. I saw him as separate from the despicable wrong he had done me.

"With this new insight, I began to feel different. It became easier to forgive. It was no longer a matter of forgetting the wrong but of placing it to one side, viewing it as separate from the one who had betrayed me.

"Slowly, forgiveness gained a foothold. It no longer seemed such an insurmountable task. Forgiveness no longer seemed a necessary evil. It remained necessary, but not an evil.

"Forgiveness gradually brought peace to me. It was then that I realized what a fool I had been. My hatred had wounded me, not the one who had betrayed me. Now, my forgiveness was healing me, not the one who had betrayed me.

"I suggest, Valerie, you think about this before you destroy yourself as I was doing."

A month passed. Valerie returned. The moment she entered the consultation room, I noted a difference in her bearing as well as in her eyes. The haunted look had disappeared, and the hard lines in her face seemed to have melted.

"I feel much better," she volunteered. "I still have a long way to go. I can see there are no shortcuts and many detours, but as my hatred ebbs, each day I feel better inside."

When she left the office, I knew she had a good start in over-coming her hatred. Valerie finally remarried and has four children who have brought her great happiness. She has confided to me that forgiveness has brought her peace.

CHAPTER 85

DOES THE MIND HAVE POWER OVER THE BODY?

It took me a long time to understand the power of mind over the body. Being confronted with odd situations opened my eyes to its power. I began to appreciate that we all do strange things at times, often not realizing what we are doing or why we do it.

Margaret's reaction to the death of her older sister, Diane, reflected her own lifelong envy of this sister. Diane had been a gracious and charming lady. Margaret had always attempted to outshine and out-do her, but she lacked Diane's looks and charm. Even in childhood, Margaret had lived in Diane's shadow.

People were gathered to attend the home funeral. In the midst of the service, Margaret dropped to the floor, apparently unconscious. The service was discontinued, and I was called.

When I arrived, Margaret had been carried into the kitchen, where she lay on the floor. Stooping over her, I checked her pulse and respirations. Both were normal, but I noticed her eyelids were fluttering ever so faintly. Reaching into my medical bag, I soaked some gauze with spirits of ammonia and covered her nose and mouth with it. Margaret held her breath as long as she could, then breathed in a full dose, and then tried again to hold her breath. Unable to do so, she struggled to free her nose and mouth from my grasp.

I leaned over her and whispered, "Promise to behave and I will remove the smelling salts."

Her eyes flew open, imploring me to release her as she nodded consent.

It seemed strange that at the time of her sister's funeral, Margaret should act up. Certainly, it was not the hot, humid day that had caused her to drop to the floor. Indeed, Margaret was seeking attention to herself and away from her sister.

She was not about to accept second place at her sister's funeral without a struggle. Her faint was her final vain attempt to gain the attention she had always sought.

I left without explaining the cause to the assembled relatives and friends. But a week later, I stopped at Margaret's house and, as we talked, although she was still somewhat miffed at my cool handling of her fainting spell, she admitted the ruse rather awkwardly. "Somehow," she explained, "I just couldn't help it. "

Yes, much of what we do and how we react may seem fraudulent to the viewer, but it is very real to the doer.

Arnold DeVoe was a minister, a straightforward man of about 40. He lived as he preached, a powerful example of someone satisfied with the simple life, free of both intrigue and wealth. Arnold's deep voice, articulate eloquence, and direct manner lent genuine inspiration to his weddings and even to his funeral services. But Arnold developed a problem — "rose fever."

Roses, of course, are out of season in this northern climate for most of the year. Imported roses are expensive. Thus, funerals and weddings are rarely ablaze with them.

It was in June of Arnold's third year at the church. The wedding was large and the roses were abundant. In the middle of the ceremony, Arnold's face turned crimson. Sweat ran down his face and neck. But he struggled on for a few minutes, then cut short his message and disappeared into his 'inner sanctum.' Minutes later, I was called to see him there.

After a brief examination, I learned that Arnold was violently allergic to roses, enough to give him a fever and a fast pulse.

Eventually, word got out of Arnold's allergy. Members of the church were considerate, and roses were voluntarily banned from wedding and funerals. But, seven years later, Arnold had a recurrence of his 'rose fever' when he was performing a funeral service for Mr. Richter.

On that cold and bleak February day, the small room in the funeral parlor was crowded and overheated. As Arnold entered the room, he glanced about at the mourners, his eyes warm with sympathy, and then stepped up onto the small dais. Although there were only two dozen or so flowers in the room, they were all roses and all close to the dais where Arnold stood to perform the service.

In his usual relaxed manner, Arnold began the service, again scanning the faces of his audience as his deep voice held their attention. His clear, incisive words made everyone feel a share in the departed's life and now in his death.

Suddenly, Arnold spied the roses. Instantly, his skin flushed scarlet. His face drew taut. His voice became harsh. Once again, as he had seven years before, Arnold struggled to continue, cut short his message, and left.

Knowing Arnold, as most did, there was questioning amazement, yet little protest. Within the hour, I was at Arnold's bedside, giving him a hypo to quiet his heart and slow his respirations. This time I sent him to the hospital.

The next day when I arrived to check on Arnold, Mr. Richter's widow and daughter, Ruth, were visiting. Arnold looked fine and felt fine. His chart revealed that his temperature, pulse, and respirations were now normal

I sat on the bed, and we four visited together for a few minutes. When Ruth and her mother were ready to leave, Ruth asked Arnold how he liked the roses that she and her mother had made especially for her father's funeral. Arnold, a man of infinite tact and astonishing reserves, hesitated and then said, "You mean you made those roses? They were beautiful. They looked like the real thing."

Arnold had been fooled like the rest of us by those roses. But it was only our eyes and perhaps our noses that were fooled. Arnold, on the other hand, a man of exceptional openness and honesty, had been completely deceived. The power of mind over body had triggered his allergic reaction just as surely as live roses themselves would have done.

Yes, we often do strange things without realizing why.

HOW SHOULD A PATIENT WITH CANCER BE APPROACHED?

Some years ago, a 50-year-old man consulted me about his stomach. Two years before, he had undergone surgery at a clinic but was unaware that he had cancer. His wife, unwisely, had held back his diagnosis, saying, "My husband will never bear up when he hears the word 'cancer.'"

As his pain increased, hospitalization became necessary. His wife insisted that I withhold the truth from him. For a week, my protests were met with stubborn resistance. The tragic picture of this man, alone in his room, alone with his thoughts, unaware of his true condition, haunted me. To make matters worse, his wife sat in the hall, frequently peeking through a crack, "to see if he was all right."

Finally, in desperation, I told her I would no linger attend her husband unless she permitted me to tell him the truth. After arguing with her at length, I finally persuaded her, but she insisted that the result would be entirely my responsibility. And so it was. Leaving her in the hall, I sat by his bed and, as gently as possible, told him he had cancer.

Within 24 hours, the man's face brightened. He sat up in bed, listened to the radio, and voiced renewed interest in life. The greatest change, however, was the disappearance of the chasm between him and his wife. With his wife's support and love and full knowledge of what he was facing, he accepted his illness. Together they shared whatever time he had left.

Dealing with such cases convinced me that the patient has the right to know, but it also convinced me that all family members have a responsibility to keep their role a positive one — to be warm, understanding, and honest. This is no time to be evasive. Doing so creates a rift between them and the patient and sets the tone of the patient's relationship with others. The aura of secrecy becomes, in the eyes of the patient, an atmosphere of conspiracy. Accepting the cancer becomes more difficult as relatives and friends shun any discussion of cancer and, later, avoid the patient. The patient becomes a lonely figure. Separated from family and friends, he or she feels shipwrecked, a person marooned on a deserted island.

*　*　*

Randy was five years old, a happy youngster whose bright blue eyes and infectious smile captivated one and all. Whenever he came to my office, he would hail the receptionist and nurse with a pleasant greeting and then engage them in tales of his dog or rabbits.

Randy had leukemia, a cancerous condition of the blood. Chemotherapy was new and was prescribed on a trial basis. In spite of this treatment, Randy's liver and spleen gradually enlarged, making his abdomen uncomfortably distended. As he became anemic, much of his exuberance faded, but he continued to greet the office force with his infectious smile.

Randy never showed signs of fear. He knew he was seriously ill, but he also knew that his parents loved him. He knew that he might not get well, but he felt secure because there was no wall of secrecy between him and his parents.

A year passed, and Randy's infectious smile became wistful and his eyes lost much of their bright look, but he still hailed the office staff with his pleasant greeting

During one of his final visits, he looked up at me and said, "Do you think God will know me? I don't even look the same to me."

Throughout Randy' illness, his parents expressed an attitude of confidence that supported their son and kept him free of fear. Somehow, they kept their distress to themselves, and Randy reflected his parents' calm demeanor

*　*　*

Over the years, I learned that relatives and friends should act natural. There is no need to hide the truth, but there is no need to dwell on it either. Visitors should bring something to, not take something from, the patient. This does not mean material gifts but the spiritual gift of bringing joy and optimism. In short, the visitor's mission should be to maintain the patient's lifeline to his past by anticipating his need to be a part of the future, whatever the length of that future may be.

A severely jaundiced woman in her early 90's was brought in by one of her daughters. Her symptoms of clay-colored stools and bright orange urine without pain suggested cancer of the pancreas or common bile duct.

"Your mother probably has cancer," I explained, "but there is a 2 percent chance that her biliary obstruction may be due to what we doctors call a 'silent stone' because there is no pain."

"But she's too old to operate, Can't something else be done?"

"Your mother will die unless the bile is released from whatever is blocking its flow. It may be, and probably is, a cancerous growth, but if it is a stone and that stone is removed, your mother will again be well."

287

After this explanation, the daughter consented. I operated and removed multiple stones blocking the flow of bile. There was no cancer. Miraculously, the elderly woman was able to walk on the fourth day. She ate well, was in excellent spirits, and, as I listened, she told me of her three pet geese. But, on the fifth day, she became depressed and her condition deteriorated.

"No one comes to see me. I'm just too old. I should have died long ago. I'm a nuisance to my children," she confided, obviously depressed that none of her 11 children had come to see her.

Later that afternoon, I drove to her farm to get the addresses of her adult children. I sent telegrams to all 11 of them, every hour on the hour. Then I visited my patient at the hospital and told her I had gone to the farm to see her geese. I assured her that they were fine, but that I thought they missed her and her special care.

The next day her children began to show up, and within three days all but one had come, some from as far away as California. This eased her feelings of loneliness. This confirmed her lifeline to her past and fulfilled her need to be part of the future. As a result, her despondency vanished abruptly. She lived to be 101 years.

* * *

Gloria was in her early 30's, a schoolteacher who enjoyed her job and made great effort to prepare each day's lesson. Gloria was also a health addict, devouring many articles on health care. She jogged two miles almost every day, played handball three times a week, and kept herself on a low-cholesterol diet. She had a trim figure.

Because of both real and imagined symptoms, Gloria came to my office every month or so. Her avid reading of health books convinced her that she was the victim of many diseases. Gloria was a strange admixture of imagination, caution and hard work. Except for respiratory infections and a stress fracture, Gloria had no serious problem until the day she came in certain she would soon die.

"I have a lump in my right breast. It has doubled in size in three months, and it's going to kill me."

"Why did you wait three months?" I asked.

"I've read about lumps in the breast. Women lose their breast, sometimes both of them, and that's horrible. I'd hate to lose mine."

"Maybe you don't have to. Let's examine yours before making such a drastic decison."

Gloria's right breast had a definitely nodular feel. The lump was two inches in diameter and, even without a biopsy, there was no doubt it was malignant. What do you say to a woman with Gloria's intense disposition?

"Gloria, I'm glad you came. This lump, most likely, is malignant, but you have probably come early enough so that the cancer can be totally removed. I feel no glands under your arm or under your collarbone. This is a good sign."

"I'm afraid, Dr. Bill—afraid you will have to mutilate my body, take my whole breast and the muscles of my chest as well. I've read a lot about that."

"Well, you know, I can't be certain what is best until a biopsy of the lump is studied. Perhaps a 'lumpectomy' can be done, which means removal of the growth and a small amount of breast tissue. This would preserve your breast."

"But I've read that three out of five patents die in less than five years after removal of their breast. Why be mutilated and then die anyhow?"

"The truth is that two out of five patients survive five years or more," I said, knowing full well that I was saying the same thing but with an optimistic interpretation of the facts.

And then I went on. "Gloria, too often women wait too long. The word 'cancer' has an ugly, fearsome ring. They are so afraid of it that they become numbed into hoping the lump will go away. Precious time is lost."

"Do you think I've waited too long?"

"I don't think so, but I must be permitted to do whatever is best for you. A 'lumpectomy' may be all that is necessary, but it may be best to remove your breast or even do a radical mastectomy, which means removing chest muscle and glands in your armpits. I can't make a decison until the biopsy is reported and the extent of your growth is detemined while you are under an anesthetic. Perhaps you would like to have a second opinion?"

"No, Dr. Bill, I'm still worried, but I'm not afraid anymore. But please don't remove the breast if you don't really have to. I've read about reconstruction of breasts and I'd prefer to keep my own." Gloria looked at me, hoping I would say something to confirm her wish to retain her breast.

"Your desire to keep your breast is understandable and I respect your wishes, but your life must also be considered. If you are going to trust me, you must trust my total judgment of your particular case, or it would be better that you seek a second opinion or even a third."

Gloria underwent a 'lumpectomy,' after which she had radiation. She still teaches school, has married and has three children.

Cancer merits not only competent treatment but also an understanding approach. Over the years, it became increasingly clear to me that the patient has the right to know his or her diagnosis and copes better knowing the truth. Even little tots, like Randy, can complete their shortened lives with greater courage when they know the truth, and in greater comfort when surrounded with love. Fear, as in Gloria's case, can lead to panic, but in some cases can be allayed with moderately positive explanations. Of course, early diagnosis is the best way to win over cancer, and an intelligent family attitude is the best ways to treat the patient.

CHAPTER 87

WHAT WAS SO SPECIAL ABOUT MAXINE?

When I first set eyes on her, it was in a supermarket. I had been married more that 20 years and no longer scanned every woman from head to foot, but I turned to look at this woman, as did every male in the store and some females too. And many took a second look. No doubt about it—Maxine Shroeder was a glowing beauty. She had large, friendly eyes, soft brown hair, and looked as though she had been poured into her dress.

Some months later, our paths crossed in a hardware store. She was busy conversing with the owner at the cash register, and again she was the focus of attention. She did not seem to notice the stares or had learned to ignore them. As she reached for a shopping bag on the floor beside her, she dropped a small package from under her arm. Being close behind her, I picked up the package and handed it to her. Our eyes met; she smiled warmly and thanked me. There was something about her that was unforgettable—something aside from her lovely face and shapely figure. It was the warm glow she cast upon one and all. My curiosity was piqued.

It was another year before I saw her again. This time I had the opportunity to delve into what made Maxine so unforgettable, what made me—and perhaps others too—recall her every look, every word, and every movement. There was no doubt she was a charmer, but I nourished the idea that there was something else and was curious to unearth what that something was. This time, I had the chance to study her at close range; she had come to my office as a patient.

"I am Maxine Schroeder," she began. "You probably don't recall, but I was one of your babies. My mother and father moved to Oregon soon after I was born. My maiden name was Tesch."

"I remember your parents. Seems to me you had an older sister."

"Yes, she moved to Ohio after she was married." Maxine not only spoke clearly, pronouncing each syllable, but also wrapped each word in an effortless smile.

"What brought you back to Ladysmith?"

"It's a long story — a story of coincidence. My husband's firm sent him here, and he had always been curious to see the area where I was born."

"Maxine, I don't mean to dig into your personal history, but sometimes that helps in understanding what makes a patient tick or stop ticking. Forgive me, and let's get down to what brought you here."

"It doesn't seem possible, but we've been here in Ladysmith for almost two years. We like it and, if my husband's firm permits, we will stay. In Oregon, I had a medical problem that was never fully answered. I was told I had Hodgkin's disease. This was three months before we left the West Coast." Maxine, who had been looking directly at me, turned away, then quickly turned back, lavished me with a generous smile, and continued.

"Lymph glands had appeared under my arms and in my groin. For six weeks, I felt weak and had bouts of fever and chills."

"Did the doctor test your blood?"

"Yes, and the laboratory reported that there were cells typical of Hodgkin's."

"Those must have been R-S cells, considered characteristic of Hodgkin's. But, Maxine, they are sometimes found in infectious mononucleosis, which is a benign disease. Have you had any chills and fever since those first six weeks?"

"No, and in the hurry and bustle of leaving Oregon, I never returned to see the doctor after the time he told me I had Hodgkin's disease."

"Have you seen a doctor here?"

"No, I've felt real well and my glands disappeared. But I'm still concerned. I've read about Hodgkin's and know it is malignant. We have three youngsters, and I want to do what's best." Maxine turned away again and, when she turned back, I couldn't help noticing that her brown eyes were moist.

"Maxine, you were right to seek medical advice. Treatment for Hodgkin's has advanced so that many cures are being made. But, of course, we can't be certain you have Hodgkin's. You say you have not had bouts of fever and chills since your first six weeks, about two years ago. This suggests that you had infectious mononucleosis. The fact that your lymph glands have spontaneously shrunk also suggests that you had infectious mononucleosis."

"Do you really think so?" Maxine's eyes seemed to brighten.

"Well, I can't be sure, but let's take another blood sample and look you over."

"Is that necessary?" Maxine gave me one of those bashful looks that many women display before being examined.

"After waiting two years, I suppose you could wait longer, but if you really want to know, we had better get it over with."

I found no enlarged lymph glands and no enlarged spleen, both findings usually present in Hodgkin's disease and in infectious mononucleosis. I sent a sample of her blood to a hematology laboratory. No abnormal cells were reported — no R-S cells.

A week later, Maxine returned to the office. "All good news," I said as soon as she entered the consultation room. "There is no evidence at present that you have Hodgkin's. I'm certain that had you reported back to your Oregon doctor, he would have come to the same conclusion."

"I'm so relieved. I can't thank you enough." She gave me the warmest smile, rose from her chair, leaned forward, and gave me an enormous hug. "When would you like me to come back?"

"Actually, I don't think that will be necessary, but if you should notice some changes, please come at once."

Maxine returned on several occasions for minor problems and for a broken arm, but her signs and symptoms of possible Hodgkin's never recurred. I often wondered what made her that something special, what gave her that extra special magnetism. She was a glowing beauty, to be sure, but something in her voice, in her smile, and in her carriage was special.

Some years passed before a partially satisfactory answer came to me. As I treated patients with terminal diseases, such as heart disease and cancer, I observed their reaction. Even though I tried to bring a positive attitude into every sickroom, patients tended to react in three distinct ways. Some just gave up. Some were bitter. Some accepted their fate but went on to live their lives as before, come what may.

Maxine had gone on to live aggressively, even though she had been told she had malignant Hodgkin's disease. She had accepted her fate without bitterness and had not given up. It was not Maxine's beauty of face or figure that gave her a special glow. Her outer glow, that special something that pervaded her entire being—her voice, her look, her smile, her bearing—came from an inner glow, a self-assurance that all is right with the world, because she had accepted her gloomy portent with optimism

As I said, this was only a partially satisfactory answer, because I still have an unanswered question: Is that inner glow something in the person's nature that makes them view life with optimism, even with a gloomy portent? Or does the gloomy portent. serve as a challenge to bring the best out of some people?

IS THERE A PERFECT PHYSICIAN?

Often, when in an introspective mood, I would ask myself if there was a perfect physician, one whose profile included perfect physical and mental health and unequivocal emotional stability. Perhaps my musings were due to a realization of my own limitations and my incomplete efforts to overcome them.

As a medical student, I was puzzled when a brilliant fellow student flunked out in his third year. He had graduated from an Ivy League college, magna cum laude, and could quote footnotes as well as whole pages from the medical text. Why had he failed?

Some years later, I was disturbed to see a physician, insecure in his medical decisions, flounder in near panic. This man was a Phi Beta Kappa and possessed an unusually receptive mind, a remarkable ability to absorb information. Why was he so insecure? And again, in a New York hospital, as I watched an operation, I saw a board certified surgeon throw surgical instruments when he became flustered. Why? All three men appeared to have more that adequate mental ability. What was lacking?

Yes, I often thought about this but never found an answer until a hunting experience suggested one. One of my close friends, Russell Banks, had invited two recently graduated foresters to join us for a day of deer hunting. Russ, an excellent woodsman and hunter, was to be our guide.

It was 6:00 on a cold November morning when we hit the woods. Two feet of snow had accumulated, and, pushed by a northeasterly wind, more snow was falling. Our progress was slow. After an hour of trudging along single file, Russ called a halt and briefed us on his plans. Using a topographical map of the area, he indicated the positions that each of the foresters would take, pointing out that these positions had the merit of safety as well as the chance for a good shot.

"Deer frequent tamarack swamps in heavy snow," Russ drawled in his typical laconic way. "You fellows are state foresters, so I assume you know the ways of the woods. You each have a map and a compass. Now you, Art, station yourself

293

here on the edge of the swamp. We'll set Stu a half-mile around the swamp. Bill and I will go through a narrow draw and then circle the swamp. We'll be back in a couple of hours or so."

After we had taken Stu to his post, Russ turned to me. "Let's rest a spell and let things settle." We found a large spruce under whose long arms we took temporary shelter from the wind and snow.

Russ had spent all of his 60 years in the woods, as a logger, trapper, fisherman, and hunter. Though without formal education, Russ combined expert woodsmen's knowledge with superb judgment. I always felt secure with him in the wild.

Art and Stu were in their early 20's. Both had attended the University of Wisconsin and graduated as foresters. At the request of an old friend, Russ had agreed to take them on this one-day hunt, although Art and Stu were strangers to both of us.

"Well, might as well start," Russ stood up, brushing off the snow. "We'll start at the top of the ravine, about 20 yards apart. Any deer nuzzling under those hemlocks will move down into the tamarack swamp. Then we'll round the swamp."

Our pace was slow, hampered by the 12- to 15-inches of new snow. An hour had passed when we spotted a large doe, accompanied by two yearlings They moved in toward the swamp. We heard a shot and hoped it wasn't Art or Stu, for only spiked bucks were legal.

Within minutes, we recognized Art, awkwardly struggling through the snow, in a near panic, his face scratched and his jacket torn.

"What's the matter?" Russ asked.

"I was lost," Art answered with a deep sigh.

"How could you be lost? You have a map and a compass."

"What good is a compass when you're lost?" the forester protested.

We didn't get any deer that day, but the young man's words often came back to me: "What good is a compass when you're lost?"

Yes, I often thought about this. Apparently, Art, the forester, was uncomfortable when confronted with unfamiliar circumstances. Though intelligent and well-trained as a forester, he was incapable of applying this knowledge in an actual situation, even though he was carrying both a map and a compass. Why? Perhaps Art's disposition was not suited to the woods. He might have been better off at a desk job.

Then I thought of the medical student who had flunked out, the Phi Beta Kappa who felt so insecure, and the board certified surgeon who threw instruments.

A simile came to mind. Like Art, each had the tools but apparently was unable to use them. Perhaps the medical student with the photographic memory could not go beyond that knowledge to apply it . The temperament of the Phi Beta Kappa physician might have been better suited to research. The board certified surgeon who threw instruments did not belong in an operating room. Perhaps he too should have been in some other specialty.

And then, I felt certain that there is no such person as a perfect physician, just as there is no perfect person. "What good is a compass when you are lost?" That expression did not make the forester a lesser person, but a lesser forester. It also became clear to me that medical knowledge in itself does not make a good physician because knowledge is useless if it cannot be applied properly

Though convinced there can be no perfect physician, I became equally convinced that a good physician needs a receptive mind to accumulate knowledge and must have the ability to use that knowledge with wisdom, compassion, and self-control, even under stress.

WHY PHYSICIANS PRACTICE DEFENSIVE MEDICINE

It was a unanimous opinion that Mary's right arm needed to be amputated at the shoulder. Slides of Mary's tumor had been examined by physicians in the oncology department of the University of Wisconsin-Madison and by cancer specialists in Minneapolis. All had agreed that the treatment of choice was to remove Mary's arm.

Mary was a charming woman in her late 30's. She had come from Ireland two years before and retained her distinctive brogue. "I'm lawyer Bill Hurley's secretary and I 'ave a lump in me wrist. The darn thing interferes with me typing. Can ya get rid of it fer me?"

I placed her right hand in my left one and felt the lump. "It's a ganglion," I said. I paused and felt it again. "I usually needle a ganglion, but this one is too close to the radial artery."

Mary pulled back her right hand and rubbed it with her left one. "It doesn't hurt overly much, Doctor. The nasty thing just bothers me. Will ya extract it for me?"

We arranged to remove the ganglion the following day. While dissecting it, I discovered it was a tumor, not a ganglion, and that it was fastened to the radial artery as well as to the extensor tendon of the thumb. After a tedious 20 minutes, the tumor was removed en masse. It seemed like a harmless growth. Perhaps a xanthoma, I thought. Without anxiety, I sent it to the state pathology laboratory for analysis.

A few days later the report came back. The tumor was a cancer, a highly malignant form of sarcoma. Telephoning the laboratory, I requested that slides of the tumor be sent to a hospital in Minneapolis in time for a pathology conference and to the University of Wisconsin oncology department. After reviewing the slides, both groups suggested immediate amputation of Mary's arm at the shoulder.

How could a small two-by-three-centimeter tumor, which looked so innocuous, be sufficient reason to remove Mary's arm? What should I do? Perplexed and deeply concerned, I consulted with Mary and her husband, David, explaining what the cancer specialists suggested as the treatment of choice.

"You mean to tell me that little peanut of a growth means Mary has to lose her arm?" David asked, staring at me with disbelief.

"I can't believe it either, David, but sarcoma is a highly noxious form of cancer and is unpredictable. No physician can detect microscopic cells that wander off from the mother cancer. I recall a football player who,in his senior year at college, had a sarcoma removed from his leg but refused to have his leg amputated. He had been advised to have it removed but wanted to become a professional player. Three months later, he died."

"Doesn't sound very good now, does it?" Mary asked, slumping in her chair and then looking at me with sad eyes. "What do you think I should do, Dr. Bill?"

"I can't decide for you, Mary. It's a difficult decision to make. For many years I waded trout streams with a friend. He doesn't wade anymore. Ten years ago he lost his left leg to a tumor like yours, but he lives a full life without it."

"But it's my whole right arm we are talking about. How can I get along without a right arm? I can't just say go ahead and take it." Mary choked on her words, sobbing uncontrollably.

David left his chair and bent over Mary. "But I don't want to lose you, Mary. You are much too precious to me." Tenderly, he raised her out of her chair and took her in his arms. "We can do it if we have to, Mary, if others can do it, so can we."

Before undertaking the removal of Mary's arm, I wanted to consult Dr. Robert Johnson, whose experience with cancer was vast and his judgment exceptional. "Perhaps we should all sleep on it." I said. "Let's wait until tomorrow before coming to a decision."

Later that day, I reached Dr. Johnson at a cancer conference in New York City. After explaining the situation, I read him the pathological report and told him of the suggested necessity for amputation. Empathetic to my reluctance to proceed with the removal of Mary's arm, he weighed his words carefully. "Bill, it looks bad. Such a young woman should not lose her arm, but remember she should not lose her life. I suggest you go into the wrist once more. Carefully dissect any tissue that can be removed in that area. However little there may be, send it to me at Madison. I will be back there tomorrow, and, after studying the tissue you send, I will call you."

When Mary and David returned the next day, I told them what Dr. Johnson had suggested. It seemed like putting off the inevitable, but at least it would give more time to make that final decision. Both agreed to the idea, and I redissected Mary's wrist and sent the tissue to Dr. Johnson.

Three days later, Robert called. "Good news, Bill. I can't find any cancer cells—none. It looks like you got them all the first time. But remember, metastases may already have taken place. Good luck."

Of course, this didn't answer the question of what I should do. I could be damned if I removed her arm, even though that was the treatment of choice, and I could be damned if I didn't. But it was not a question of legalities. It was a question of what was best for Mary. Once again, I talked it over with Mary and David, repeating to them what Dr. Johnson had said.

"What does that mean?" Mary asked, "Does that mean it's safe to keep my arm?"

"No, not really, Mary. No doctor could promise that, but it does mean there's less chance that the cancer has spread." I hesitated. Mary looked at David, anticipating he would say something, but he didn't.

I continued, speaking very slowly, not wanting my works to be misunderstood. "If you were my daughter, I would suggest keeping your arm. But even if you were my daughter, I couldn't make the decision for you. Only you, Mary, have the right to make the decision."

Thirty years have passed. Mary has her right arm. Had I removed it, I would have followed the accepted treatment of choice. But I did not do so. Had the cancer taken her life, I would have been guilty of not following the usual procedure. Such are the difficult decisions physicians are called on to make, because medical science is not an exact science.

While great achievements are continuing to be made in medicine and surgery, there are too many individual vagaries of response for medical and surgical treatments to be called an exact science. It is important that patients appreciate this fact. And, in this day of multiple medico-legal suits, it would be a blessing if lawyers took this fact into account.

Although laboratory tests can be suggestive and at times confirmative, they do not produce exact diagnoses. While computers are becoming increasingly helpful, they will never change medical science into an exact science in spite of impressions to the contrary. From his or her practice, every doctor can produce examples of why medicine and surgery are not exact sciences. The responses to drugs vary from individual to individual. Even aspirin shows this variation. It is very helpful for some people while others cannot tolerate it.

We know that a person's disposition also can affect his or her state of health and response to medicine and surgery. One does not have to be a physician to recognize that some individuals face sickness and accidents with hope while others face them with despair. Realizing this, an experienced physician focuses part of his attention on the patient's individual make-up and treats each patient accordingly. Such is the art of medicine, rather than the exact science of medicine.

This difference in the make-up of people is a good reason for patients to have a choice of physicians, since physicians also have varied dispositions. Even if all physicians had equal professional abilities, their treatment of patients would not be exactly the same. Some patients respond better to a positive-minded physician who prescribes treatment in an authoritative manner. Other patients demand a thorough explanation. Personalities, will it or not, enter into the treatment package.

Specialization has added to the quality of medical and surgical care as a whole, yet even among the highest echelons of medical experience, medical and surgical care is not an exact science.

Barney was as redheaded and freckled as anyone I have ever encountered. He was in his early teens when he developed a separation of the upper growth centers of both hip bones. This condition is like fracturing both hips and is called slipped femoral epiphyses. I confined him to bed until I could arrange for Dr. Malvin Nydahl, an orthopedic surgeon, to come to Ladysmith. When he came a week later, my colleagues and I had several cases which required his surgical skills.

It was late afternoon before Dr. Nydahl started Barney's operation. When he completed transfixing Barney's left hip with a surgical nail, Dr. Nydahl was exhausted and decided he had had enough for the day. With that, he announced to the surgical team, "Dr. Bauer will do the right hip next Monday."

Having nailed several adult fractured hips, I felt confident to do the operation. Everything seemed to go well.

After Barney left the hospital, I saw him regularly. When he reached the stage of gradual weight bearing with the help of crutches, there were no untoward signs or symptoms. On his sixth-month visit, however, I noticed he favored his left hip. An X-ray indicated that the upper femoral epiphysis of his left hip had slipped again. I contacted Dr. Nydahl, who eventually replaced Barney's left hip.

Why did the left hip break down, the one the specialist had done? Why not the right hip, the one I had done? Why? There is no logical explanation. It's just the way things happen because medical science is not an exact science. It would be a blessing if lawyers took this fact into account before advising their clients to sue.

All physicians are constantly learning as medical experience accrues. In a real sense, physicians in toto are like a huge medical computer, absorbing factual experiences from the entire medical world. Exposure to improving medical and surgical procedures is available to physicians through lectures, textbooks and journals, and continuing education courses. These bring them up to date on new advances. But these new advances are also subject to change. For years, endometrial cancer of the uterus was treated with surgery alone. Then trials of radiation therapy alone proved equally effective. Finally, a combination of surgery and radiation developed with better results. Surgery for cancer of the breast has also changed appreciably. Lumpectomies have not completely replaced simple or radical mastectomies but have proved beneficial in some cases. These facts further demonstrate that medical science is not an exact science and reveal the need for the physician to exercise individual judgment.

Sometimes drugs and treatments with the most promise bring unforeseen results. A synthetic female hormone, DES (diethylstilbestrol), was once considered of potential value to prevent spontaneous abortions. In the 1940's and 1950's, no physician and no drug company suspected that DES would increase the possibility of cervical cancer in the daughters of mothers who had received this drug during pregnancy, nor that it would increase the sexual aberrations in both male and female offspring. Many thoughtful, well-trained, and well-read physicians gave DES to their patients threatened with spontaneous abortions. How could these physicians have predicted the long-term results? They were not clairvoyant. Why should these physicians be held responsible for the disastrous long-term effects of a drug given in good faith over 30 years ago? Yet, many of these physicians have been sued for malpractice. Medicine is not an exact science.

DES also has definite advantages for some males afflicted with protsatic cancer. But only for some. How can a physician predict which ones?

One of my patients with prostatic cancer lost 60 pounds and had metastases to his pelvic bones, lumbar vertebrae, ribs, and skull. In the X-ray, these bones looked as if they were full of 'moth holes.' After a frank discussion of the facts, the patient consented to castration and promised to take DES daily. Fourteen months later, the 'moth holes' had disappeared and his weight had been regained. Was it the castration? Was it the DES? Was it the combination? The answer is "we don't know." Responses vary. Patients I have treated with one or both had varied responses, many with no improvement at all. Results are unpredictable. Medical science is not an exact science.

We physicians are too often damned if we do and damned if we don't. With the constant need to follow the accepted treatment of choice to avoid suit, we are practicing defensive medicine and are losing our ability to treat our patients as individuals.

And that ability to make individual judgments should not be lost. It can be very important.

* * *

Mrs. Kustik and her husband came from Czechoslovakia. She was a gentle woman who seldom spoke harshly, but when aroused swore in Slovak. With little education but a strong mind, she ruled the roost with a kind but firm hand. Her children learned to eat everything placed before them. "Waste not, want not" was her motto. Chores were shared by all, as she insisted, "No one eats unless he works."

In spite of poor times (the Depression years), the family did not lack for essentials. A rifle was always handy to furnish meat, for within rifle range were deer, squirrels, rabbits, and partridge. Need, not game season, determined when the rifle was used. A large, well-tended garden furnished an assortment of vegetables, many of which were canned for winter use.

Mrs. Kustik's two adversaries were her diabetes and her ample testing of her own cooking. As the years rolled on, the combination developed serious consequences for her. There was little warning. Her weight had increased and her breath had become shorter. One morning, vice-like pains suddenly seized her chest, and within two hours her right leg had become black. Pulsation in the leg was completely absent, due to a blood clot.

What to do? Amputation of the 70-year-old woman's leg would probably kill her because of her coronary occlusion. On the other hand, the dead leg would kill her if not removed. It was obvious—I could be damned if I did and damned if I didn't.

After a consultation with two of her children, thoroughly weighing the probabilities with them, I consulted another physician. We agreed that Mrs. Kustik's only chance for survival was to amputate her leg. We detailed the exact procedure we would take so that we could complete the operation in the shortest amount of time and with the least amount of trauma.

The procedure went well and she did recover, returning to her home as matriarch of her family. She made meals as before but from a wheelchair. Grudgingly, she submitted to a more stringent diet and took her insulin with more regularity, but stubbornly refused to try a prosthesis.

Such are the difficult decisions physicians are called on to make, once again proving that medical science is not an exact science and that the physician can be damned if he does and damned if he doesn't.

CHAPTER 90

DO WE HAVE THE RIGHT TO DIE WITH DIGNITY ?

Advanced medical technology keeps alive many people who formerly would have died. This presents a problem. Although valuable and productive months and even years are added to the lives of some seriously ill patients, there are others kept alive with hopeless outlooks. Although their hearts are kept beating and their lungs kept breathing, their minds are dead. There is no hope of their ever enjoying quality living again. There are others whose minds are alert but whose bodies are wracked with terminal disease. For them, there is also no hope of quality life again.

To live or not to live? To die or not to die? These are questions the patient, the relatives, and the physician must ask themselves. What rights does the patient have to die in peace? To die with dignity? Spouses, parents, sons, and daughters — what can they do to prevent unnecessary suffering and unwarranted prolonging of life? And what is the proper role of the physician?

Philosophical, religious, cultural, medical, and social consideration are all part of arriving at a specific decision. What is really best to do? Who among us would play God? Is the patient in a truly terminal phase of his life? If a decision is made to let a patient die, honestly believing this is best, will that decision be made easier the next time, and perhaps less carefully made? Will the decision be unduly influenced by sympathy for the patient?

On the other hand, in the fear of playing God, of making a judgment of life and death, will we permit some patients to suffer an endless procession of agonizingly painful days and nights? And families to watch this interminable suffering of their loved ones? There are already many cases where a husband or wife felt obliged to stop their spouse's suffering by cutting off life support systems or even taking more drastic action. Are these truly acts of murder or acts of mercy activated by love?

Jake Logan was a lumberjack of prodigious proportions. His hands, arms, legs, chest, and neck were huge. He enjoyed crushing the hands of anyone foolish enough to place their hand in his. Yes, he was an enormous man with a reputation for such strength that few men had the audacity to cross him. Even in his 60's, his powerful frame remained as a hallmark of his lumberjack days and prevented many a man from confronting him.

Jake was 64 when cancer assailed him. At first, he paid little attention to the initial warnings. His appetite failed him, his zest for life evaporated, and he just didn't seem to care. His wife finally brought him in for medical attention.

"Jake is not himself," she said. "He's been this way for two or three months."

"I'm all right," Jake rumbled in his deep voice. "Just off me feed."

"Yes, and crankier than you have ever been. And Dr. Bill, he's lost an awful lot of weight."

Even though I hadn't seen Jake for several years, it was obvious that he had lost weight. His cheekbones were more prominent, his eyes more deeply set, and in most places his skin hung loosely. A sallow complexion had replaced his usual ruddy one and a wan look his usual 'I am master of all' appearance.

Jake had cancer of the liver that had already spread widely and within a week made hospitalization necessary. But even in the hospital, there was little that could be done for this once unusually strong man and his very concerned wife except to comfort them and to relieve the pains that rapidly spread throughout Jake's frame—pains that even this macho man could not tolerate.

For three months he lay in bed, unable to do anything for himself. During the last month, his only source of nourishment was intravenous feedings given at the insistence of two sons who did not share their mother's request not to use heroic means of life support. Jake was a pitiful sight . His large frame, once superbly covered with 250 pounds of flesh, was reduced to a skeleton of less than 100 pounds. Daily, his wife tortured herself to view this skeleton with his hollow, unseeing eyes, and his ever-open unspeaking mouth, with the full realization that nothing could be done for this husband of 40 years. There was no way of knowing when his misery would end.

Many similar tragic cases come to mind, when the human heart agonized to make the proper decision but feared to play God, and when the human heart was torn asunder by the battle to satisfy cultural, religious, medical, and social customs — the battle that has never yet been won, for there are no easy answers. There are too many questions that hunger for answers. We put a dog out of his misery, but watch a loved one suffer. We don't want the dog to suffer; we also don't want our loved one to suffer, but the forces of cultural, religious, medical, and social customs influence us. Does our culture accept the shutting off of all life-sustaining equipment? Does our religion permit the discontinuance of this equipment? Is the doctor certain our loved one's condition is terminal, that there is no hope? In the final analysis, we all must ask ourselves, "Am I ready to make such a decision?"

But there is much more to be taken into consideration. If society appears ready to accept the concept of removing all life-sustaining efforts, under what circumstances? And who will make the final decision? And who will justify it? If such decisions become accepted, will they become accepted with such ease that there will be no soul-searching, that such decisions will open the door to greed and fraud? Will there develop such laxity in making these decisions that it may lead to extermination of those no longer able to contribute — the handicapped and the infirm and the elderly?

There are no simplistic answers and we should not expect them, for this question of whether or not to remove all life-sustaining efforts is not a simple one and deserves our most thoughtful consideration. Making such a decision is intrinsically tied up with all the gains man has made in developing tolerance and compassion for the underdog, the less fortunate, the invalid, the aged, the infirm. Without a substantially responsible method of making such a decision, society could lose those humanitarian gains that men have fought and died for and return to its 'survival of the fittest' pattern of life. With certainty, we should seek an appropriate answer to prevent unnecessary suffering, particularly long-term suffering of those with terminal disease. But with equal certainty, we should not lose the strides mankind has made in tolerance and compassion over the centuries. In trying to ease the suffering of the terminally ill and allowing them to die with dignity, we are exercising compassion, but we can be trapped into creating a monster that permits careless decision making and even wanton extermination, as was done by the Nazis.

It seems warranted to suggest that "To Die With Dignity" committees be established in sufficient numbers to properly serve all areas of each state. Out of the pool of each state's physicians and lawyers, two of each could be selected on a rotating basis as the need arises. Each county judge would act to help select four local citizens, following the usual custom for selection of a jury, to complete the committee. The eight individuals would be called to make the final decision, and the relatives could make their desires known at a hearing of such a committee. The hearing could also be attended by the family physician and the family pastor.

Does this seem like a lot of trouble? We go to a lot more trouble to quibble over property rights. Certainly the right to sustain life and the right to die in peace with dignity deserve equal consideration.

This chapter was published in the *American Medical Association News* (the *AMA News*), the *Wisconsin Medical Journal,* and also the *Florida Medical Journal* by request.

PART FIVE

In writing this book, I have relived many of my medical adventures. Now that the book is in its final stages, I have the same ambivalent feelings I had when I retired. At that time, I felt sad that my years of practice were over, but happy to have had such a privilege. Now, I feel sad that the writing of this book is about to end, but happy to have relived those adventures.

I find it fitting to close this book with four chapters to express my gratitude to my profession, my concerns for its future and to share the words of a patient which show the heartwarming relationships I enjoyed.

Table of Contents

Part Five

THE HERITAGE OF MEDICAL CARE

Each generation of doctors brings to medical care not only new faces and new enthusiasm but also new concepts of treatments and new tools. Each generation learns from those who came before and adds its knowledge for those who follow. The legacy of medical care is sound and worthy of respect.

My father was a physician. Two brothers and a sister were physicians. Two of my children are physicians. This suggests a genetic inheritance. Perhaps so, but a genetic inheritance does not a physician make. My strongest influence came in my daily contacts with the experienced physicians in our rural area. They faced their medical challenges with courage and skill. What I learned from them cannot be found in textbooks, and, unfortunately, little of it is taught in medical schools.

For more than four decades, I climbed the stairs to my second floor office, drove through backwoods roads making home calls, and left my warm bed to make emergency calls and deliver babies. In the footsteps of my predecessors, I kept my fees low. For the first 20 years, my office fee was $1.00. By the early '60's, it had risen to $2.00 a visit, and in the mid-'70's, because of higher salaries and the increased cost of supplies and utilities, it became necessary to raise my office fee to $4.00. But even this proved inadequate. On his annual December visit, my certified public accountant informed me that I was losing money on more than 70 percent of my patients.

"How come?" I asked.

"Seventy percent of your patients are on Medicare," he said, "and Medicare only pays you $3.00 a visit. Analysis of your cost figures shows that it costs you $3.39 to process each patient. If you don't raise your fees, you will have to close your office."

I felt compelled to write an article, "Medicare is Forcing Me to Close my Office." Following publication of this article in *World Medical News*, I received responses from doctors in many states.

Senators Proxmire and Nelson, Wisconsin senators in Washington, also wrote, offering an explanation of why my Medicare payments were so low: "Medicare payments are based on established fees. Since your fees are low, your percentage prescribed by law is also low. Young doctors starting practice immediately establish their fees on a higher level, resulting in higher payments from Medicare." They promised to do something to relieve the problem.

Their explanation was simple, but the relief they promised came too late. Matt, the CPA, was right. The problem eventually led to the closing of my office, but for two years I kept it open by accepting a position in the emergency room of a city hospital, 60 miles from home. I worked 12 to 15 hours a day, three days a week. It paid well. I plowed the money back into my private practice, which I continued the remainder of the week. However, the dual role became too exhausting for a man of my age. The long hours of professional work plus the many hours on the road took their toll. Reluctantly, I closed my office and gave up my emergency room work as well.

My final days in the office were filled with emotion. It wasn't only my patients who had moist eyes and choked voices. I, too, was finding the good-byes difficult.

A local newspaper's spread about my retirement seemed excessive and even embarrassed me. Nevertheless, I enjoyed it, except for the pictures. "That couldn't be me," I said to my wife. "I look too old."

Closing the office meant sorting over the many years of accumulated files, X-rays and patients' records. It also meant sorting out mementos of my practice — books, gifts from patients, and wise adages. Actually, this bittersweet task took several months to complete. One hour, two at the most, was all I could take at one time. Provocative memories slowed the pace as I relived many a moment of my medical career.

I also had decisions to make. Should I completely retire, or should I continue to see former patients by appointment? I asked myself, "Where has the time gone?" I couldn't believe it. I was now a senior physician. Some of my peers had already retired; others were on the verge of retirement. How could I just quit? How could I shut myself off from all my patients, from work that consumed and delighted me?

I thought back to the physicians who had preceded me, those who had pioneered this area and had left such a rich legacy of medical care. As a young physician, I had learned to respect these men. Long before my arrival, they had tilled these medical fields with courage, leaving the soil fertile for the skills of future physicians. In their day, they had treated much trauma, for this had been a busy lumbering area. Somehow they had managed without our modern equipment and know-how. Antibiotics and even sulfa drugs were not in their arsenal. They depended on their alert and creative minds and their caring hearts to draw from their patients that extra something that often makes the difference between success and failure. While we did not always see eye-to-eye with them, my peers and I absorbed much from these pioneer physicians and always showed them respect, for they left a heritage worthy of emulation.

Thoughts of retirement continued to plague me. Many young physicians had entered our community. Some had left. Some had remained. Was I ready to turn over to these young physicians the legacy of medical care?

In January 1980, a bombshell exploded. One of the young physicians, who had been in the community only a few years, made public derogatory remarks about past medical care in Rusk County. His views were printed in various Wisconsin newspapers:

> *The medical care in Rusk County Hospital was appalling and atrocious. In the last five years, an unheralded revolution in health care has occurred. We now have the youngest, most qualified medical staff of any hospital of comparable size in Wisconsin and perhaps in the nation. We have unique problems in that our rural population is older than the state and national average.*

Aside from his lack of humility, we can fault him for his lack of simple reasoning. How did our rural population get older than the state and national average if the medical care was so poor?

I received numerous phone calls from irate citizens, shocked by this young physician's arrogance. I was persuaded to reply:

> *I object to the remarks made by . . . on two counts. His remarks were derogatory to the community that supports him and to the physicians and nurses who preceded him. By the many calls I have received, it appears my objections are shared by many in the community.*
>
> *Of course, there should be improvement in medical services. Accumulated knowledge of medical experiences should enable physicians to give, and entitle patients to receive, better medical care. Each generation of physicians should add to, not detract from, the quality of medical care.*
>
> *In addition, improved equipment has been made available by an improved economy and generous donors.*
>
> *An unmistakable arrogance is exhibited in labeling "past medical care as atrocious," saying that "five years ago, conditions were appalling."*
>
> *When it becomes necessary to gain stature by knocking someone else and patting oneself on the back, something is definitely wrong.*
>
> *We are fortunate, indeed, to have conscientious new medical personnel. But it is about time that some of them appreciate the efforts made by physicians and nurses who preceded them and by the community as a whole.*

Shortly after my letter appeared in various Wisconsin newspapers, seven young physicians, members of the Rusk County Medical Society, sent a letter of apology to each senior physician. Although this was a gracious gesture and deserving of credit, the shadow of this young physician's remarks hung heavy over our community for some time.

About this time, still uncertain whether or not to completely retire, I was haunted by the memories of physicians who had pioneered this area. Though they had long since departed, I often saw their faces and recalled special characteristics of each. I remembered one of them who, when exhausted, would plop himself down in a patient's house to take a nap rather than return home to answer a busy telephone. Another who appeared to be a strange combination of composure and uneasiness, was, according to one of his patients, a lovable old grouch. A third was a master of epigrammatic expressions. Among his many descriptive commentaries was "shifty as a shit-house rat."

As I mused over these former colleagues, I wondered what had made these men, these hardy medical pioneers, retire? One had died of cancer. Another had a nervous breakdown. Still another had a stroke. In truth, all had been forced to retire. Why did they hang on so long? Undoubtedly, they enjoyed having a finger in the medical pie, as I did.

Sometimes, half-asleep, mulling over the situation, I'd ask myself whether these old-timers were now in a land where decision making was no longer required? A land where no one became sick? Where no one had accidents? Where no one needed surgery? If such a realm existed for them, were they happy without the need to make such decisions? I wondered if they missed the daily concerns of their practice.

As a result of these frequent musings, I vowed to hang on to a limited form of practice, to see only former patients and only by appointment, but to be ready to give that up if it became necessary. I also realized what a marvelous medical heritage had been mine, handed down from these pioneer physicians. I hoped that those who followed would carry on this medical legacy with competence and appreciation for the nurses and physicians who had preceded them.

CHAPTER 92

"HOW COME YOU LOST YOURSELF IN NORTHERN WISCONSIN?"

It was June 1984, the 50th anniversary of my graduation from Williams College. For the most part, the college looked unchanged — a small college town tucked into the Berkshire Mountains of northwestern Massachusetts. It was we, my classmates and I, who had changed. Faces once flushed with youthful exuberance were now deeply lined. Bodies once sleek and firm, for the most part were now padded. It took lengthy scrutiny to distinguish old friends. But then, for the moment, it seemed we became young again. We tackled the dummies on the football field and the problems of the classrooms.

We questioned each other about marriage, children, business, and profession. One in my group was president of a large bank, one a chief executive of an international firm; another an eminent heart surgeon. When it came my turn, I told them I was a country doctor.

The bank president looked at me quizzically. "How come you lost yourself in northern Wisconsin?" he asked. "Whatever made you do that, Bill ?"

At the time I said very little, surrounded as I was by such a distinguished group, but since then I have given it a lot of thought. For those many years, without fame or fortune, I have been happy with my work and family. There have been problems, of course, but never a moment of boredom. And for those 50 years I have been blessed with the special beauty of all four seasons in the country.

No, I had not lost myself in northern Wisconsin — I had found myself.

REFLECTIONS OF FIFTY YEARS

During my 50 years as a country doctor, many truths were revealed to me. Those years were interwoven with the threads of joy, hope, learning, and humility. When things went well, a sense of fulfillment became my joy. Hope, often born of necessity, sparked the treatment of my patients. Learning was a daily experience. Humility rose as a strength with the appreciation that the physician treats, but God heals.

I learned that becoming a physician is not taught in medical school. Training in the understanding of disease and exposure to up-to-date treatments alone do not qualify young men and women as good physicians. Just as having children does not automatically make us good parents, having patients does not automatically make us good physicians. To become a good physician takes time, patience, and genuine concern.

The process is slow. The excitement of success is balanced by the frustration of failure. One patient's appreciation is offset by another patient's dissatisfaction. Practicing medicine is an unending cycle of attainment and disappointment. Yet the physician, alert to the needs of his patients, accumulates growth in his medical skills like a snowball rolling downhill.

I learned that while I would not trade my lifetime of diverse medical adventures with anyone, present day specialization and group practice make good sense for two reasons: Accumulated knowledge has become too massive for any one individual to absorb or assimilate, and group practice provides the physician more time to achieve proper balance between his marriage to medicine and his marriage to wife and family.

I learned that there is a great need for tort reform by our courts to reduce medico-legal suits and thus alleviate the physician's need to practice defensive medicine. But that will happen only if we as physicians recoup our warm patient-physician relationships. Improvement in such vital relationships will come about only when we doctors touch more deeply our patients' hearts and reach less deeply into their pockets. We must avail ourselves of the advantages of medical technology without creating an image of mechanistic robots.

During half a century of practice, my medical adventures in northern Wisconsin added so much to my storehouse of knowledge, broadened my outlook, increased my tolerance, and taught me the satisfaction of giving. But more than anything, this 50 years of interacting with people revealed to me how much all of us need one another.

*This chapter was given as a short talk when I was honored at the dinner for doctors who had practiced for 50 years. It was also later published in the *Wisconsin Medical Journal* in April 1990.

CHAPTER 94

EULOGY to The MEDICAL LIFE of a COUNTRY DOCTOR

In 1981 I was operated on for cancer of the colon. Relatives, neighbors, friends, and patients responded with visits, calls, and letters. Patients I had not seen in years wrote or dropped in.

One day, the following letter arrived. It brought tears to my eyes. No words ever pleased me more. The memories of a career that was never spectacular but very rewarding are etched in these words of affection:

> *Dear Doctor Bill,*
>
> *It is the bleakest time of the year. We have been thinking of you this month, hoping for the very best outcome of your surgery. Remembering visits to your office for our minor colds, ear infections, broken bones — where not only were our bodies mended and healed, but our souls and minds were searched as well.*
>
> *And there were many things you said — that we didn't want to hear.*
>
> *And we complained — loud and clear — but were the better for it, I think.*
>
> *It is important that you know that even now, in your difficult time, you continue to be our model of strength and compassion.*
>
> *It is important that you know of our love.*
>
> *We are the babies you delivered, the parents you advised, the elderly you comforted.*
>
> *Your side of the bleachers is packed!*

Dear Doctor Bill,

It is the bleakest time of the year.

We have been thinking of you this last month, hoping for the very best outcomes of your surgery

- Remembering visits to your office for our minor colds, ear infections, broken bones - where not only were our bodies were mended and healed but our souls and minds were searched as well.

And there were many things you said - that we didn't want to hear

And we complained - loud & clear - but were the better for it, I think.

It is important that you know that even now, in your difficult time, you continue to be our model of strength and compassion.

It is important that you know of our love.

We are the babies you delivered, the parents you advised, the elderly you comforted.

Your side of the bleachers are packed!